# MENTAL CAPACITY LAW, SEXUAL RELATIONSHIPS, AND INTIMACY

# Law, Society, Policy

*Series Editor:* **Rosie Harding**,
University of Birmingham

---

*Law, Society, Policy* offers an outlet for high quality, socio-legal research monographs and edited collections with the potential for policy impact.

**Scan the code below to discover new and forthcoming titles in the series, or visit:**

bristoluniversitypress.co.uk/law-society-policy

# MENTAL CAPACITY LAW, SEXUAL RELATIONSHIPS, AND INTIMACY

Edited by
Beverley Clough and Laura Pritchard-Jones

With a Foreword by
Kirsty Keywood and Margaret Flynn

BRISTOL UNIVERSITY PRESS

First published in Great Britain in 2024 by

Bristol University Press
University of Bristol
1–9 Old Park Hill
Bristol
BS2 8BB
UK
t: +44 (0)117 374 6645
e: bup-info@bristol.ac.uk

Details of international sales and distribution partners are available at bristoluniversitypress.co.uk



British Library Cataloguing in Publication Data
A catalogue record for this book is available from the British Library

ISBN 978-1-5292-3562-3 hardcover
ISBN 978-1-5292-3563-0 ePub
ISBN 978-1-5292-3564-7 ePdf



Cover design: Andrew Corbett
Front cover image: Shutterstock/ppeter9476
Bristol University Press uses environmentally responsible print partners.
Printed and bound in Great Britain by CPI Group (UK) Ltd, Croydon, CR0 4YY

FSC
www.fsc.org
MIX
Paper | Supporting responsible forestry
FSC® C013604

To Dave, James and Edie
and
To Nain, Taid and Lil

# Contents

# Series Editor's Preface

The Law, Society, Policy series publishes high-quality, socio-legal research monographs and edited collections with the potential for policy impact. Cutting across the traditional divides of legal scholarship, Law, Society, Policy offers an interdisciplinary, policy-engaged approach to socio-legal research which explores law in its social and political contexts with a particular focus on the place of law in everyday life.

The series seeks to take an explicitly society-first view of socio-legal studies, with a focus on the ways that law shapes social life, and the constitutive nature of law and society. International in scope, engaging with domestic, international and global legal and regulatory frameworks, texts in the Law, Society, Policy series engage with the full range of socio-legal topics and themes.

# Notes on Contributors

**Neil Allen** has two super daughters (for which he can take little credit) and, in the time he has spare from fatherhood, is a Barrister [39essex.com] at 39 Essex Chambers, Senior Lecturer at the University of Manchester, and founder of LPS Law Ltd [lpslaw.co.uk]. With particular interests in human rights, mental health and incapacity law, he is consistently ranked as a leading barrister in the Court of Protection. Neil has been involved in a number of the reported cases in the field of sexual relationships and intimacy, including *SSJ v A Local Authority* (sex workers), *Re AA* (autoerotic asphyxiation) and *Re A* (internet and social media). He also teaches undergraduate and postgraduate students, regularly delivers professional training to a variety of audiences and enjoys writing about the law.

**Claire Bates** has a dual role, as founder and leader of the National Supported Loving Network and as an honorary research associate at the University of Kent's Tizard Centre and Manchester Metropolitan University. She has worked with people with learning disabilities for over two decades in various roles, establishing and leading the National Supported Loving Network, which promotes good practice through guidance, research and education surrounding sexuality and intimate relationships within social care. Her publications include *Sexuality and Learning Disability: Practical Approaches to Providing Positive Support* (Pavilion Publishing, 2008).

**Karen Brennan** is Associate Professor in Law at the University of Essex. Her research and teaching interests lie in criminal justice, with a particular focus on socio-historical and gendered issues connected with criminalisation in the context of pregnancy/childbirth and motherhood. She has published extensively on the topic of maternal infanticide. Her research interests also include abortion and obstetric violence. She is co-editor (with E. Milne) of *100 Years of the Infanticide Act: Legacy, Impact and Future Directions* (Hart Publishing, 2023); and *Women and Criminal Justice System: Failing Victims and Offenders?* (Palgrave Macmillan, 2018).

**Beverley Clough** is Professor of Law and Social Justice at Manchester Law School, Manchester Metropolitan University. Her research explores the intersections of healthcare law and social care law through a feminist disability studies lens.

**Lorraine Currie** is a mental capacity freelance consultant, currently working as an associate for West Midlands Association of Directors of Adult Social Services (ADASS) and the Social Care Institute for Excellence. She is a regular trainer, blog writer and a visiting lecturer at Keele University. Lorraine has written a number of Mental Capacity Act/Deprivation of Liberty Safeguards (MCA/DoLS)-related guidance tools mainly for the Local Government Association and ADASS. Lorraine's research interests are mental capacity, supported decision making and brain injury.

**Alan Cusack** is Associate Professor of Law at the University of Limerick, where he also holds the position of Director of Policing Studies. He is a qualified solicitor and a graduate of University College Cork (BCL, LLM, PhD), University College Dublin (Dip. Emp.) and the Law Society of Ireland (Solicitor, 2012). His research on the intersection of vulnerability and the criminal process has been widely published in national and international journals. He is a co-author of *Criminal Law in Ireland* (Clarus Press, 2021) and is currently completing a monograph entitled *Victims of Crime with Intellectual Disabilities and the Criminal Process: Adversarial Procedure on Trial* (Routledge, forthcoming 2025). He has acted as an expert advisor to the Minister for Justice, Garda Commissioner, the European Commission, Rape Crisis Network Ireland and the Department of Justice and he has provided expert analysis on the treatment of vulnerable witnesses for national media outlets in Ireland.

**Allegra Enefer** is training to become a barrister. She graduated from the London School of Economics (LLB, first class) and completed her Bar Vocational Studies at the City Law School. Her research interests are in socio-legal theory and medical law and ethics. Her work has previously been published in the *International Journal of Law and Psychiatry* and the *LSE Law Review*.

**Andrea Hollomotz** is Associate Professor in Sociology and Social Policy at the University of Leeds and came to academia from a social work and social care background. Her academic work focuses on the sociological study of disability and interpersonal violence. She aspires to enable a deeper understanding of the needs of those who have been hurt and those who hurt others, to inform service responses that can help to break the circle of offending, as well as to make suggestions on the design of inclusive services that can enable healing and recovery from interpersonal violence. She also aims to inspire upstream thinking about social change that can help to reduce disabled peoples' increased risks of being targeted.

**Jaime Lindsey** is Associate Professor at the School of Law at the University of Reading. Her research interests include healthcare law, family law, access to justice and dispute resolution. She currently holds an Economic and Social Research Council New Investigator Award for a project on 'Mediation of Medical Treatment Disputes: A Therapeutic Justice Model'. Her monograph, *Reimagining the Court of Protection: Access to Justice in Mental Capacity Law* (Cambridge University Press, 2022) was awarded the Hart Socio-Legal Studies Association (SLSA) early career book prize 2023 and was shortlisted for the Society of Legal Scholars Peter Birks prize for outstanding legal scholarship 2023. Jaime is a member of the SLSA, a non-practising solicitor and an academic fellow of the Middle Temple.

**Hannah Morgan** is Associate Professor in Social Policy and Disability at the University of Leeds. She is a member of the university's Centre for Disability Studies and organiser of the Leeds Disability Studies Conference. Her research focuses on disabled people's experiences of health, social care and welfare services, professional practice and education and the development of Disability Studies and its relationship with the disabled people's movement. She co-edited *Disability, Spaces and Places of Policy Exclusion* (Routledge, 2014) and co-authored *Social Work, Cats and Rocket Science: Stories of Making a Difference* (Jessica Kingsley Publishers, 2020).

**Carmelle Peisah** is an old age and consultation-liaison psychiatrist; family and systems therapist; Conjoint Professor, University of New South Wales; Clinical Professor, University Sydney; president-founder of Capacity Australia (Australian Centre for Capacity, Ethics, and Prevention of Exploitation of People with Disabilities (ACCEPD); 2021 recognised by Expertscape as a World Expert in human rights (in the top 0.1% of scholars writing about human rights in the past ten years; ranked 5th in Australia); previously a professional member of the former New South Wales Guardianship Tribunal (now NCAT); an expert witness on capacity issues (over 300 cases both locally and internationally); and co-author of the e-text *Capacity and the Law* https://austlii.community/wiki/Books/CapacityAndTheLaw/.

**Laura Pritchard-Jones** is Senior Lecturer in the School of Law at Keele University. Her research interests are broadly within adult social welfare law, mental disability and mental health law, and adult safeguarding. She has published widely on these topics, including co-authoring one of the leading practitioner textbooks on adult safeguarding.

**Alex Ruck Keene KC (Hon)** is an experienced barrister, writer and educator. His practice at 39 Essex Chambers is focused on mental capacity and mental health law. He also writes extensively in the field, and is the creator of the website http://www.mentalcapacitylawandpolicy.org.uk/, providing resources and expert commentary on some of the most difficult mental capacity issues. He is a visiting professor at King's College London, a visiting senior lecturer at the Institute of Psychiatry, Psychology and Neuroscience, King's College London and a research affiliate at the Essex Autonomy Project, University of Essex.

**Ralph Sandland** is Professor of Law and Difference in the School of Law, University of Nottingham. His research interests include mental health and mental disability law, family law, gender and sexuality, and legal history and he has published widely in these areas. He is co-author, with Peter Bartlett of *Mental Health Law, Policy and Practice* (Oxford University Press, 4th edn 2014) and is currently working on a new edition of this text. He is also currently writing a history of sexuality and the law.

**Oluwatoyin Sorinmade** is a consultant in old age psychiatry, with special interest in mental health law, especially the Mental Capacity Act (England and Wales), as well as in empowering the decisional autonomy of older adults and enabling people to live well with dementia. His research interests are in human rights, mental health law and improving the quality of lives of older adults. He has published in the field of old age psychiatry, mental health law and human rights, and on subjects relating to mental health law, especially as they affect the older adult population.

**Becky Squires** is Principal Social Worker for Adults, and Senior Manager for Governance and Practice with Westmorland and Furness Council. She also lectures in Social Work at Lancaster University. Becky is a qualified Approved Mental Health Professional and Best Interests Assessor and leads on best practice, co-production, work with carers, and DoLS. She has published work on social pedagogy and relationship-based practice (2023) and social work in rural communities (2024).

# Acknowledgements

This edited collection began life as a seminar hosted at Keele University in 2022, generously funded by the Socio-Legal Studies Association, the School of Law at Keele University and the Centre for Disability Studies at the University of Leeds. The editors would like to thank the organisations which funded the event; without this, this edited collection would not have been possible. The editors would also like to give their unreserved thanks to the contributors and authors who feature in the collection for all their reflections at the workshop and in the process of drafting the chapters. The richness of the collection is a product of these conversations and contributors' careful engagement with the issues. Finally, we extend our thanks to Bristol University Press for their diligence and support in bringing this collection to fruition, as well as to the anonymous reviewers for their insightful comments and feedback.

# Foreword

*Kirsty Keywood, Senior Lecturer, Centre for Social Ethics and Policy, University of Manchester*

*Margaret Flynn, Chair of the National Mental Capacity Forum*

This book was hatched in May 2022 at Keele University by Beverley Clough and Laura Pritchard-Jones. Characterised by a willingness to think across disciplines and time, the Keele event focused on the delicate and at times controversial terrain of sex, sexuality, intimacy and their legal footholds. It took for granted the necessity of conversations across disciplinary boundaries and involved clinicians, social workers, lawyers, student researchers and the relatives of people with compromised mental capacity. We were pleased to be invited to contribute to this volume, since it returned us to work we first undertook over 20 years ago. Back then, we had wanted to understand the healthcare decisions of adults with intellectual disabilities. Our findings confirmed the limited control people had over their bodies and over decisions about their lives. This has found subsequent reference points in our reviewing work, research and self-advocacy.

This volume describes a shifting legal landscape and what it means for the health and social care professionals who are supporting people with cognitive impairments in relation to intimate relationships. Readers are alerted to questions such as:

- What is a good intimate relationship versus a bad one, and to what extent is it appropriate for these to be interrogated by the law?
- Ought the concept of mental capacity to be the determinant for the lawful exercise of sexual agency?
- What sexual and emotional practices constitute the decision-making 'matter' in mental capacity law, and how does this impact on how capacity is assessed?
- Is it appropriate to consider lifelong celibacy as the correct legal response to a person who is considered to lack capacity in relation to sexual intimacy?
- Must consent to having sex always accept that the potential partner must also be consenting?

Readers seeking simple answers will be disappointed. Contexts matter, and variations and hazards in the lives and opportunities of men and women with mental disabilities are multiple, as are the social structures within which identities are negotiated and produced. These contexts alert us to some pressing questions about how sexual identity and intimacy is understood and supported. Without knowing the world-views and lines of authority within their families, it is possible that beliefs and traditions result in explicit efforts to shield children, young people and adults from sex education and, more specifically, sexual expression. Do people with cognitive impairments share expectations of relationships, marriage and parenthood with their family members? Are restrictions placed on potential and actual sexual activities? Are they their parents' companions and care-givers? How will anyone know and take action if their rights are not prioritised or even known? Sexual agency is influenced not only by family, of course. Legal and political institutions – alongside social and cultural practices – operate to delimit the terms on which people are recognised as legitimate sexual beings. In examining the legal parameters of sexual agency, this book serves as an important and timely reminder that law is not value neutral, either in its motivations or in its impacts. How the law frames sexual autonomy tells us something about power, ideology and their differential impacts on individuals and communities.

It is impossible to talk about sexual agency and mental disability without also acknowledging the necessary implication of race, gender and class, for example. It is plausible that the statutory embargo on the sexual relations of women – and not men – with intellectual disabilities under the Criminal Law Amendment Act 1885 has impacted on their families and care providers through the generations, with concerns about sex coalescing around the risk of pregnancy and procreation. Eugenic fears, premised on a preoccupation with social purity in the service of nation building, were salient in shaping the Mental Deficiency Act 1913 and subsequent policies of institutional, sexual segregation. Through such statutory interventions, mental disability law has gifted a profusion of crude and pejorative classification terms. As the spaces within which the law's jurisdiction over the sexual lives of people with mental disabilities have expanded over the years to accommodate issues of marriage, parenthood and sexual capacity, the terminologies have changed, but many of the underlying assumptions persist.

If our own sexual expressions and intimacies were subject to the scrutiny familiar to people with compromised decision-making capacity, we might be very willing to support a redistribution of advantage. We might experience outrage that our treasured human bonds were subject to unseemly prying, while acknowledging that there is possibly a case for 'advance decisions as to intimacy'. When the former Associate Justice Supreme Court of the United States, Sandra Day O'Connor, learned that her husband had entered into a relationship with another resident in his care facility – he had Alzheimer's – his wife's reported contentment at this new relationship was breath-taking and humane.[1] As the authors delve into the contexts that shape preferences, desires and the possibilities of law and social justice, an agenda for further action and reflection may be discerned. Primarily, we must take seriously the wishes and aspirations of people in relation to sexual intimacy. The stakes are high because those who appear bent on shoring up opposition to sexual expression deny our shared humanness. The bodily and emotional lives of people who require support in every aspect of their days are vulnerable to being rendered invisible. For example, the invasion of intimate bodily spaces in the cause of managing double incontinence cannot be solely constructed as a private concern. Perceptions of extreme difference in respect of those with more extensive support needs as compared to people with less conspicuous needs call out for explicit engagement and challenge.

Compounding these perceptions, we note that chronically soaring levels of vacancies and low pay within a dysfunctional social care market are not conducive to providing decent and humane support around sexual intimacy. As this book reveals, sustained and consistent reflection is important among researchers, professionals and families in creating the necessary conditions to enable people to articulate their aspirations for affiliation, friendships, relationships and sexual expression. Families and support staff may require assistance to enable their relatives and the people they support to express their desires and have their sexuality accorded respect. Law and policy are essential in meeting these demands for assistance and in negotiating the tensions these generate when implemented alongside duties to protect individuals from abuse and exploitation. In sum, the task of supporting people to live 'gloriously ordinary' lives, in line with the paradigm-shifting ethos of the United Nations Convention on the Rights of Persons with Disabilities, is an unignorable backdrop to the chapters in this volume. In confronting and teasing out the multiple and overlapping challenges generated by this task, this book offers a vital and impressive contribution to the literature.

1 https://www.nytimes.com/2023/12/05/opinion/sandra-day-oconnor-marriage.html (accessed 19 February 2024).

# Introduction

*Beverley Clough and Laura Pritchard-Jones*

Sexual and intimate relationships for anyone can be challenging, emotional and rewarding. People with intellectual or cognitive disabilities, however, have often been denied opportunities to develop such relationships, thanks to a historical legal framework that considered them to be 'defectives', 'monsters'[1] and in need of confinement (Sandland, 2013), and professional practice that has been – and, in many ways, arguably continues to be – considerably risk averse (Bartlett, 2010). More recent developments in the law, in part driven by the empowering ethos of the United Nations Convention on the Rights of Persons with Disabilities (UNCRPD), have been transformative. In England and Wales, the legal framework contained in the Mental Capacity Act 2005 (MCA) and associated case law has attempted to give a clearer steer on how to assess a person's capacity to make decisions about sexual relationships, as well as other types of decisions that may also be a feature of intimate relationships, such as contact with other individuals, and the use of social media and the internet. Within this legal framework, however, supporting people with decision making about intimate relationships remains complex, daunting and requires a balancing of many principles, including how best to promote a person's right to have sexual or intimate relationships, and the extent to which they should be protected from abusive or exploitative intimate relationships, or be prevented from possibly abusing others themselves.

In England and Wales, it is these ideas that recent developments in the case law have had to grapple with. In *A Local Authority v JB*[2] (*JB*), the court was faced with a situation involving a 36-year-old man who had a 'complex diagnosis' of autistic spectrum disorder and impaired cognition. He had

[1] Language such as 'defectives' and 'monsters' are not terms in use today and are rightly recognised as offensive and dehumanising. However, language such as this is used on occasions in this collection where historical legislation and literature are being discussed.

[2] [2019] EWCOP 39.

been living in a supported residential placement for the last five years, under close supervision which significantly curtailed his freedom to socialise with others. This close supervision was put in place purportedly to prevent him from behaving in sexually inappropriate ways towards women. As Roberts J put it in the Court of Protection judgment,

> The primary thrust of the evidence is that JB lacks the insight or ability to communicate appropriately with women to whom he is attracted. On occasions his advances have lacked appropriate social inhibition and, whilst he has never been charged with (let alone convicted of) any criminal offence, there is a concern that his behaviour, if unrestrained, may result in his exposure to the criminal justice system and risk to potentially vulnerable females.[3]

JB objected to these restrictions and, like many people, expressed his desire to have sex and find a girlfriend. Given the level of restrictions placed on him, JB's case raises profound questions about the law and how it can – and should – be used in situations like this; situations where most people would face no obstructions to such a fundamental aspect of human life. How should the law respond in these situations? Is it the role of law to pre-emptively intervene to prevent sexual relations, particularly where there is concern about risk, either for the individual or potential sexual partners? How does and should law enable, shape or curtail sexual relationships and intimacy in the context of mental capacity?

In December 2021, the Supreme Court delivered their judgment in this case and, with it, invited renewed engagement with the issues surrounding mental capacity to consent to sex. This was the first case involving the question of capacity to consent to sex to reach the Supreme Court, and thus provided an opportunity for the highest civil court in the UK to provide an authoritative steer on an issue that has vexed professionals and the judiciary for many years. As will be discussed later, the Supreme Court held that to be deemed to retain mental capacity to engage in sex, a person (P) must (among other things) understand that the other person must consent to that sexual activity and can withdraw that consent at any point. This was a significant step, going beyond the previous case law which, as will be seen later, focused primarily on more abstract and mechanistic aspects of sexual intercourse. In many ways, however, and as this edited collection shows, the case raises more questions than answers, and is by no means the end of the matter. This collection brings together academics, practitioners and third-sector organisations to reflect on how we got to this point, the

[3] *A Local Authority v JB* [2019] EWCOP 39, para 3.

conceptual and practical challenges posed by the legal developments, and where we go next.

## Emerging issues in law and practice

The Mental Capacity Act 2005 is central to practice among many professionals such as social workers, nurses, occupational therapists and medical practitioners. Issues arising under the Act are thus by no means simply doctrinal or academic ones, but often have very real implications for professionals and for the people they support through their professional roles. The assessment of mental capacity in the context of sexual and intimate decision making has become a perennially difficult issue for practitioners, driven in no small part by the ebbs and flows in the law's attempts to define the test for capacity for sex in recent times. The legislation outlines that mental capacity is assessed in a 'decision and time specific' way. In effect, people do not lack capacity in relation to all decisions in a global sense or all of the time. A person is deemed to lack mental capacity if they are unable to make a particular decision, at a particular time, due to an impairment of, or a disturbance in the functioning of, the mind or brain (s2(1)). Section 3 states that they are unable to make the decision if they are unable to understand the information relevant to it, to retain that information, to use or weigh it, or to communicate the decision. If an individual is deemed to lack mental capacity, then any decision made must be made in their best interests – outlined in section 4 – and this must, among other things, involve a consideration of what the person wants: their wishes, feelings, values and beliefs. However, the stakes are high in this area of decision making. If a person lacks capacity to make decisions about sex, then under section 27 of the Act no best interests decision can be made for them to have sex, and it would be a criminal offence under the Sexual Offences Act 2003 for anyone to have a sexual relationship with them. It is for this reason that there are legitimate concerns about proposals for advance consent to intimacy,[4] or substituted decision making[5] for sexual or intimate decisions; ideas discussed in later chapters in this collection. Such proposals could, under the current legal framework, be considered a licence to commit sexual offences against

[4] This proposal is one which would allow for people to make advance statements or declarations about intimacy or sexual decision making in the event that they – at some later date – lack capacity to make those decisions, such as in the event that they develop dementia.

[5] This is where another person would be authorised to make sexual or intimate decisions on behalf of another person who lacks capacity to make those decisions themselves. As already mentioned, this is currently expressly forbidden by section 27 of the Mental Capacity Act 2005.

a person who lacks mental capacity for that decision and would therefore also sit uncomfortably with section 27 of the MCA. Such a concern was highlighted in the recent case of *Local Authority A v ZZ*,[6] in which Burrows J noted that,

> For historical reasons, sex and marriage are decisions that the law dictates cannot be made on behalf of a person unable to make the decision for himself. If Peter lacks capacity to consent to sexual relations, no one, this Court included can make a best interests decision on his behalf. He is simply unable to have sex. The Local Authority will have to use their best efforts to ensure that he does not have sex. The same is true of marriage. This is because consent is simply a basic prerequisite for both sex and marriage, and substitute consent is seen as repugnant.[7]

It is clear, then, that the finely balanced nature of decisions in this area, the significant consequences of the capacity assessment resulting in potential over-criminalisation of disabled people and their partners, the difficulties of breaking down a complex and often highly personal interaction, as well as the fact that supporting adults with sexual and intimate relationships is about much more than just the MCA, pose several issues for law and practice.

On the one hand, it is undoubtedly the case that disabled adults have the right to sexual and intimate relationships; these should be promoted, fostered and supported. Such a right is enshrined legally not only in Article 8 of the European Convention on Human Rights, but also through the operation of the UNCRPD. As will be seen further in the later chapters in this edited collection, there is crucial importance in social work and healthcare professionals supporting disabled adults to have the relationships they want, and that social history tells us they have so long been denied. However, as many professionals will recount, there is also a tension here. Disabled adults, statistically, are at risk of sexual abuse (Hughes et al, 2012; Tomsa et al, 2021). In England, for example, between April 2022 and March 2023, 9,640 of all concluded section 42 enquiries involved an allegation of sexual abuse or sexual exploitation (NHS Digital, 2023). Moreover, Article 16 of the UNCRPD requires member states to put in place mechanisms by which disabled adults can be safeguarded from abuse or exploitation. The tension that therefore arises in this area – and as seen from the factual matrices behind much of the case law in this area (Lindsey, 2020) – is navigating the question as to how professionals should support sex lives among disabled adults, while

6 [2023] EWOP 61.

7 *Ibid.*, para 44.

also being conscious of the fact that some sexual relationships are abusive or exploitative. How can professionals balance their ethical obligations both to support and simultaneously to protect? Or, to put it another way, how can they be mindful of supporting the good relationships, while protecting from the bad? Perhaps at an even more basic level, what is – and who should decide what is – a good intimate relationship, as compared to a bad one?

## The relevant information

One of the biggest drivers for renewed engagement by the courts with issues around sex and capacity has been a desire to confront what should be considered relevant information under the MCA. The way in which information is used and framed in issues relating to sexual capacity is an issue that has emerged throughout much of the post-MCA case law, and often because it is seen to provide the dividing line between relationships that are abusive and those which are not. Information is crucial to any capacity assessment in this regard, as it is important to know what information is relevant to that decision for the purposes of section 3. As will be seen later, this has proven to be a tricky exercise in the capacity and sex case law in two ways: is consent relevant information, and what role does information about particular sexual partners play in this process?

One of the earliest cases in which the issue of capacity to consent to sex was considered was in the pre-MCA case of *X City Council v MB and others*,[8] a case concerned primarily with capacity to consent to marriage. Munby J, as he then was, heard arguments pertaining to consent to sex[9] as part of this, and began to reflect in the judgment on 'How then is one to assess whether someone has the capacity to consent to sexual relations, the ability to choose whether or not to engage in sexual activity?'[10] He went on to suggest,

> Does the person have sufficient knowledge and understanding of the nature and character – the sexual nature and character – of the act of sexual intercourse, and of the reasonably foreseeable consequences of sexual intercourse, have the capacity to choose whether or not to engage in it, the capacity to decide whether to give or withhold

8 [2006] EWHC 168 (Fam).

9 As will be seen later, the Court of Appeal and Supreme Court in *A Local Authority v JB* shifted the terminology away from 'consent to sex', and instead held that the question should be whether a person has capacity to 'engage in sex'. However, given that *X City Council v MB* pre-dates those decisions, this collection has left the contemporaneous language – consent to sex – in place.

10 *Ibid.*, para 68.

> consent to sexual intercourse (and, where relevant, to communicate their choice to their spouse)?[11]

The issue again came to be considered by Munby J in *Local Authority X v MM*[12] (*MM*). It is in this case that we begin to see the emergence of what was to become one of the core questions for the courts to grapple with in later cases: is capacity to make decisions about sexual relationships *act specific* or *person specific*? In effect – and in very pragmatic terms – when professionals are assessing a person's capacity to make decisions about sexual relationships, do they assess the person's ability to understand information just about sexual intercourse in the abstract, or about sex with a particular person? As this edited collection will show, this question has particular importance where there are concerns about sexual exploitation or abuse, and the Supreme Court's decision in *JB* has gone some way towards clarifying this. In *MM*, Munby J roundly supported an act-specific test, with the information relevant to the decision being framed in terms of the mechanics of the sexual activity, rather than the individual, or any possible sexual partners.[13]

This act-specific versus person-specific debate since took centre stage in the subsequent case law. Broadly, there was a concern that a person-specific test might entail significant encroachment on peoples' abilities to develop and maintain sexual relationships with partners of their choice. On the other hand, a more abstract act-specific approach has the potential to overlook and entrench the controlling influence that particular individuals might have on a person whose capacity is in question. In effect, as Lindsey has highlighted, the law here has the potential to both over and under protect (Lindsey, 2020).

As Baroness Hale (as she then was) put it in the criminal law context, 'it is difficult to think of an activity which is more person- and situation-specific than sexual relations'.[14] The act-specific approach in the civil case law – both in its potentially artificial focus on the mechanics and medical issues involved in sex, as well as its abstractedness – tended to overlook this. Despite this, the act-specific approach was further reiterated in the civil case law on capacity to consent to sex under the MCA, driven in some ways by a concern with the pragmatic issue that should someone be deemed to lack capacity, they would effectively have to be prevented from having sexual relationships until they had attained this capacity. There was a clear and openly stated concern, then, to set a 'low threshold' so as not to intrude on sexual autonomy, as reiterated in the Court of Appeal in *IM v LM*;[15] however, concerns were

[11] *Ibid.*, para 84.

[12] [2007] EWHC 2003 (Fam).

[13] *Ibid.*, para 86.

[14] *R v Cooper* [2009] UKHL 42, para 27.

[15] [2014] EWCA Civ 37.

raised as to whether such an approach in fact 'asked the right questions' (Clough, 2014), or potentially left abusive partners and situations to persist outside of the realm of mental capacity law.

In response to this early case law, academic literature engaged with ideas of vulnerability in order to analyse the ways that mental capacity law was responding to these questions of sexual abuse and sexual autonomy (Clough, 2014; Herring and Wall, 2015). Much of this built on the work of Martha Fineman and an approach to vulnerability which challenged ideas of particular groups (such as disabled people, older people, women, children) being vulnerable, and instead positioned vulnerability as a universal human condition, arguing for the state to be responsive to this in order to foster resilience (Fineman, 2010). Alongside other feminist literatures, such as that on relational autonomy and care theory (Nedelsky, 2012; Mackenzie, 2014), these critiques drew attention the problematic ideal of autonomy which underpinned the case law here, and which often resulted in the obscuring of structural and social sources of harm by hinging intervention on an assessment of an individual's mental capacity in an all-or-nothing way. This approach resonated in many ways with debates as to the social model of disability versus an individual or medical model, with the social model urging a focus on structural and societal causes of harm, rather than shifting the focus to individuals and individualising legal and state responses (Clough, 2017). These themes of vulnerability and the social model of disability will be returned to throughout the collection, and are particularly prominent in Squires and Morgan (Chapter 5), and Hollmotz's (Chapter 7) chapters.

Despite the authoritative statement provided by *IM v LM*, there continued to be judicial and academic disquiet as to the application of the test in practice and the implications of it for judicial reasoning.[16] The most recent authoritative proclamations on this issue came in December 2021, when the Supreme Court handed down judgment in *A Local Authority v JB*.[17] In *JB*, the issue was posed differently. Unlike previous cases, which centred on the information required to be understood in order to *consent* to sex, both the Court of Appeal and Supreme Court held that the issue was about *engaging* in sex. To put it differently, mental capacity and sex is not concerned whether the person has capacity to *consent* to sex, but to *engage* in sexual relationships. As Baker LJ put it in the Court of Appeal judgment, 'giving consent to sexual relations is only part of the decision-making process. The fundamental decision is whether to engage in sexual relations'.[18] Moreover, the Supreme Court also held that relevant information under section 3 of

[16] See, for example the judgment of Cobb J in *Derbyshire CC v AC* [2014] EWCOP 38.

[17] [2021] UKSC 52.

[18] [2020] EWCA Civ 275, para 92.

the Mental Capacity Act 2005 when it comes to issues about sex involves an understanding that the other person engaged in sexual activity must be able to, and does in fact, from their words and conduct, consent to such activity before, and throughout.

This shift in emphasis moves away from seeing people with disabilities as passive actors in sexual encounters, instead positioning them as actively engaging in, and initiators of, a sexual relationship. In this regard, this aspect of the judgment has been welcomed for centralising the importance of consent in sexual relationships (Lindsey and Harding, 2021; Subhi, 2021). In some ways this might be seen as a natural development of the case law and something which is almost inevitable once the focus shifts from 'consent to' to 'engaging in', bringing with it a recognition of interpersonal dynamics. However, this does raise a number of critical issues, as will be discussed further later in this chapter and throughout the collection. The case has brought the civil and criminal law into closer alignment in relation to capacity to consent to sex, deeming that information relevant to the decision (in relation to which capacity is assessed) includes knowledge that the other person must be consenting and does indeed consent. As Baker LJ put it,

> The Mental Capacity Act and the Court of Protection do not exist in a vacuum. They are part of a wider system of law and justice. Sexual relations between two people can only take place with the full and ongoing consent of both parties. This principle has acquired greater recognition in recent years within society at large and within the justice system. The greater recognition has occurred principally in the criminal and family courts, but it must extend across the whole justice system.[19]

We might question whether the recognition of relationality and attention to the social and interpersonal context evident here is a wholly positive step. Questions as to the ability of the mental capacity framework to adequately attend to the complexities of interpersonal relations and intimacy necessarily come to the fore. This is particularly important when we consider the ways that the boundaries of civil and criminal law have become blurred by the recent case law, something which is reflected on by Lindsey and Brennan (Chapter 3) in their chapter in this collection.

A further issue raised by this shift from 'consent to' to 'engaging in' sexual relations is the scope that this has for significant interferences in the lives of people with intellectual disabilities and cognitive impairments. The possibility of discrimination here was robustly dismissed by Lord Stephens in *JB*, stating that,

[19] *A Local Authority v JB* [2020] EWCA Civ 735, para 6.

> Mr McKendrick also submitted that sexual activity, and decisions about engaging in sexual relations for a person of full capacity, are largely visceral rather than cerebral, owing more to instinct and emotion than to analysis. On this basis he argued that to include as part of the information relevant to the decision the fact that the other person must have the capacity to consent to the sexual activity and must in fact consent before and throughout the sexual activity imposes a discriminatory cerebral analysis on the potentially incapacitous. I reject that submission. As the Court of Appeal observed, at para 96, 'amongst the matters which *every person* engaging in sexual relations must think about is whether the other person is consenting' (emphasis added). If that is properly viewed as cerebral or as involving a degree of analysis, a decision to engage in sexual relations is necessarily cerebral or analytical to that extent.[20]

Here, the suggestion that *everyone* engaging with sexual relations must think about whether the other is consenting is seen to prevent any discriminatory consequences of the judgment. However, the ways that the law is utilised in day-to-day practice may result in discriminatory outcomes. The MCA is explicit in applying only to individuals with 'an impairment or disorder in the functioning of the mind or brain', and so those falling outside of this will be unlikely to be subject to the assessment of their capacity to 'engage' in sexual relations in this way. Moreover, the legal landscape in this area has the potential to artificially 'silo' decisions in a manner that is not reflective of the ways that many people's decisions are usually made (Pritchard-Jones, 2021). For example, a person may retain capacity to engage in sex with a person, but simultaneously not to have contact with them; an issue that arose in *A Local Authority v AW*.[21]

In terms of the previous debates as to whether capacity in this area is act or person specific, the decision of the Supreme Court suggested that when there is no identifiable partner, it must be act specific and generic. However, the Court did go on to say that there may be circumstances where person-specific information is relevant to the decision, particularly where the person is known, as such information would be 'relevant' for the purposes of section 3. In effect, the Supreme Court attempted to take the matter back to the very basics of the MCA: the question to be asked is 'what is the matter to be decided here?' While this enables some flexibility into the legal approach and its translation into practice by frontline professionals tasked with implementing it, this may invite uncertainty in the application of the

[20] *A Local Authority v JB* [2021] UKSC 52, para 96, emphasis in original.

[21] [2020] EWCOP 24.

assessment in practice, creating difficulties for different professionals and carers, as well as opening up space for more normative moral judgements. Moreover, the ability to take this into consideration provides a system whereby mental capacity assessments in this area can acknowledge, for example, abusive relationships, where either it is the person whose capacity is in question who is being or has been abused,[22] or they are at risk of sexually abusing another person (as was the case in *JB*). In doing this, it necessarily therefore requires a better understanding among professionals implementing the Act as to what an abusive sexual relationship, or sexual exploitation, looks like in practice.

The ability of the Mental Capacity Act 2005 to encompass the protection of others as part of assessing capacity is not without problems, but, as Lord Stephens outlined in the Supreme Court decision,

> The information relevant to the decision includes information about the 'reasonably foreseeable consequences' of a decision, or of failing to make a decision: section 3(4). These consequences are not limited to the 'reasonably foreseeable consequences' for P, but can extend to consequences for others. This again illustrates that the information relevant to the decision must be identified within the factual context of each case. In this case there are reasonably foreseeable consequences for JB of a decision to engage in sexual relations, such as imprisonment for sexual assault or rape if the other person does not consent. There are also reasonably foreseeable harmful consequences to persons whom JB might sexually assault or rape.[23]

This raises significant issues as to the underpinning rationale of mental capacity legislation, from one purportedly focused on balancing the empowerment and protection of the person who may lack capacity, to one which encompasses the protection of others in society, and one that it appears not all judges are comfortable with. As one Court of Protection judge recently noted, 'although the issue of the consent of others to sexual relations has entered the list of relevant information, the Court of Protection must not allow the desire to protect others unduly to influence a clear-eyed assessment of P's capacity'.[24] Perhaps by way of explanation as to why

22 See, for example: *Hull City Council v KF* [2022] EWCOP 33; *Leicester City Council v MPZ* [2019] EWCOP 64.

23 *A Local Authority v JB* [2021] UKSC 52, para 73.

24 *PN v Durham County Council and others* [2023] EWCOP 44, para 11. 'P' is a letter often used in case law and literature to denote the person who may or may not lack capacity under the MCA. This point has been further reiterated in *A Local Authority v ZZ* [2023] EWCOP 61, para 49, Per Burrows J.

some may be uncomfortable with this protection imperative, it is worth reiterating the implications of a finding of incapacity here; the individual involved will in effect be prevented from having sex, often through intense supervision of their day-to-day lives and with significant restrictions on their liberty. Questions as to the legitimacy of the civil law effectively imposing restrictions on liberty that are otherwise the preserve of the criminal law – and without the formal processes that the criminal law contains – require critical consideration. Moreover, the case law raises important considerations for how the various professionals and informal carers might make these assessments of 'risk' on a day-to-day basis, given the significance of the consequences which will flow from the capacity assessment. It is to some of these questions that this edited collection turns.

## Outline of structure and chapters

The issues in this area are often complex legally, practically and ethically. This edited collection draws on perspectives from a range of disciplines in order to explore some of these issues. Part I is focused on some of the complex legal questions that have arisen historically, and contemporaneously. In Chapter 1 Sandland explores the historical dimensions to legal regulation of sexuality and intimacy for people with disabilities and demonstrates how normative social and psychological ideas about cognitive impairments fed into these legal developments. In this regard, the chapter provides the groundwork for exploring some of the more contemporaneous facets to legal regulation and professional practice that ensue in the subsequent chapters. In doing so, it also highlights many of the societal assumptions that underpinned the control of this aspect of the lives of people with disabilities for so many years and provides a benchmark for assessing whether – notwithstanding the progress made under the Mental Capacity Act and practice in recent years – such societal assumptions have, indeed, entirely dissipated. Ruck Keene, Enefer and Cusack's Chapter 2 then explores in further detail some of the issues that have arisen under the Supreme Court judgment in *JB*. More specifically, they consider the fundamental clash that often arises between promoting the rights of people with disabilities to have sexual lives, and the need for consent to be true consent. Building on the previous discussions, in Chapter 3 Lindsey and Brennan explore in more detail the boundaries between the civil and criminal law in this area, and the extent to which such legal domains can, or should, be considered as silos, or whether a hybrid approach might be more beneficial. In Chapter 4, the concluding chapter in Part I, Bates offers reflections on the implications of these debates in practice for those individuals and organisations working to support adults with disabilities to have sexual relationships while also navigating the complexities of consent in practice.

Part II focuses in more detail on a wider array of challenges in practice for those working to support adults, as well as what could – or should – be done from a professional perspective moving forward. Much has been written in recent years on the importance of taking a person-centred approach to support – and particularly health and social work practice – with disabled people. The particular strengths of these later chapters lie in their ability to allow us to question whether the law in its current guise is adequately equipped to allow for such a person-centred approach, or is too restrictive, or focused on disability at the expense of sexual violence. In Chapter 5 Squires and Morgan continue this exploration through an analysis of the extent to which such a person-centred approach can be translated into social work practice with disabled people through an improvement in legal, emotional, relational and ethical literacies. Sorinmade and Peisah's chapter (Chapter 6) focuses on the rights of people living with dementia to sexual and intimate lives from a psychiatric perspective. Dementia and the impact this has on a person's memories can present particularly complex ethical questions, which often go undiscussed. Moreover, many adults with dementia may live in care homes, which creates further barriers to sexual relationships. Sorinmade and Peisah argue that more can and should be done to promote this fundamental right among people living with dementia, which requires a shift away from a medical view of the condition, towards one which situates it within its social context, but may also have profound questions for the extent to which the law allows for such an approach. In Chapter 7 Hollomotz draws on findings of qualitative research to explore the extent to which forces beyond *mental* incapacity are also at play here. In particular, she argues that a focus on social incapacities – social forces around disabled adults – exacerbate their experience of interpersonal violence. This raises legitimate questions as to whether the law – in its almost exclusive focus on disturbances in the functioning of the mind or brain – masks some of these broader forces at play in situations where women are subjected to sexual violence; forces such as sexism, disablism and the internalisation of blame. In Chapter 8 Currie and Allen draw on their significant experience as a social worker, Deprivation of Liberty Safeguards expert, and Best Interests Assessor (Currie) and as a barrister and academic (Allen), to reflect on the issues raised in these later chapters and the extent to which the arguments raised might have real implications for practitioners navigating this complex, ethically fraught and challenging domain.

## References

Bartlett, P. (2010) 'Sex, dementia, capacity and care homes', *Liverpool Law Review*, 31(2), 137–154.

Clough, B. (2014) 'Vulnerability and capacity to consent to sex – asking the right questions?' *Child & Family Law Quarterly*, 26, 371–397.

Clough, B. (2017) 'Disability and vulnerability: challenging the capacity/ incapacity binary', *Social Policy and Society*, 16(3), 469–481.

Fineman, M. (2010) 'The vulnerable subject and the responsive state', *Emory Law Journal*, 30, 251–275.

Herring, J. and Wall, J. (2015) 'Autonomy, capacity and vulnerable adults: filling the gaps in the Mental Capacity Act', *Legal Studies*, 35, 698–719.

Hughes, K., Bellis, M.A., Jones, L., Wood., S., Bates, G., Eckley, L., McCoy, E., Mikton, C., Shakespeare, T. and Officer, A. (2012) 'Prevalence and risk of violence against adults with disabilities: a systematic review and meta-analysis of observational studies', *The Lancet*, 379(9826), 1621–1629.

Lindsey, J. (2020) 'Protecting vulnerable adults from abuse: under-protection and over-protection in adult safeguarding and mental capacity law', *Child and Family Law Quarterly*, 32, 157–175.

Lindsey, J. and Harding, R. (2021) 'Capabilities, capacity, and consent: sexual intimacy in the Court of Protection', *Journal of Law and Society*, 48(1), 60–83.

Mackenzie, C. (2014) 'The importance of relational autonomy and capabilities for an ethics of vulnerability', in C. Mackenzie, W. Rogers and S. Dodds (eds), *Vulnerability: New essays in ethics and feminist philosophy*. Oxford: Oxford University Press, pp 33–59.

Nedelsky, J. (2012) *Laws relations: A relational theory of self, autonomy and the law.* Oxford: Oxford University Press.

NHS Digital. (2023) *Safeguarding Adults, England, 2022–23*. Available at: https://digital.nhs.uk/data-and-information/publications/statistical/safeguarding-adults/2022-23 (Accessed 11 May 2024).

Pritchard-Jones, L. (2021) '*A Local Authority v JB* [2020] EWCA Civ 735 and *A Local Authority v AW* [2020] EWCOP 24: rethinking sexual capacity?', *Medical Law Review*, 29(1), 143–156.

Sandland, R. (2013) 'Sex and capacity: the management of monsters?', *Modern Law Review*, 76(6), 981–1009.

Subhi, E. (2021) 'A Local Authority v JB [2020] EWCA Civ 735; [2019] EWCOP 39', *Feminist Legal Studies*, 29, 267–276.

Tomsa, R., Gugtu, S., Cojocaru, D., Gutiérrez-Bermejo, B., Flores, N. and Jenaro, C. (2021) 'Prevalence of sexual abuse in adults with intellectual disability: systematic review and meta-analysis.' *International Journal of Environmental Research and Public Health,* 18(4), 1980–1997.

PART I

# Legal Developments

1

# Historical Perspectives on Law, Sexual Intimacy and Capacity

*Ralph Sandland*

## Introduction

In this chapter the principal aim is to analyse the law around sex and capacity which was repealed and replaced by the Sexual Offences Act 2003 and Mental Capacity Act 2005. This law is to be found in a spasmodic trail of criminal case law, punctuated and undermined from the late 19th century onwards by a statutory embargo on sexual activity involving, initially, 'idiots' and 'imbeciles' and, later, (some) 'mental defectives'.[1] Initially, this embargo extended only to females and only to sexual intercourse, but it was extended in both respects by legislation in the second half of the 20th century. I will argue that this historical analysis suggests that the legacy inherited by the modern law involved more than the need to strike an appropriate balance between protection and sexual autonomy, which was the main preoccupation of the Law Commission (1995, para. 5.13) and Parliament[2] at the time of the

1 This is the terminology of the time, and was used by psychiatrists and other medical professionals, politicians and the general public, as well as being found in legislation, such as the Idiots Act 1885 and the Mental Deficiency Act 1913, which defines these terms for legal purposes in section 1. Much of this language was replaced in legislation in the latter half of the 20th century (although with language which to modern eyes is equally problematic), but the term 'defective', as discussed later in the chapter, was not finally removed from the law until 2003. In the interests of historical and legal accuracy, this chapter will use the language current at the time of the law it discusses. This should not in any way be taken to imply, however, that this language is acceptable to the modern reader, or indeed, the modern author.

2 See, for example, Lord Falconer, then Lord Chancellor, opening the second reading debate on the Sexual Offences Bill in the House of Lords, 13 February 2002, Hansard (2002)

2003 Act. The law as it stood at the start of the 21st century was patchy at best in terms of substantive content, but what is equally if not more striking about this history is that it reflected systematic discrimination against persons with mental disabilities of such depth that the very humanity of persons so categorised was thereby put into question.

## The criminal law on sex and capacity, 1845–85

The law finally replaced in 2003 begins in the mid-19th century, with a slight revision of the common law definition of rape. The law at the time (and indeed until 1976)[3] required the presence of force and resistance before a court would find that a rape had occurred. This situation was modified in *R v William Camplin*,[4] and it is this modification which marks the beginning of a concern with capacity issues. Camplin was convicted for the rape of a girl of 13, but the decision was reserved by the trial judge, Parke B, for a point of law to be decided by the Court for Crown Cases Reserved (which heard appeals on points of law at this time). The argument of counsel for the defendant was that, as there had been no actual or threatened force and no resistance, no rape had occurred. Camplin had given the girl alcohol and had intercourse with her when she was insensible with drink. His evidence was that he gave her alcohol to free up her inhibitions but not for the purpose of rendering her insensible.

The Court for Crown Cases Reserved upheld the conviction, taking the view that where there had been some 'fraud' or deception by which the victim had been tricked or manipulated into a situation which obviated the need for force and precluded the possibility of resistance, any subsequent sexual intercourse constituted rape. In the report of the case at (1845) 1 Denison 89 at 91, reference was made to a summary by Parke B of the views of the appellate judges in favour of upholding the conviction, in which it is stated that 'several thought that the crime of rape is committed by violating a woman when she is in a state of insensibility, and has no power over her will, *whether such state is caused by the man or not*, the accused knowing that she is in that state' (emphasis added). While it would not, strictly speaking, be correct to say that the significance of *Camplin* is that the presence of force

[HL] volume 644, column 774: 'Existing legislation has offered inadequate redress when [people with a mental disorder or learning disability] are sexually abused. It is essential the Bill remedies this, while recognising the rights of people with disabilities to a full life, including a sexual life.'

3 Section 1(1) Sexual Offences (Amendment) Act 1976 inserted a consent-based definition into section 1 Sexual Offences Act 1956.

4 (1845) I Cox Criminal Cases 220, (1845) 1 Denison 89. Neither source contains a full verbatim report and each contains text not present in the other.

and physical resistance is demoted from being a constituent of the actus reus[5] to being evidence that the intercourse occurred without the consent of the victim, the decision did move the issue of consent closer to centre stage. There was, as Smith and Hogan (1988, p 433) put it in their textbook on crime, 'a subtle change of emphasis' in the law with this case.

In the course of argument in *Camplin*, Lord Denman observed that 'A question also arose, in the case of a female idiot, whether the absence of and the impossibility of consent would not be sufficient? but I believe it was not decided'.[6] At that time, there was no clear legal definition of an 'idiot', and the term was often used interchangeably with 'imbecile', but in 1820 the French alienist Esquirol had developed a typology of idiocy and imbecility that was to prove increasingly influential throughout the 19th century. According to Esquirol (1845, p 470), there are two degrees of imbecility and three of idiocy. Imbeciles have some intellectual capacity, indicated by their level of articulacy: 'In the first degree of imbecility, speech is free and easy. In the second, it is less easy, and the vocabulary is more circumscribed', whereas 'In the first degree of idiocy, properly so called, the idiot uses merely words and short phrases. Idiots of the second degree, articulate only monosyllables, or certain cries'. In either case, such idiots 'have a very small number of limited ideas, beside their passions for the supply of instinctive wants … Reason does not control their actions; which are few, and repeated, either from habit or the force of imitation' (Esquirol, 1845, p 448). There are 'merely the rudiments of intelligence, and instinct controls all the faculties' (Esquirol, 1845, p 454). Idiots of the third, and lowest, degree are not merely intellectually subhuman: 'They are below the brute; for animals possess the instinct for self-preservation and

---

5 The 'actus reus' of a crime is the criminal act. In 1845, the actus reus of rape was an act of sexual intercourse by force and in the face of resistance from the victim. These days, the actus reus of rape is an act of sexual intercourse without the consent of the other person, and the presence or absence of force and resistance is no longer relevant. Actus reus is contrasted with 'mens rea', which is the state of mind the offender must be shown to have. For a conviction, it must, depending on the offence, be shown that the accused person intended to do what they did, or that they were reckless as to the consequences of their actions. For a conviction for rape these days, for example, it must be shown that the accused person intended to have sexual intercourse knowing that this was without the consent of their victim, or was reckless (did not care) as to whether or not there was consent.

6 I Cox Criminal Cases 220 at 221. Unfortunately I have been unable to locate this case. It may be *R v Samuel Street*, although from a much earlier date, 27 August 1725. Here, a man was indicted for the rape of a female idiot but acquitted by a jury for want of evidence, and instead he was to be tried for a misdemeanour (presumably assault), but there is no record of the final outcome. Available at https://www.oldbaileyonline. (All references in this chapter from this source were last accessed 19 June 2023.)

reproduction. Idiots do not possess this instinct, and have no sense of their existence' (Esquirol, 1845, p 467).

The decision in *Camplin* as explained by Parke B certainly seemed to indicate that a female idiot of whatever degree, as permanently insensible and unable to make a reasoned decision, could be the victim of a rape even where no force was used. The issue arose in the following year, in *R v Ryan*.[7] Ryan was indicted for the rape of a female idiot who, 'when asked questions in the witness-box, was evidently unconscious of their purport, and not in a condition to understand right from wrong'. This seems fairly clearly to indicate that she could not give or refuse consent as a matter of reason or conscious decision. The judge, Platt B, nonetheless sought from her father information about her character, who gave evidence, which the judge accepted, that his daughter had habits of 'decency and propriety'. The implication of this seems to be that she would not have consented to intercourse, seen at the time to be only marginally decent and proper even within marriage, and not at all outside of marriage. But Platt B nonetheless told the jury that

> The question is, did the connection take place with her consent? It seems that she was in a condition incapable of judging, and it is important to consider whether a young person, in such a state of incapacity, was likely to consent to the embraces of this man; because if her habits, however irresponsible she might be, were loose and indecent, there might be a probability of such consent being given and a jury might not find it safe to conclude that she was not a willing party. But here the presumption is, that the young woman would not have consented.

We can see the influence of the ideas articulated by Esquirol in this statement. In terms of conscious decision making, the question – the 'capacity question', we would say these days – is whether the person in question is 'incapable of judging'.

Although low on substantive content, here is the start of a test for capacity, at least in the context of the crime of rape, and there seems to be little doubt that on this measure the complainant lacked capacity to consent. But, as can be seen, there is also the possibility of consent as the manifestation of her 'habits': that is, as became clear in later case law, an instinctive consent. So this case, following *Camplin* in that it focused on the presence or absence of consent rather than of force, also set up a twin-track mechanism for

---

7 II Cox C.C. (1846–1848) 115. The report occupies only this one page, and all subsequent quotes from the case are found there.

detecting the presence or absence of consent: one based on reason and one based on instinct (and, as will be seen in later chapters, this distinction continues to have purchase today: the Law Commission report (2000: para. 4.59), on which the modern law is based, recognised a distinction between the 'cerebral' and the 'visceral', as does subsequent caselaw).[8]

In cases following *Ryan*, it became established that where there was no consent either reasoned or instinctive, rape was the appropriate charge. The defendant was convicted of rape on this basis in *R v Richard Fletcher.*[9] In this case a girl of 13, Jane Jones, described as 'an idiot girl' by counsel for the appellant and 'of imbecile mind', 'weak intellect', 'incapable of distinguishing right from wrong' and lacking 'sufficient intelligence to be sworn' to act as a witness by Hill J, the trial judge, at 131, had a sexual encounter with the defendant. Although Jane did not resist, she later protested that Fletcher had hurt her. Fletcher was convicted on the basis that he had carnal knowledge of Jane by force and without her consent, the jury being of the opinion that she was 'incapable of giving consent, or of exercising any judgment on the matter', this being the test explained to them by Hill J at 132.

Fletcher appealed on the basis that the law was said to require that the sexual intercourse had been against the will of the complainant, rather than without her consent. This argument was rejected. The Court of Criminal Appeal, citing *Ryan*, held at 134 that the test was 'without her consent' rather than 'against her will': an easier test for the prosecution to satisfy, as a conviction was appropriate where there had been no positive acquiescence, whereas to demonstrate that the sexual encounter was against the will of the complainant entails showing in addition that the complainant offered some resistance. On this basis, the court decided that the conviction should stand because there was no evidence either of reasoned consent or of the operation of animal instincts, but 'rather to the contrary' in the view of Lord Campbell, who also explained at 134 that, compared to *Camplin*, 'the only difference being in this case that pointed out, that here the prosecutrix[10] was not capable of giving consent. But then the prisoner knew her condition at the time.' Here, the court endorsed the suggestion which had been mooted in *Camplin* (see earlier); that it did not matter whether or not the defendant caused the victim's lack of capacity. From that point on, it was enough for a conviction to show that the defendant knew that his victim was not in a position to give consent. Although this is not really 'fraud', as

[8] See, for example, *R v C* [2009] UKHL 42 per Baroness Hale at para 15; *A Local Authority v H* [2012] EWHC 49 (COP); and most recently, *A Local Authority v JB* [2021] UKSC 52: see chapters by Lindsey and Brennan (Chapter 3), and Ruck Keene, Enefer, and Cusack (Chapter 2) in this volume.

[9] (1859) VIII Cox C.C. 131.

[10] This is an old-fashioned term for a female complainant or victim.

the defendant had not misled or tricked his victim into a position where she lacked capacity, his behaviour was equally morally reprehensible and therefore equally criminally culpable.

There is, however, little discussion here of the appropriate test for capacity to consent to sexual relations, apart from the statement of Hill J to the jury that it should convict if of the view that intercourse had taken place and Jane was 'incapable of giving consent, or of exercising any judgment on the matter'. A later case in which a conviction for the rape of an 'apparent idiot' was upheld on appeal because there had, the victim's idiocy (or most probably, imbecility, in Esquirol's terms) notwithstanding, been a valid refusal to consent, unfortunately did not discuss the test for capacity at all.[11] Hill J's form of words was applied in subsequent cases with little elaboration: in *R v Robert Barratt*,[12] the question, answered affirmatively by Kelly CB at 500 with the agreement of the rest of the court, was whether the complainant 'was in such a state of idiotcy as to be incapable of expressing either consent or dissent', resulting in a conviction for rape, upheld on appeal. By the mid-1870s, then, a test for capacity to consent to sexual relations was in existence, but in a very basic form, lacking any real substantive content.

Meanwhile, in cases where there was no reasoned consent but animal instincts were found to have been or to possibly have been aroused, defendants were either found not guilty by a jury (as in *R v Israel* (1857))[13] or had a conviction for rape overturned on appeal (as in *R v Charles Fletcher*).[14] In *Charles Fletcher*, Fletcher was convicted for the rape of a 16-year-old idiot girl,[15] Fanny Churchill, despite his claim that Fanny had given consent, and despite the medical evidence, at 248, that Fanny '[a]lthough only sixteen years old ... was a fully developed woman; and that strong animal instincts might exist, notwithstanding her imbecile condition'. Following conviction, the trial judge, Keating J, reserved the case as there was, at 249, 'no evidence against the prisoner, except the fact of connection and the imbecile state of the girl'. The Court of Criminal Appeal quashed Fletcher's conviction.

---

11 See *R v Pressy* from December 1867, XI Cox C.C. (1868–1870) 635.

12 (1873) XII Cox C.C. (1871–1874) 498.

13 This case was not reported in the law reports but can be found in the Proceedings of the Old Bailey, third session, 1856–57, 259, available at Old Bailey Proceedings Online www.oldbaileyonline.org. In *R v Richard Fletcher* in 1859, Wiles J, apparently referring to *Israel*, described the prosecutrix in that case as having 'animal instincts of a strong tendency': *Fletcher* (1859) VIII Cox C.C. 131 at p 134.

14 (1866) X Cox C.C. (1864–1867) 248.

15 As in the previous *Fletcher* case, there is slippage between the terms 'idiot' and 'imbecile' here. In his statement of the case reserved for decision by the Court of Criminal Appeal the trial judge, Keating J, referred to Fanny as 'an idiot girl' and as being of 'imbecile condition' (X Cox C.C. (1864–1867) 248, 248) and as being in 'an imbecile state' (249); Pollock CB refers to Fanny as being an 'idiot' on three occasions in his judgment (249).

Giving judgment, Pollock CB held, at 249, that 'we are all of the opinion that some evidence of that allegation [of rape] as a fact ought to be given before a conviction can be obtained'. In other words, here again, although there was no evidence of reasoned consent, the possibility of instinctive consent rendered the conviction unsatisfactory. In this period from the 1840s to the 1870s, then, the law had begun to recognise that the issue was more about consent and capacity than whether physical force had been used, but it had also, problematically, recognised that consent could be given on an 'instinctive' basis.

## The statutory embargo on sexual relations with an idiot, imbecile or mental defective, 1885–2003

Parliament addressed the decision in *Charles Fletcher*, described by Mead and Bodkin (1885, p 49) as 'a defect in the law',[16] 20 years later in the form of section 5(2) of the Criminal Law Amendment Act 1885. This provision marked the start of a statutory embargo, continued and developed by later legislation, which survived into the 21st century, rendering the issue of capacity to consent irrelevant for significant numbers of people. In this section I trace that statutory history.

Section 5(2) of the 1885 Act made it an offence[17] for any person who

> (2) Unlawfully and carnally knows,[18] or attempts to have unlawful carnal knowledge of any female idiot or imbecile woman or girl, under circumstances which do not amount to rape, but which prove that the offender knew at the time of the commission of the offence that the woman or girl was an idiot or imbecile …

Despite providing legal protection to idiot and imbecile women and girls, this provision endorsed the notion of instinctive consent, accepting that its presence meant that the crime of rape could not be made out. Esquirol's explanation of idiocy is thereby endorsed (and explicitly so by Mead and Bodkin, 1885, pp 47–8), but only imprecisely, because the section applies to all idiot or imbecile women, whether or not actually possessing capacity to give or refuse a non-instinctive consent. The effect was to remove the

[16] The decision also received harsh criticism from the Irish Court for Crown Cases Reserved in *R v Dee* (1884) 15 Cox CC 579.

[17] But only a misdemeanour, with a maximum sentence of two years' imprisonment, with or without hard labour.

[18] Defined by section 63 Offences Against the Person Act 1861 to require 'Proof of Penetration only'.

right to a sexual life from at least some, and perhaps many, women who were in fact able to make their own decisions in this regard.

In subsequent years, the core concept of idiot/imbecile was extended and developed further, to capture also the newly created categories of the 'feeble-minded' and the 'morally imbecile' by and through the discourse leading to the Mental Deficiency Act 1913 (hereafter MDA) (see Thomson, 1998; Jackson, 2000; Sandland, 2013). Section 1 MDA, which defined these four categories as subsets of the general category of the 'mentally defective', essentially endorsed Esquirol's understandings of idiots – 'persons so deeply defective in mind from birth or from an early age as to be unable to guard themselves against common physical dangers' – and imbeciles – characterised by mental defectiveness 'not amounting to idiocy, yet so pronounced that they are incapable of managing themselves or their affairs'. The 'feeble-minded' exhibited 'mental defectiveness not amounting to imbecility, yet so pronounced that they require care, supervision, and control for their own protection or for the protection of others'. Finally, 'moral imbeciles' were defined as 'persons who from an early age display some permanent mental defect coupled with strong vicious or criminal propensities on which punishment has had little or no deterrent effect', and are closer to modern concepts of personality disorder than to learning disabilities.

Section 56(1)(a) of the MDA contained a new offence, to sit alongside section 5(2) of the 1885 Act, which continued in force, committed by any person

(a) who unlawfully and carnally knows, or attempts to have unlawful carnal knowledge of, any [mentally defective] woman or girl under care or treatment in an Institution or Certified House or Approved Home, or whilst placed out on licence therefrom or under guardianship under this Act.

Such a person was, however, provided by section 56(1)(a) with a defence, if able to prove 'that he did not know, and had no reason to suspect, that the woman or girl was a defective.'[19] This stacks the odds more sharply against an accused person as compared to the offence under section 5(2) of the 1885 Act, because under that provision it was for the Crown to prove that the offender knew at the time of the commission of the offence that the woman or girl was an idiot or imbecile, which apparently caused problems in securing convictions (Wormald and Wormald, 1913, p 83), whereas under section

[19] Section 56(1) created further offences, concerned to prohibit the exploitation of a defective woman through her prostitution, or abduction out of the possession of 'her parent or any other person having the lawful care or charge of her' for purposes of sexual exploitation.

56(1)(a) of the MDA it was for the offender to prove that he did not know, and had no reason to suspect, that the woman or girl was a defective. This is made more hazardous still for the offender, because although idiocy or imbecility might fairly readily be detected, feeble-mindedness and, especially, moral imbecility, were less easy to detect (Wormald and Wormald, 1913, p 10). However, as the offence under section 56(1)(a) of the MDA was committed only in respect of sexual intercourse with a mentally defective woman who was subject to some degree of control or supervision under that Act, the question perhaps was whether the defendant knew that the MDA was in play in respect of the woman in question, as much as whether he knew that she was a mental defective.

Beyond the technical legal questions, it is important to appreciate that the underlying basis of the offence in the MDA was not the same as that in the 1885 Act. The latter, if problematic because of its limited reach and its acceptance of the 'animal instincts' doctrine, was nonetheless concerned primarily to protect the vulnerable and punish the morally repugnant exploitation by men of female idiots and imbeciles. The MDA, by contrast, put that protectionist impulse in tension with a fear of the mentally defective, which was articulated as a moral panic about the 'disastrous consequences' for society and civilisation in general of the feeble-minded in particular 'being allowed to repeat their type … increasing the ranks of the degenerate and wastrel classes' (Wormald and Wormald, 1913, p 6) and the MDA was concerned with protecting society at large from the mentally defective as a class, as much as with providing care and protection to mentally defective individuals. This panic was mired in eugenic thinking, albeit that in the version that was finally enacted in 1913, the worst excesses of eugenics-based thinking, and provision for the sterilisation of defectives, had been removed from the MDA (Sandland, 2013). It is not surprising that in this socio-political climate, in which mentally defective women were constructed in contradictory terms, as a moment of undecidability – simultaneously 'asexual childlike innocents' and 'hypersexual eugenic burdens' (Denno, 1997, p 324) – there was little appetite to develop a test for capacity to consent to sexual activity.

The offences from 1885 and 1913 were subsequently re-enacted as sections 7 and 8 respectively of the Sexual Offences Act 1956 in substantially the same terms, the only difference being that the phrase 'unlawful sexual intercourse' replaced 'unlawful carnal knowledge'. The 1956 Act also contained a number of further sexual offences against defective persons, extending the reach of the statutory presumption of incapacity for those defined as defective. Section 14(4) provided that 'A woman who is a defective cannot in law give any consent which would prevent an act being an assault for the purposes of this section, but a person is only to be treated as guilty of an indecent assault on a defective by reasons of that incapacity to consent, if that person knew or had reason to suspect her to be a defective', and section 15(3) provided a comparable offence against a male defective.[20] These offences,[21] as with the offence by then contained in section 7, were not limited by the requirement that the defective person in question was subject to the powers under the MDA. But they were also broader than the offence in section 7 in that they were not limited to situations where the offender knew that their victim was an idiot or imbecile. Rather, they extended also to situations where there was either knowledge or reason to so suspect the presence of idiocy or imbecility.

The definition of 'defective', although redrafted in 1956, remained essentially as it had been in 1913.[22] As such, the 1956 Act marked a significant expansion of autonomy-removing intervention in terms of the breadth of the categories of actors and behaviours subject to the embargo. Further reform was soon in coming, however. Three years later, the Mental Health Act 1959 repealed all existing statutes concerning mental deficiency. Idiocy, imbecility, feeble-mindedness and moral imbecility/deficiency were all divested of any legal significance at this time.[23] The offence of unlawful carnal knowledge of a mentally defective woman subject to detention or community supervision under the MDA was repealed[24] and the offence first introduced by the 1885 Act, now found in section 7 of the 1956 Act, was revised and extended[25] to encompass the broader category of 'defective' so that it now reads:

[20] When male homosexuality was partially decriminalised by the Sexual Offences Act 1967, section 1(3) of that Act made clear that a defective or severely subnormal man could not give a valid consent to a homosexual act and that any other man who engaged in such an act with a defective, knowing or suspecting that was the case, was guilty of an offence.

[21] The offences concerned to prevent the abduction, abuse or exploitation of a defective woman through her prostitution were also re-enacted, by sections 9, 21, 27 and 29 of the 1956 Act.

[22] Section 45(1) of the 1956 Act defined 'defective' to mean, first, a person exhibiting 'mental defectiveness which is of such a degree that he requires care, supervision and control for his own protection or for the protection of others', which approximated most closely to the 1913 definition of 'feeble-minded'. In the new definition this necessarily extended to idiots and imbeciles as being terms which imply even greater need for protection than the feeble-minded. Secondly, the section 45(1) definition applied to any person exhibiting 'mental defectiveness coupled with strongly vicious or criminal propensities and who requires care, supervision and control for the protection of others' who 'requires care, supervision and control for his own protection or for the protection of others' is clearly modelled on moral imbeciles (who had become 'moral defectives' by virtue of section 1(1) Mental Deficiency Act 1927, although with no change in the definition).

[23] Section 1 and Schedule 8 Mental Health Act 1959.

[24] Section 127 and Schedule 8 Mental Health Act 1959.

[25] By section 127(1) Mental Health Act 1959.

(1) It is an offence, subject to the exception mentioned in this section for a man to have unlawful sexual intercourse with a woman who is a defective.
(2) A man is not guilty of an offence under this section because he has unlawful sexual intercourse with a woman if he does not know and has no reason to suspect her to be a defective.

In breaking the link between unlawful carnal knowledge/sexual intercourse and being subject to detention or community supervision that had been introduced by the MDA, the scope of the offence was broadened, as now intercourse with *any* 'defective' woman was criminalised, but at the same time the scope of the term 'defective' was narrowed.

This was achieved by the insertion[26] of a new section 45, on the meaning of 'defective', into the 1956 Act, which provided that: 'In this Act defective means a person suffering from severe subnormality within the meaning of the Mental Health Act, 1959.' This was in turn later replaced by schedule 3, paragraph 29 Mental Health (Amendment) Act 1982: 'In section 45 for the words from "severe subnormality" onwards there shall be substituted the words "a state of arrested or incomplete development of mind which includes severe impairment of intelligence and social functioning".'

Now, only those suffering from 'severe subnormality', later 'severe impairment of intelligence and social functioning' were covered by the statutory embargo on sexual activity, and in *R v Hall*,[27] which concerned offences under section 14(4) of the 1956 Act, it was established that severity is judged by reference to 'normally developed members of the public' rather than by reference to other mentally impaired persons, with the consequence that the number of those defined in law as 'defective' was much reduced, as compared to the situation in 1956.

The law continued in this form until all relevant sections of the 1956 Act were repealed by schedule 7 of the Sexual Offences Act 2003, by which time it was the only place in the legislative landscape that the term 'defective' still had currency, having been removed from broader mental health and mental capacity law by the 1959 Act. As such, the vestiges of the 1913 policy, of controlling the breeding potential of the mentally deficient population through the control of their sexual activity, could still be found at the start of the 21st century. Any argument that the law was designed, at any point before 2003, primarily to protect individuals is undermined by the fact that it applied to 'defectives' as a class, irrespective of the potential capacity of any individual to make their own decisions in respect of sexual activity and intimacy.

26 Also by section 127(1) of the 1959 Act.

27 (1988) 86 Cr. App. R. 159.

## Capacity and consent in the criminal courts, 1885–2003

The 1885 Act created a new offence, but the old offences continued to apply. After 1885, if a female idiot or imbecile lacked sufficient capacity – reasoned or instinctive – to consent to or refuse sexual intercourse, then it continued to be appropriate, unless the defendant and victim were married to each other,[28] to charge the defendant with rape (Mead and Bodkin, 1885, p 49).[29] Moreover, as already seen, the protection offered by section 5(2) of the 1885 Act extended only to female idiots and imbeciles and only to unlawful carnal knowledge (rape). No other form of sexual assault was covered until the 1950s, and the MDA applied only to female defectives detained in, or released from, hospital on licence or subject to guardianship under that Act. Although this amounted to a considerable number of women – at least 50,000 by 1939, according to Thomson (1998, p 2) – most defectives were not subject to the MDA. As such, many vulnerable women were in fact outside the statutory embargo. Moreover, both of these Acts applied only to females: mentally defective men and boys were not protected until the passage of the Sexual Offences Acts of 1956 and 1967.

In all of these situations, sexual activity was a possibility and hence there was a need for a legal test of capacity to consent not based on animal instincts. Yet the criterion of being 'incapable of judging' expressed in *Ryan* barely developed beyond the bare bones laid down in that case. In *Fletcher* in 1859, it was said that Jane Jones was 'incapable … of exercising any judgment on the matter' by reason of a defect of understanding, that is, her state of idiocy. This case, together with the much later decision in *Lang*[30] (in which it was held that the question for the jury was whether the 'understanding and knowledge' of an alleged victim of rape 'were such that she was not in a position to decide whether to consent or resist'), was cited as still representing the current law by the Law Commission (1995, p 53) in its Consultation Paper *Consent in the Criminal Law* published in 1995. This indicates how little the law developed subsequently.

What is missing in the case law is any consideration of the substance of the test: issues which are now seen as crucial, such as understanding that sexual activity is a choice and can be rejected, or that intercourse can

---

28 It is a separate question whether an idiot or imbecile could contract a valid marriage in the first place (see later), although no doubt many did in fact enter marriages.

29 See, for example, *R v William Stafford*, 25 February 1907, in which the defendant, who pleaded guilty to the attempted rape and indecent assault of Florence Summerfield 'knowing that at the time she was an idiot or imbecile', was sentenced to six months' imprisonment with hard labour (available at www.oldbaileyonline.org).

30 (1976) 62 Cr. App. R. 50.

lead to pregnancy or to the transmission of sexually transmitted diseases (STDs), were not considered in *Fletcher*. Apart from *Lang*, there is very little subsequent case law, and what there is, is not very illuminating. The only directly relevant authority is *R v Frederick Briden*, decided on 19 November 1906.[31] The defendant had sexual intercourse with a young woman, Jane de Fries, and was indicted for the offence under section 5(2) of the 1885 Act. Although it is not clear from the brief report of the case, there must have been some dispute as to whether Jane could properly be defined as an idiot or imbecile as the statute required, because the court considered the issue and counsel for the prosecution provided a number of authorities on the definition of an 'imbecile'. These included that offered by Maudsley ('weakness of mind, owing to defective moral development': 1906, p 66); that contained in the Oxford English Dictionary ('mentally weak; of weak character and will, through want of mental power'); and the direction given in 'a recent case' at Bodmin Assizes by Kennedy J, who told the jury that 'there must be such weakness that under the will of the man there was no chance for the woman; the woman must be incapable of resisting persuasion, of exercising an act of her own will, or of giving or withholding her consent'. Lamley Smith J, the trial judge in *Briden*, put that same direction to the jury 'and in considering that, the jury should consider two questions: (1) was the woman an imbecile? And (2) did the prisoner know it?'

In *Briden*, as in the Bodmin case, both questions were answered affirmatively. The defendant was convicted of the offence under section 5(2) and sentenced to four months' imprisonment. This case is less helpful than it could be, because again there is no consideration of substantive content of the test for capacity, and the issue is constructed more in terms of relative strength of will, which is an issue already structured by a gendered power dynamic which obscures the capacity issue. It does seem that some substantive content can be extrapolated from elsewhere in the law of rape. For example, in the well-known decisions in *R v William Case*[32] and *R v Flattery*,[33] the defendant, who had told the complainant with whom he engaged in sexual intercourse that what he proposed was a surgical intervention, was guilty of rape; as was the singing teacher in *R v Williams*,[34] who told his victim that intercourse was a procedure to improve her singing ability. In these cases, the complainant did not understand the nature or quality of the act or its sexual nature. This, it can be deemed, must therefore form part of the test of capacity, relevant to whether, in the words used in *Fletcher*, the complainant

31 Unreported but available at www.oldbaileyonline.org.
32 (1850) 1 Denison 580.
33 [1887] 2 QBD 410.
34 [1923] 1 KB 340.

can be said to be 'incapable of giving consent, or of exercising any judgment on the matter'. But beyond that, things are vague.

By the end of the 20th century, the situation in the UK contrasted sharply with that in other common law jurisdictions. Case law going back as far as 1913 could be found in America, in which year the Georgia Court of Appeal in *Morrow v State*[35] judged and found capacity to consent to sexual activity by considering the individual in question's abilities to read and write and their work history. In 1941, an Oklahoma court in *Hacker v State*[36] reversed a rape conviction based on ability to consent where the mentally retarded[37] victim could read, write and count; and in 1965 in *People v Blunt*[38] the Illinois Appeal Court decided that an alleged rape victim had capacity to give or refuse consent, based on her ability to prepare meals, do domestic work and travel alone. By the mid-1990s a number of different tests of capacity were being used in American courts. Sundram and Stavis (1993, p 451) identified three, the most common of which asked if the person in question understood the sexual nature of the acts involved and their possible consequences of pregnancy or STD transmission, while in some states it had also to be shown that the person in question understood the moral dimensions of sexual activity. In a smaller number of states, a narrower approach was taken, which asked only if the person in question understood the sexual and voluntary nature of the act, but not the possible risks and consequences of sexual conduct.

A few years later, Denno (1997, pp 344–5) identified six tests, including, as well as the three mentioned earlier: an expanded version of the first test which looks to see if the complainant understood the broader circumstances, including for example the intent of the perpetrator, as well as the nature and consequences of the act; a test which asks only if the complainant could exercise judgement regarding consent; and finally an approach which does not include a test of capacity as such but which looks at 'evidence of the victim's disability as a means of determining capacity to consent'. Exactly why there is this history of the development of capacity tests in the USA but not in the UK is not clear, but it may be because in the UK courts were concerned only with protection and not at all with enabling persons with learning disabilities with sufficient capacity to engage in consensual sexual activity.

---

35 (1913) 79 S.E. 63.

36 (1941) 118 P.2d 408.

37 This term came to replace 'idiot' and 'imbecile' in medical and official discourses in the early decades of the 20th century. It was itself subsequently replaced with 'intellectual disability'; in some instances, such as US federal law on social security, only relatively recently: see US Government Social Security Administration (2013, p 46499).

38 (1965) 212 N.E.2d 719.

In Australia, in *R v Morgan*,[39] a rape case, the trial judge had directed the jury that to have capacity the alleged victim must understand the concept of virginity and its loss, including both the moral dimensions and the idea that sexual activity might be regarded by some as 'naughty', as well as the physical dimensions, in particular the likely rupture of the hymen; that sexual intercourse involves a unique degree of intimacy; and that intercourse may result in pregnancy. The defendant was convicted and successfully appealed on the basis of a misdirection, the Supreme Court of Victoria at pp 341–2 holding that the trial judge's direction required too detailed knowledge of the complainant. To find capacity lacking,

> it must be proved that [the complainant] has not sufficient knowledge or understanding to comprehend (a) that what is proposed to be done is the physical fact of penetration of her body by the male organ or, if that is not proved, (b) that the act of penetration proposed is one of sexual connection as distinct from an act of a totally different character.

Although to be found to have capacity, 'That knowledge or understanding need not, of course, be a complete or sophisticated one. It is enough that she has sufficient "rudimentary knowledge" of what the act comprises and of its character to enable her to decide whether to give or withhold consent.'

The emergence of these tests in the criminal law of various jurisdictions reflected work done by psychologists and sexologists on the determination of capacity, such as the development for example of the Socio-Sexual Knowledge and Attitude Test (SSKAT) by Wish and colleagues (1980), and this in turn reflected changing attitudes towards persons raising concerns about mental capacity from around the middle of the 20th century. This attitudinal shift, as Baroness Hale noted in *R v C*[40] at paragraph 8, had seen the implementation of policies of deinstitutionalisation and 'normalisation' in the UK as elsewhere but, as she also noted, at paragraphs 9–10, had not in England and Wales, as we have seen, extended to matters of sexual autonomy.

This goes some way to explaining why legal developments elsewhere were not mirrored in England and Wales, but this cannot be the whole story. Baroness Hale made the further point, at paragraph 10, that the 1956 Act provisions were not only over-inclusive, as already discussed, but also under-inclusive, as they did not extend to 'people with other mental disorders[41] which might well mean that they lacked the capacity to make a genuine choice about their sexual relationships'. And, as discussed

[39] [1970] VR 337.

[40] [2009] UKHL 42.

[41] By which she means mental illnesses rather than developmental disabilities.

earlier, after the narrowing of the definition of 'defective' in 1959, most people with developmental disabilities – all those who were not classified as 'severely subnormal' or having a 'severe impairment of intelligence and social functioning', who amount to no more than 5 or 6 per cent of the total 'defective' population (Reed, 1997, pp 801–2) – were beyond the scope of the embargo on sexual activity. In these circumstances, the lack of any development of the components of a test for capacity in England and Wales is puzzling, especially when contrasted to the post-2003 situation, because, as later chapters will show, there has been a constant stream of case law in the 21st century.

Part of the answer seems to be that, when there was the opportunity for the judicial development of a test, it was not taken. A case in point is one of the last criminal cases before the coming into force of the Sexual Offences Act 2003, *R v K. L.*[42] M, aged 29, had a diagnosis of Prader-Willi syndrome, one aspect of which was significant developmental disability. She had spent all her life in residential accommodation, the last several years in a care home where she had her own room and her own key, but she had difficulty with simple tasks such as dressing or bathing and was in receipt of 24-hour care. Sometime in December 1999 M became pregnant. When interviewed by a police officer, on video and in the presence of a senior member of staff from the care home, she had given only monosyllabic answers to questions put to her. The Court of Appeal noted at paragraphs 9–10 that 'Her verbal functioning is evidently very limited indeed … her comprehension was indeed of the most limited kind and that her behaviour was childlike'. M did not know how she had become pregnant or who the father was. She denied that any man had been in her bed or that she had taken her clothes off in the presence of a man. She did not have a boyfriend and did not like boys. Subsequently, K.L., a member of staff at the care home, confessed that he was the father, but claimed that despite her diagnosis, of which he was aware, M had not only consented to, but had initiated, sexual contact on several occasions and that in his view she had capacity to do so.

K.L., who had pleaded guilty to three counts of unlawful sexual intercourse with a defective woman under section 7 of the 1956 Act, was also convicted following a trial of three counts of rape. He appealed on various grounds, to do with the admissibility of video evidence and the direction given by the judge to the jury, but the ground most relevant to the present discussion concerns evidence which had been given on M's capacity to decide to engage in sexual activity by Mr A, a consultant psychologist. Mr A gave evidence, at paragraph 14, that M had 'a mental age of little more than that of a child of some three-and-a-half years of age', her IQ was very low (below 50), she was

[42] [2002] EWCA Crim 2171.

in the bottom 0.013 per cent of the population for intellectual functioning and below average in community self-sufficiency. In Mr A's view, M had a severe impairment of mental functioning and lacked capacity to consent to sexual relations. K.L. argued that Mr A in giving this evidence had usurped the role of the jury as to findings of fact.

The Court of Appeal, noting that the giving of opinions by experts is common, held at paragraph 24 that this did not usurp the role of the jury in this case because 'the judge made it clear that it was for the jury to decide that issue and the judge made it clear that the jury were not bound to accept the expert evidence'. What can be seen here is how, in the context of a criminal trial, the issue of law – the legal test for capacity to engage in sexual relations – got folded into the issue of fact, of whether the complainant had capacity or not. The careful guarding of the role of the jury by both trial judge and appellate court meant that the chance to develop a capacity test was not taken. Instead, the attitude of the courts here as elsewhere in criminal law has been that the words in question are common words and do not need judicial or expert elaboration.[43]

## The civil law on sexual activity and capacity to consent before the Mental Capacity Act 2005

Surprising as it may seem, there is no discussion in a civil court of how capacity to consent to sexual relations is to be assessed before *X City Council v MB*,[44] decided in the period between the completion of the passage through Parliament of the Mental Capacity Act 2005 in April 2005 and its coming into force in October 2007. This was a case primarily about capacity to marry, but the judge, Munby J, decided at paragraph 64 that, as marriage 'must be understood as providing the parties to the marriage with the right to choose whether to engage in sexual activity within that union', it was also necessary to consider the test for capacity to engage in sexual relations. However, surveying the field, all that he could find was the 'now very elderly English cases on the subject' discussed already in the second part of this chapter. He declined, at paragraph 73, to follow these cases, which he found 'not particularly illuminating' and 'in any event disfigured by acceptance of the doctrine … that a mentally disordered person can legally consent to sexual activity if their "animal instincts" take over'.

[43] This tendency goes back at least as far as the 19th century. For example, it was held in *R v Goode* 7 A. & E. 536 the question of whether the prosecutrix was or was not an idiot/imbecile could under the 1885 Act be decided by the jury by reference to her appearance and demeanour in court without recourse to expert evidence (see Mead and Bodkin, 1885, p 49). See also, for example, *R v Rivett* (1950) 34 Cr. App. R. 87.

[44] [2006] EWHC 168 (Fam).

It might be thought in lieu of direct authority that some assistance could be derived by looking at the law on capacity to marry or to consummate a marriage, but the law in those areas is little more developed than the test for capacity to engage in sexual activity as explained in the 1859 *Fletcher* decision. For example, Sir John Nicholl, in *Browning v Reane*,[45] held that whether 'from ideotcy or lunacy, or from both combined', a person lacks capacity to marry if 'incapable of understanding the nature of the contract itself, and incapable, from mental imbecillity, to take care of his or her own person and property'. The required level of understanding was discussed in several 19th-century cases following *Browning*, culminating in the decision in *Durham v Durham*,[46] with Sir James Hannen holding at p 82 that:

> the contract of marriage is a very simple one, which does not require a high degree of intelligence to comprehend. It is an engagement between a man and woman to live together, and love one another as husband and wife, to the exclusion of all others … a mere comprehension of the words of the promises exchanged is not sufficient. The mind of one of the parties may be capable of understanding the language used, but may yet be affected by such delusions, or other symptoms of insanity, as may satisfy the tribunal that there was not a real appreciation of the engagement apparently entered into.

Although this test was further discussed in later case law and to some extent finessed by decisions in the 20th century such as the well-known case of *In the Estate of Park deceased, Park v Park*,[47] it remains essentially unchanged today, and was cited as such by Munby J in 2004 in his detailed historical review of the law on capacity to marry in *Sheffield City Council v E*.[48] It does little to clarify the appropriate content of the test for capacity to consent to sexual relations, confining itself instead to requiring that understanding must be 'real', with no further elaboration of what that entails.

The law on capacity to consummate a marriage is similarly unhelpful. Capacity here is usually understood to raise issues of physical rather than intellectual ability or understanding. There are cases, such as *G v G*,[49] *H v H*[50] and *Dickinson v Dickinson*[51] which refer to incapacity caused not by some 'structural impediment' but instead by 'the influence of hysteria' on

45 (1812) 2 Phill Ecc 69, at p 70.
46 (1885) 10 PD 80.
47 [1954] P 89.
48 [2005] Fam. 326.
49 (1871) L.R. 2 P. & D. 287.
50 (1873) L.R. 3 P. & D. 126.
51 [1913] P. 198.

the wife. But there is nothing in the judgment in any of these cases which even approaches a test for capacity. In the absence of any direct domestic authority, Munby J in *MB* elected to apply the approach taken by the Supreme Court of Victoria in *Morgan*, which, as discussed earlier, involves knowledge or understanding of the nature and sexual character of the act in question, finding at paragraph 74 that this 'stands as an essentially correct summary and statement of the common law rule'. And, as already discussed, and as Munby J noted, at paragraph 68, this chimes with the authorities of *Case*, *Flattery* and *Williams*, albeit that those cases were concerned with fraud rather than capacity as such.

As to why there is no legal development after the mid-19th-century case law discussed earlier, the common law rule that a husband cannot rape his wife, which meant that neither consent nor capacity had any relevance to sex within marriage, may be relevant. So too may be the social censure on sex outside marriage and the lack of any sexual education which pertained well into the 20th century. And certainly, after the 1913 embargo there would be no prospect of a care provider or local authority seeking guidance from a civil court as to the potential to consent to sex of any person in their charge, which is a situation we have seen in the post-2003 Act case law. However, it seems implausible that for a century and a half there was no sexual encounter, or no encounter where there was some concern about the capacity of one of the parties to consent, which does seem to indicate that the 1885 Act and the subsequent legislation discussed earlier effectively shut down any further development of the common law. We are left with the suspicion that there is a hidden history, either of consensual sexual activity but more likely of the abuse of those lacking or of uncertain capacity, hidden behind the discourses of asexuality and promiscuity which, albeit contradictory of each other, structured the MDA and the subsequent law.

## Conclusion

This chapter has provided a survey of the law of capacity to consent to sexual relations and intimacy from the mid-19th century to the start of the modern law in the early 21st century. What is most striking is the underdevelopment of the law, even by the end of this period. On the rare occasions when the issue was before a court, detailed judicial analysis is invariably lacking at any point before the 2006 decision in *MB*, with successive judges content to see the presence or absence of capacity as a question of fact, to be left to juries, rather than as questions of law, requiring the elaboration of the various elements that we now take as axiomatic in assessing capacity.

Beyond this, a significant part of the explanation for this underdevelopment lies in the acceptance: (i) by 19th-century judges of very questionable contemporary theories of intellectual disability, which corrupted the development of the law with the notion of instinctive consent; and (ii) by the legislature in the early 20th century of that same notion, coupled with eugenic-based concerns about the supposedly dangerous and disastrous social, economic, political and moral consequences of uncontrolled reproduction by the mentally defective. The result was that significant swathes of the population were assumed to lack capacity to give a reasoned consent, or make their own sexual choices, and so were in effect rendered asexual by the law, even as that asexuality, and that law, was haunted by a fear of the hypersexual mental defective. Although not explicitly endorsed by later parliaments, nonetheless subsequent reform of mental disability law and the law of sexual offences left these assumptions unaddressed and unchallenged throughout the 20th century.

As already noted, however, the reform process which led to the Acts of 2003 and 2005 was premised in part at least on the view that the law should, wherever possible, enable and facilitate 'a full life, including a sexual life'[52] for persons with intellectual disabilities. These days, the law bears the influence of human rights discourse, as well as the language (if not always the practice) of deinstitutionalisation and normalisation, including the normalisation of sexual relationships.[53] Nonetheless, one question for subsequent chapters in this volume is whether the status-based and discriminatory construction of the intellectually disabled discussed in this chapter has been consigned to history or whether it continues to have currency in the 21st century, the claimed focus on the individual in both criminal and civil law capacity tests notwithstanding.

## References

Denno, D.W. (1997) 'Sexuality, rape and mental retardation', *University of Illinois Law Review*, 1997(2), 315–434.

Esquirol, J.E.D. (1845) *Mental maladies*, trans E.K. Hunt, Philadelphia, PA: Lea and Blanchard. First published in French in 1820 as *Des Maladies mentales*.

Jackson, M. (2000) *The borderland of imbecility: Medicine, society and the fabrication of the feeble minded in late Victorian and Edwardian England*, Manchester: Manchester University Press.

Law Commission (1995) *Criminal Law: Consent in the criminal law: a consultation paper*, Consultation Paper No 139. https://www.lawcom.gov.uk/app/uploads/2016/08/No.139-Criminal-Law-Consent-in-the-Criminal-Law-A-Consultation-Paper.pdf (Accessed 19 June 2023).

Law Commission (2000) *Consent in sex offences: A report to the Home Office Sex Offences Review*, London: Law Commission, 2000.

[52] Lord Falconer, see footnote 1.

[53] See Squires and Morgan, Chapter 5 in this volume.

Maudsley, H. (1906) *Responsibility in mental disease* (6th edn), London: Kegan Paul, Trench, Trubner and Co. https://wellcomecollection.org/works/h2t3pnpj/items?canvas=11 (Accessed 19 June 2023).

Mead, F. and Bodkin, A.H. (1885) *The Criminal Law Amendment Act, 1885: With introduction, notes, and index*, London: Shaw and Sons.

Reed, E.J. (1997) 'Criminal law and the capacity of mentally retarded persons to consent to sexual activity', *Virginia Law Review*, 83(4), 799–827.

Sandland, R. (2013) 'Concubitu prohibere vago: sex and the idiot girl 1846–1913', *Feminist Legal Studies*, 21, 81–108.

Smith, J.C. and Hogan, B. (1988) *Criminal law* (6th edn), London: Butterworths.

Sundram, C.J. and Stavis, P.F. (1993) 'Sexual behavior and mental retardation', *Mental and Physical Disability Law Reporter*, 17(4), 448–457.

Thomson, M. (1998) *The problem of mental deficiency: Eugenics, democracy and social policy in Britain c.1870–1959*, Oxford: Clarendon Press.

U.S. Government Social Security Administration (2013) 78:148 *Federal Register Rules and Regulations* https://www.govinfo.gov/content/pkg/FR-2013-08-01/pdf/2013-18552.pdf (Accessed 19 June 2023).

Wish, J.R., Edmonson, B. and Fiechtl McCombs, K. (1980) *The socio-sexual knowledge and attitude test*, Wood Dale, IL: Stoelting.

Wormald, J. and Wormald, S. (1913) *A guide to the Mental Deficiency Act 1913*, London: P.S. King and Son (reprinted by Gale: Farmington Hills, MI, 2010).

2

# Sexual Capacity: Are There Questions the Law Should Not Ask?

*Alex Ruck Keene, Allegra Enefer and Alan Cusack*

## Introduction

Since the mid-2010s, the courts in England and Wales have been determining questions of sexual decision-making capacity, by reference not to the question of whether a person consented to a specific encounter, but to whether the person is capable of consenting to sexual activity. Consequently, the courts have reached further and further into the bedroom, with profound implications for the rights of those with cognitive impairments to express themselves sexually. In 2021, the question of how courts should consider the question of sexual decision-making capacity finally reached the Supreme Court in the case of *A Local Authority v JB* [2021] UKSC 52 (*JB*). In this chapter, we explore the clash of principles the case illuminates between the need for sexual consent to be true consent, and the need to support the exercise of sexual expression by those with cognitive impairments. We examine why the clash is so fundamental, including by reference to sometimes forgotten debates preceding legislation in both England and Wales and, for comparison, Ireland, and human rights arguments. Recognising that, whether or not it was inevitable that the law would assert an interest in questions of sexual decision-making capacity, it has now done so, we set out a way in which it may be possible to approach matters which may not eliminate, but may at least mitigate, the clash of principles that arises in consequence of the law's involvement.

## *JB*: the case and its implications

*JB*'s case concerned a 38-year-old man with several physical and cognitive impairments, in whose life the local authority had significant involvement. Unlike many of the previous cases in this context, the concern on the part of the local authority was not that JB might not be able to give consent to sexual activity proposed by others (as often arises in the context of potential exploitation or abuse). Rather, the concern was that JB would be at risk of engaging in a course of sexual activity that might not have the consent of a prospective sexual partner. Indeed, on the evidence before the court (which had not at the time of the case been the subject of judicial determination), it was quite clear that JB was actively seeking to initiate sexual activity, potentially with women who either would not, or could not, give consent.

Faced with numerous concerns regarding JB's capacity in a range of matters – including, in particular, his capacity 'to consent to sexual activity' – the local authority applied to the Court of Protection for a series of declarations. While, by the date of the relevant hearing, all interested parties had reached agreement on the majority of issues relating to JB's capacity, two fundamental legal questions remained to be addressed. The first was whether, for purposes of the Mental Capacity Act 2005 (MCA), the test was one of consenting to sexual relations (as courts before the Court of Appeal in *JB* had understood), or whether it was to decide to engage in sexual relations. The Supreme Court agreed with the Court of Appeal that the 'matter' in question was the decision to engage in sexual relations.[1]

The second legal question was whether, in order to have capacity to decide to engage in sexual relations, JB needed to understand not only that he could give or withhold consent, but also that *the other person* must be able to consent and give and maintain consent throughout. Expert evidence was adduced to indicate that, by virtue of his Autistic Spectrum Disorder, JB could not understand, use or weigh this information.[2]

The critical question was therefore whether the information about the consent of the other person was legally relevant to a decision to engage in sexual relations for purposes of the capacity test contained in sections 2–3 Mental Capacity Act 2005. If it was legally relevant, then, assuming that, upon further examination by the first instance judge to which the case was

---

1 *JB* at para 90.

2 It is perhaps important to note that matters were proceeding expressly on the interim basis provided for under section 48 Mental Capacity Act 2005, that is, that there was reason to believe that JB lacked the capacity to decide whether to engage in sexual relations (see *JB* at para 4). The expert evidence had therefore not formally been adopted by any court to reach its own determination of JB's capacity.

remitted, JB could not understand, use, or weigh it, two consequences would flow:

(1) JB would not have the requisite mental capacity to make the decision to engage in sexual relations;
(2) No other person would be entitled to make this decision on his behalf, as section 27(1)(b) Mental Capacity Act 2005 provides that nothing in the Act permits a decision to consent to have sexual relations to be made on behalf of a person. This meant, in turn, that JB would – to quote Lord Stephens (who gave the Supreme Court's sole judgment) – be 'deprived of all sexual relations'.[3]

Due to the framing of the issue, and perhaps in a starker fashion than in any previous case, the Supreme Court's attention was drawn sharply to the normative nature of the classification of information as legally relevant or irrelevant. Put another way: to identify the information that is legally relevant to a decision, one must make a choice as to which information *ought* to be considered relevant.

Lord Stephens held (at paragraph 96) that: 'amongst the matters which every person engaging in sexual relations *must* think about is whether the other person is consenting [...] If that is properly viewed as cerebral or as involving a degree of analysis, a decision to engage in sexual relations is necessarily cerebral or analytical to that extent' (emphasis added, and different emphasis in the original removed).

Once that approach was adopted, it flowed inexorably that JB would lack capacity to decide to engage in sexual relations if he could not, in fact, understand, use, or weigh the information. Unless JB could be supported to gain the ability to do so (and it is important to emphasise that the local authority responsible for his care made clear that it was seeking to provide that support), then there would be an all but insurmountable legal barrier standing in the way of JB ever acting upon his strongly expressed desire to find a sexual partner.[4]

Further, the test as clarified by the Supreme Court impacts indirectly upon many in situations far removed from those of JB: in particular those who, unlike JB, are in relationships which have (or may have) a sexual component. This was a matter to which the Supreme Court were entirely alive. In particular, they were at pains to disagree with the statement of the Court of Appeal in *In re M (An Adult) (Capacity: Consent to Sexual Relations)*[5]

3 *JB* at para 1.
4 The term 'sexual partner' is used carefully, and in line with the framing of matters at para 23 of the judgment.
5 [2014] EWCA Civ 37, [2015] Fam 61, at para 77.

that capacity to consent to sexual relations can *only* be assessed on a general and non-specific basis. Such a restriction on the formulation of the 'matter' was, Lord Stephens considered:

> contrary to the open-textured nature of section 2(1) MCA. A general and non-specific basis is not the only appropriate formulation in respect of sexual relations as even in that context, 'the matter' can be person-specific where it involves, for instance, sexual relations between a couple who have been in a long-standing relationship where one of them develops dementia or sustains a significant traumatic brain injury. It could also be person-specific in the case of sexual relations between two individuals who are mutually attracted to one another but who both have impairments of the functioning of their minds.[6]

Approaching matters in that way meant that the information relevant to the decision could depend upon the characteristics of the prospective partner. For instance, the risks of pregnancy would not be relevant to a decision in respect of sexual relations with a person of the same sex.[7]

This 'tailoring' of the information could undoubtedly lessen the impact of the Supreme Court's decision in some cases. For instance, Lord Stephens identified that '[t]here may, for example, be no reasonably foreseeable consequence of a sexually transmitted disease in a long-standing monogamous relationship where one partner has developed dementia'.[8] This might open the door to a more flexible approach in such situations, although at the cost of judgments being made about the quality of such relationships (Ruck Keene and Price, forthcoming). The process of refining an understanding of the consequences of sexual relations could also lead to situations where the bar appears to be raised in relation to a specific partner. In *Hull City Council v KF* [2022] EWCOP 33, the first reported post-*JB* decision concerning sexual capacity, the judge found that, while KF was in principle capable of making decisions to engage in sexual relations, she could not decide upon sexual relations with a violent and abusive partner. Further, Lord Stephens identified that the reasonably foreseeable consequences that formed part of the relevant information (under section 3(4) MCA 2005) could extend to consequences for others. This means, in turn, that if, on the facts of the case, engaging in sexual relations with another could cause serious consequences for that other person (for example, pregnancy, the threat of a

6 *JB* at para 71.

7 *JB* at para 71, endorsing *A Local Authority v TZ* [2013] EWCOP 2322, [2013] COPLR 477 at para 55.

8 *Ibid*.

sexually transmitted disease, and so on), such consequences would have to be understood by the individual whose capacity is in question.

We deliberately do not seek to comment upon whether the outcome in respect of JB's own specific case is 'good' or 'bad'. In part, this is given the involvement of one of us, Alex Ruck Keene, in the case itself. However, and more importantly, this was because, as the Supreme Court were at pains to emphasise, no final decisions had actually been taken in relation to JB's capacity in this regard at the point that the case was remitted back to the first instance judge.[9]

That having been said, we suggest that it is difficult to see any other way in which the Supreme Court could have answered the questions posed of it in JB's case. Once the forensic spotlight has been turned on the 'matter' that has to be considered from a capacity perspective, we suggest that it becomes clear that looking purely at the question of whether a person can consent (as courts had done before *JB*) is an approach which ignores the fact that those with cognitive impairments are not merely passive recipients of the sexual interests of others, but are equally likely to wish to express themselves sexually. Conversely, it seems difficult to see how the Supreme Court could reach any other conclusion but that those with cognitive impairments wishing to express themselves sexually have to be able to understand the need for consent on the part of any putative sexual partner.

In the next two sections we examine the clash of principles which the case exposed; in the section following, we examine them through a human rights lens; and in the last section we ask a more radical question as to whether the law in fact has any place here at all.

## An irreconcilable clash?

JB's case exposes what might be thought to represent an irreconcilable clash between two fundamental principles. On one hand, enshrined primarily (but not exclusively) in the criminal law, is the principle that sexual consent must be true consent, freely given and truly maintained by both parties throughout the course of sexual activity. On the other, is a principle (the precise legal location of which is perhaps less obvious[10]) of supporting the entitlement to sexual expression of those with cognitive impairments. In other words, we can see this clash as concretising the tension between the rather woollier principles of 'protection' and 'empowerment' that are so often identified as being in play in the context of those with cognitive impairments.

---

[9] See *JB* at para 121.

[10] To the extent it is located in human rights law, we consider this later, in the section 'Human rights to the rescue?'

Before we address this clash further, we need to address one potential objection to our framing of the position. It might be suggested that the Supreme Court were not saying anything at all about the question of what it means to give consent to sexual relations, as opposed to the (different) question of whether a person can have capacity to make decisions about initiating sexual relations. At paragraph 112, Lord Stephens noted that, for the purpose of the criminal law:[11]

> the primary issue would relate to P's capacity to 'consent to' not to 'engage in' sexual relations. These are two different concepts. The capacity to 'engage in' sexual relations encompasses both P as the initiator of those relations and P as the person consenting to sexual relations initiated by another. The information relevant to a decision whether to initiate sexual relations includes the fact that the other person must have the ability to consent to the sexual activity and must in fact consent before and throughout the sexual activity. That is not information relevant to an evaluation of whether P has the capacity to 'consent to' sexual relations initiated by another person. [...]. I do not consider that the criminal law requires that a complainant understands that their assailant must have the capacity to consent and in fact consents before the complainant can be considered to have capacity.

However, a person will usually be in the Schrödinger's cat position of being both a potential 'consent-giver' and a potential initiator. As Lord Stephens noted at paragraph 90:

> It may be helpful to observe that the terminology of a capacity to decide to 'engage in' sexual relations embraces both (i) P's capacity to consent to sexual relations initiated by the other party and (ii) P's capacity to understand that, in relation to sexual relations initiated by P, the other party must be able to consent to sexual relations and must in fact be consenting, and consenting throughout, to the sexual relations.

A necessary component of capacity to decide to engage in sexual relations being the ability to understand, retain, use and weigh the fact of the other's consent, the clash of principles we identified at the outset of this section is therefore present when matters are looked at through the prism of the MCA 2005, which requires a focus on whether the person

[11] Specifically, the Sexual Offences Act 2003, which is the governing statute in England and Wales.

currently has or lacks the capacity to make the relevant decision, rather than through the rear-view mirror of the criminal law, which looks at whether the person in fact gave consent sufficient to make the act in question legal. Importantly, this clash persists regardless of whether the individual concerned is a person who is deemed to pose a risk to others (such as JB), or – by contrast – is someone whose sexual expression is regarded as meriting support.

If JB's case brought this clash of principles to the fore, it is important to note that it is one that has been lurking beneath the surface, if primarily viewed through a criminal law lens, for many years. Space precludes a detailed examination of the evolution of the Sexual Offences Act 2003 (SOA 2003) (see Chapter 1 by Sandland in this volume; Ruck Keene and Enefer, 2022), now the governing criminal statute – but it can be identified as setting out a framework which is tilted definitively towards protection. A similar theme can then be traced, in the parallel field of civil law, in the evolution of the case law decided under the MCA 2005 (Ruck Keene and Enefer, 2022). For our purposes, however, we particularly want to emphasise that, as identified by both the Law Commission (Law Commission, 2000) and the Independent Review of Sex Offences (Home Office, 2000) there might have been a different route, and – radically – that there might have been a route in which the law played far less of a role. Before we turn in the last section to that more radical route, and what it might mean going forward, it is helpful, to ensure against parochialism, that we first examine how the same dilemmas have been addressed in a different jurisdiction and, next, whether human rights-informed approaches can lead the way out.

## Another perspective: the position in Ireland

While a factual scenario of the magnitude of *JB* has yet to come before Irish courts, the dilemma posed by the case – in terms of seeking to reconcile the legal requirement of consent with a desire to support exercises of sexual expression by persons with cognitive impairments – is nevertheless all too familiar to Ireland. Indeed, as far back as 2005, McCormack et al (2005) noted, in the context of campaigning for a new legislative model to safeguard the sexual agency of persons with intellectual disabilities, that 'getting the right balance between protection from exploitation and abuse, and the right to experience one's sexuality in a positive environment, will be the litmus test for such legislation' (McCormack et al, 2005, p 226). A cursory review of Ireland's statute book, however, would suggest that Irish policy makers – much like their counterparts across the Irish Sea – have not always succeeded in satisfying this exacting litmus test.

For a start, Irish policy makers have largely refused to engage with this topic in the civil field, opting instead to resolve the question almost entirely through the retrospective prism of the criminal law.[12] And yet, the ability of Ireland's criminal law to fulfil this function is far from certain.[13] Indeed, prior to the introduction of the Criminal Law (Sexual Offences) Act 2017 (CL(SO)A 2017), individuals with a 'mental impairment' were faced with the threat of criminal prosecution under Irish law if they engaged in sexual intercourse or buggery with a person to whom they were not married.[14] Aside from its obvious perpetuation of pathological and pejorative terminology, the relevant provision was criticised on grounds that it 'both under-criminalises and over-criminalises this sensitive area of sexual activity' (Kilcommins, Edwards and O'Sullivan, 2014, p 695). It was, ironically, the under-criminalisation of this area which led to calls for reform, following the decision in *The People (DPP) v XY*,[15] where a trial judge felt compelled to direct a jury to acquit a defendant who stood accused of forcing a woman with an intellectual disability to perform an act of oral sex in circumstances where this sexual conduct fell outside the scope of the relevant provision and could not be prosecuted under any wider legislation (Cusack, 2015).

To address this lacuna, Ireland's Law Reform Commission recommended an overhaul of the legislative landscape so as to ensure that any criminalising provisions would apply to a wider range of sexually abusive behaviour (Law Reform Commission, 2013). In addition, and in an approach that largely followed the model proposed by the Law Commission in England and Wales, the report advocated for the recognition of a defence in cases involving a sexual act between two equally vulnerable persons in circumstances where there was an absence of exploitation on the part of an accused, irrespective of the decision-making capacity of the other.[16]

This proposal, however, was quickly rejected by the Department of Justice, which was concerned that an accused might be afforded a valid defence to an allegation of sexual wrongdoing by demonstrating that there was

[12] Most notably, the Law Reform Commission in its 2005 Consultation Paper on Vulnerable Adults and the Law: Capacity, declared: 'This Consultation Paper is concerned with law on capacity as it impacts on decision-making capacity in a civil law context. However, when considering personal relationship issues, capacity to enter into a sexual relationship is a matter which is ruled by the criminal law.'

[13] See generally, Cusack (2015).

[14] By operation of s 5 Criminal Law (Sexual Offences) Act 1993.

[15] *The People (DPP) v XY* (Central Criminal Court, 15 November 2010; *The Irish Times*, 16 November 2010).

[16] This novel defence would not be restricted exclusively to cases where the sexual contact was apparently consensual in nature; rather, it would have a wider application in all cases involving an absence of exploitation by an accused.

no exploitation underpinning or preceding the sexual encounter, thereby effectively sidestepping the issue of consent.[17]

Following a stakeholder consultation, the CL(SO)A 2017 was introduced, which repealed section 5 of the 1993 Act and aligned Irish law (to a large extent) with the protectionist model embodied in the SOA 2003 in England and Wales. Under the 2017 Act, it became an offence for any person to engage in a 'sexual act' with an individual who does not have the capacity to consent to the act by reason of an intellectual disability, mental disability or mental illness (that is, where he or she is a 'protected person') in circumstances where the assailant knows or is reckless as to whether or not the complainant lacks capacity.[18]

The legislation adopts a functional test for capacity whereby the issue of whether or not a person is to be regarded as a 'protected person' under the Act is determined exclusively by focusing on his or her ability to give informed consent.[19] If the person cannot consent to a sexual act (that is, he or she is a 'protected person'), then, as is the case under the SOA 2003,[20] questions of consent are irrelevant: the only possible defence to such an action is to show that an accused subjectively did not know, and was not reckless with respect to whether or not, the complainant was a 'protected person' (that is, a vulnerable person who lacked capacity to consent to sex). In such a case, however, a statutory presumption exists to the effect that an accused knew, or was reckless as to whether or not, the complainant was a 'protected person'.[21] Accordingly, unless an accused can establish a defence of insanity under the Criminal Law (Insanity) Act 2006, it will fall entirely upon him to prove (to the standard of a reasonable doubt) that he did not know, and that he was not reckless, as to whether or not the complainant was classified as a 'protected person' (under the statutory functional test).

---

17 Department of Justice, 2014 at p 9: 'There would be serious concerns that making lack of consent contingent on exploitation or abuse would confuse the issue and undermine the basic principle of consent.'

18 Criminal Law (Sexual Offences) Act 2017, s 21(1). Additionally, it is an offence, pursuant to s 21(2) of the Criminal Law (Sexual Offences) Act 2017 to 'invite, induce, counsel or incite a protected person to engage in a sexual act knowing that that person is a protected person or being reckless as to whether that person is a protected person'.

19 *Ibid.* at s 21(7) provides as follows: 'For the purposes of this section, a person lacks the capacity to consent to a sexual act if he or she is, by reason of a mental or intellectual disability or a mental illness, incapable of—(a) understanding the nature, or the reasonably foreseeable consequences, of that act, (b) evaluating relevant information for the purposes of deciding whether or not to engage in that act, or (c) communicating his or her consent to that act by speech, sign language or otherwise.'

20 Sexual Offences Act 2003, s 30(1)(d).

21 Criminal Law (Sexual Offences) Act 2017, s 21(3).

Given the high evidential burden that the new legislative framework imposes upon defendants, it is likely to informally fall once more (as was the case under the 1993 regime) upon Ireland's Director of Public Prosecutions to protect those with intellectual disability who are accused of engaging in a sexual act with a 'protected person' by exercising a discretion not to prosecute such cases. It might be thought that such discretion is the only way in which to navigate the otherwise impossible tensions in play; it might equally be thought that this is to risk continuing the potential to over-criminalise expressions of sexual agency among two persons with intellectual disabilities. In this regard, the 2017 Act can be seen, in many respects, to mimic the criminalising, exclusionary protectionist spirit of the SOA 2003. And yet, as the *JB* case has revealed, the forward-looking mechanics of a *civil law* response – with an emphasis on the need to understand, use and weigh information – are equally unlikely to provide an easy solution to the plight of persons with cognitive impairments in Ireland. In advocating a human rights-focused approach to this sensitive area, Flynn has criticised the 2017 enactment for representing a missed opportunity by Ireland's legislature to embrace a disability-neutral approach to this issue which would avoid perpetuating individualised notions of personal tragedy (Flynn, 2017). But do human rights necessarily provide the answer?

## Human rights to the rescue?

Human rights arguments were given relatively short shrift by the Supreme Court in *JB*, in part because of the way in which the case had been formulated.[22] Some might therefore argue that analysing matters through the prism of the European Convention on Human Rights (ECHR) and/or United Nations Convention on the Rights of Persons with Disabilities (CRPD) might allow the clash of principles to be avoided. In this section, we examine whether this is so.

Firstly, it is important to emphasise that Article 8 ECHR (which enshrines a 'right to respect for private and family life') 'cannot be understood as guaranteeing a right as such to establish a relationship with one particular person'.[23] Nor, whether by asserting 'sexual rights' or otherwise, could JB (or anyone else) assert any right to be supported or facilitated to have sexual relations with a person who is unwilling. Article 8(1) ECHR guarantees the right to protection against unjustified interference by the state in mutually

[22] The Supreme Court refused permission to bring a standalone ground of appeal based upon Article 8 ECHR (see paras 117–119). The position in relation to the CRPD is addressed later.

[23] *Evers v Germany* [2020] ECHR 356 at para 54.

consensual sexual activity: it cannot be read as guaranteeing a right on behalf of a person to sex.[24]

Article 8(1) ECHR imposes upon the State – including the Court of Protection – the positive obligation to secure the 'physical and moral integrity'[25] of the person, including against sexual activity to which they are incapable of consenting. This obligation can arise even where the individual appears either not to be distressed by the situation or where they appear actively to take pleasure from the sexual contact. As Munby J made clear in *Re MM (Local Authority X v MM and KM)*:[26]

> the State is entitled to control even seemingly consensual sexual acts in private where it is necessary to 'safeguard … against exploitation and corruption … those who are especially vulnerable because they are young, weak in body or mind, inexperienced, or in a state of special physical, official or economic dependence'.[27]

Indeed, under this construction of Article 8 ECHR, not only is the State *entitled* to intervene, but the state may be under a *positive* obligation to do so.[28]

Strasbourg jurisprudence has repeatedly emphasised the importance of sexual acts as being truly consensual. While the primary focus has been upon mechanisms to prosecute *after* non-consensual sexual activity has taken place,[29] the systemic obligation to protect in such circumstances is not solely the function of the criminal justice system. It can also involve the civil justice system where the remedies available under that system afford sufficient protection.[30] The Strasbourg Court has also emphasised (through the prism of the prohibition on torture enshrined in Article 3 ECHR, but of equal applicability to Article 8) the obligations upon the state to ensure: 'effective protection, in particular, of … vulnerable persons

---

24 See also the discussion, in relation to any obligations upon the state arising out of Article 8 ECHR in the context of paid sex work and those with disabilities: *Secretary of State for Justice v A Local Authority & Ors* [2021] EWCA Civ 1527, [2021] 3 WLR 1425 at paras 52–60.

25 The descriptive phrase used since *X v The Netherlands* (1968) 8 EHRR 235, such integrity including the sexual life of the individual.

26 [2009] 1 FLR 443.

27 At para 128, citing *Dudgeon v United Kingdom* (1982) 4 EHRR 149 at para 49.

28 See para 129, citing *X v The Netherlands* (1968) 8 EHRR 235.

29 See, for example, *MC v Bulgaria* (2005) 40 EHRR 20 at para 166: 'In accordance with contemporary standards and trends in that area, the member States' positive obligations under Articles 3 and 8 of the Convention must be seen as requiring the penalisation and effective prosecution of any non-consensual sexual act, including in the absence of physical resistance by the victim.'

30 *S v Sweden* (2014) 58 EHRR 36 at para 85.

includ[ing] to take reasonable steps to prevent ill-treatment of which the authorities had or ought to have had knowledge', in circumstances where: 'in the case of people in a vulnerable position, including people with disabilities, [...] the authorities must show *particular vigilance and afford increased protection* in view of the fact that such individuals' capacity or willingness to pursue a complaint will often be impaired' (added emphasis).[31]

If, as in England and Wales, civil law remedies – including in the form of the mechanisms available under the MCA 2005 – can secure against the risk that an individual will take part in sexual activity to which that person cannot consent, then deployment of such remedies would offer protection for that person for Strasbourg purposes. This approach explains the decision of Sir Mark Hedley in *CH v A Metropolitan Council*.[32] That case concerned a situation where, during the course of fertility treatment being sought by a man with a learning disability and his wife, a psychologist considered that the man lacked capacity to consent to sexual relations. The wife was advised by the local authority that she must abstain from sexual intercourse with her husband as that would, given his incapacity to consent, comprise a serious sexual offence under sections 30–31 Sexual Offences Act 2003. The psychologist had made clear that the man needed a course of sex education to assist him to achieve the necessary capacity, but the local authority did not implement it until proceedings were brought in the Court of Protection by the man's sister. The local authority conceded that it had breached the man's rights under the ECHR by failing to provide him with the support necessary to gain capacity to consent to sexual relations. However, Sir Mark Hedley, endorsing the award of damages, made clear that: (1) the initial safeguarding steps taken upon the basis of an understanding that the man lacked that capacity were 'inevitable' having regard to the provisions of the criminal law; and (2) the initial 'incursions on the conjugal relations of the husband and wife' were justifiable by reference to Article 8(2) ECHR.[33]

In *Sandwell Metropolitan Borough Council v RG and Others*,[34] although not referring to the ECHR, Holman J applied, in effect, the same approach on a 'real time' basis. Holman J held that, in consequence of a declaration that a man lacked capacity to consent to sexual relations it 'will be the *duty* of the local authority, as his carers, to take all reasonable steps to prevent him being the victim of a criminal act' (emphasis added)[35] and to supervise contact between the man and the woman to whom he had been married

31 *IC v Romania* (2019) 68 EHRR 13 at para 51 (concerning rape of a 14-year-old with learning disabilities). See also in this regard, by analogy, Heri (2020).

32 [2017] EWCOP 12, [2017] COPLR 341.

33 *CH* at para 12.

34 [2013] EWCOP 2373, [2013] COPLR 64.

35 *Sandwell* at para 24.

in an arranged marriage to the extent necessary to ensure that there was no sexual touching between them.

In respect of the person themselves, it should be noted that the courts have sought to implement this protective obligation even where the person *has* capacity to make decisions in relation to sexual relations, if it is considered that they lack capacity to judge whether a prospective sexual partner could cause them risk.[36]

As already identified, the obligation to protect is not limited to situations where the person appears to be subject to coercion or other form of abuse. Indeed, in the context of forced marriage (which can give rise to similar issues as those under consideration here[37]), the domestic courts have grappled with how best to protect the person from themselves where there is a clear risk that they will be exposed to Article 3 ECHR ill-treatment.[38]

Moving outwards from the person themselves, the obligation to protect under the ECHR arises in relation to those who might be victims of sexual assault (broadly defined) against the risk to them from a person who was incapable of understanding the need for sexual activity to be mutually consensual. Again, this obligation is imposed upon the State as a whole, by section 6 Human Rights Act 1998. This can arise in the context of determining capacity. As the Supreme Court held in *JB*: 'the court as a public authority [bound by the HRA 1998], in determining what information is relevant to the decision, must include reasonably foreseeable adverse consequences for P and for members of the public. In practice, by doing so, the court under the MCA protects members of the public.'[39]

In respect of JB's own case, Lord Stephens contemplated that the legitimate aims for any interference with JB's Article 8 rights would include the protection of both mental and physical health of others, the protection of the rights and freedom of others as well as the prevention of disorder or crime.[40]

The protective obligation can (and in practice does) arise much more obviously in relation to the steps taken by public authorities, with the sanction of the Court of Protection, to control the residence, care and

36 See *A Local Authority v TZ (No.2)* [2014] EWCOP 973, [2014] COPLR 159, 'filtering' the question through the prism of TZ's lack of capacity to make decisions as to contact, and hence the court's jurisdiction to make decisions as to contact on his behalf.

37 For two reasons: (a) forced marriage will occur if the person lacks capacity to marry, irrespective of the motives or conduct of the other person; and (b) capacity to marry has traditionally been linked to capacity to consent to/make decisions about sexual relations.

38 See *Re K (Forced Marriage: Passport Order)* [2020] EWCA Civ 190, [2020] Fam 283, Sir Andrew McFarlane expressly using the concept of protecting the person from themselves (see para 36).

39 *JB* at para 92.

40 *JB* at para 119.

contact arrangements for the person if they lack capacity in those domains. The Court of Protection can undoubtedly take into account the potential for risk to others as part of its determination as to what steps to take in the name of the person's best interests (at least so long as it can identify that there will be a 'knock-on' adverse consequence to the person of taking a step that might harm others).[41] While perhaps not immediately obvious from the Supreme Court's judgment, this situation arose directly in the *JB* case, where the Court of Protection had previously endorsed a care plan with significant restrictions upon JB including, one-to-one supervision when out in the community and when in the presence of women, on the basis (agreed by the Official Solicitor on his behalf) that JB lacked capacity make to decisions – among other matters – about contact with others.[42]

The ECHR does not, therefore, appear to provide any answer to the dilemma.

What about the CRPD? This treaty, concluded in 2006 and ratified by the United Kingdom in 2009, seeks to bring about a radical change in the approach adopted in the social, political and legal arenas to those with disabilities (see, for an overview, Series, 2019). With its focus on securing equality for those with disabilities, including in the field of legal capacity, does the CRPD provide a way to cut through debates mired in history?

We note, immediately, that *JB* case itself confirms that the CRPD will not be seen by the English courts as providing the answer, Lord Stephens re-emphasising that, as an unincorporated international treaty, the CRPD is of only limited relevance to the courts in England and Wales.[43] Indeed, the Supreme Court went further. In refusing permission to bring a standalone ground of appeal based on the CPRD (raised for the first time before the Supreme Court), Lord Stephens nonetheless made clear that he did not consider that ruling by the Court of Appeal had created a separate standard of capacity for people with disabilities. There was no discrimination contrary to the CRPD, he considered, because the Court of Appeal's test applied equally to everyone in society.[44]

However, more fundamentally, it is not obvious that the CRPD does more than reframe the clash of principles, for three reasons. First, Article 23(1) CRPD obliges states parties to the CRPD to take effective and appropriate measures to eliminate discrimination against persons with disabilities in all matters relating to marriage, family, parenthood and

41 See, for instance, *Birmingham City Council v SR; Lancashire County Council v JTA* [2019] EWCOP 28, [2020] 3 All ER 438 at para 41.

42 *JB* at paras 2 and 11.

43 See *JB* at para 120, *R (SC, CB and 8 children) v Secretary of State for Work and Pensions & Ors* [2021] UKSC 26, [2021] 3 WLR 428 at paras 77 and 84.

44 *JB* at para 120.

relationships, on an equal basis with others. 'Relationships' here includes the expression of sexual desire (Filala-Butora, 2018, pp 634–5 and 639). However, it cannot be said that Article 23(1) imposes an obligation upon the State to facilitate or support the imposition upon another of sexual desire expressed by a person with disabilities, irrespective of whether the other person is consenting.

Second, to determine whether a person is consenting, it is essentially impossible to escape the functional concept of capacity criticised by the Committee on the Rights of Persons with Disabilities[45] as incompatible with the equal enjoyment of the right to legal capacity guaranteed by Article 12 CRPD. As one of the leading advocates for the position adopted by the Committee has noted in the course of developing a model for sexual relations compliant with the right to legal capacity contained in Article 12 CRPD: '[i]t is, of course, important to ensure that all parties in any sexual activity are agreeing to that sexual activity. That agreement cannot exist without the parties having the decision-making skills necessary to *understand*, to some extent, what the nature of the sexual activity is' (Arstein-Kerslake, 2015, emphasis added).

It is undoubtedly possible to bolster and support these decision-making skills, and it may be possible to seek to strip out some of the information currently accepted as necessary by the courts in England and Wales, but on any view there will be those who simply cannot achieve this understanding. What is to happen at that point?

Third, Article 16 CRPD materially provides that: 'States Parties shall take all appropriate legislative, administrative, social, educational and other measures to protect persons with disabilities, both within and outside the home, from all forms of exploitation, violence and abuse, including their gender-based aspects.'

It is important to note that 'protection' encompasses *prevention* not merely ex post facto *punishment*[46] of exploitation, violence and/or abuse against those with disabilities. Article 16 therefore appears to point to the same outcome as reached under the ECHR: (1) the protection of a person from themselves if they cannot give appropriate consent to an act initiated by others (if it is accepted that non-consensual sexual activity itself represents a harm to the person); and (2) the protection of others unable to give that consent from the actions of a person unable to recognise the need for such consent.

45 See Ruck Keene, Kane, Kim and Owen (2019).

46 Addressed, separately, in Article 16(5), which provides that: 'States Parties shall put in place effective legislation and policies, including women- and child-focused legislation and policies, to ensure that instances of exploitation, violence and abuse against persons with disabilities are identified, investigated and, where appropriate, prosecuted.'

Some might argue that the observations already made do not engage with the point that it appears that it is only in respect of those with disabilities that questions of the ability to consent are asked. However, the problem arises where – for whatever reason (including to discharge obligations under Article 16 CRPD) – the questions *have* been asked. At that point, therefore, the CRPD – as with the ECHR – might recast the language within which a choice has to be made, but does not ultimately avoid the need to make a choice – protection or empowerment. Both also, ultimately, appear to point towards a protectionist regulatory model rather than one based on empowerment. In the next section, we therefore ask whether there is (or could be) any other way in which to avoid this choice being required at all.

## Asking a different question?

As we noted earlier, the prospect of viewing sexual relations in the context of cognitive impairment as 'outside the law' (Home Office, 2000) has been considered, only to be rejected. Both in the criminal and now in the civil field, the law has firmly intruded itself, and questions of sexual activity in this context may appear to be entirely 'juridified'.[47] Sexual activity in the context of cognitive impairment is seen both as a legitimate area for the law to be concerned with, and for people and bodies to have recourse to the law to resolve the dilemmas that arise.

Juridification is notoriously difficult to reverse; and there may be very sound reasons why we would not wish to seek entirely to reverse it. As the (English) Independent Review of Sex Offences noted (Home Office, 2000), it 'seems wrong' for the criminal law to withdraw completely for two reasons.

First, such a non-interventionist approach would appear to be obviously wrong in situations where one of the two participants[48] has a cognitive impairment which (1) appeared to put them in a situation where they were incapable of understanding what the other proposed; and (2) where the situation caused them distress or harm. This situation is addressed, more or less effectively, by the criminalising provisions of the SOA 2003 in England and Wales and the CL(SO)A 2017 in Ireland.

Second, this strategy would also seem wrong in a situation where (1) one of the participants had a cognitive impairment which rendered them incapable of understanding the harm that they might cause by initiating sexual relations with a person who was not in fact consenting; and (2) initiated or continued

---

[47] Habermas (1987), and, specifically with reference to issues in the context of capacity, Series and Nilsson (2018) at p 351.

[48] It is of course entirely possible for there to be more than two participants, but for present purposes we focus on the most commonly occurring situation.

sexual relations with a person who was not consenting and did cause them harm. At that point, however, the criminal law (at least as conventionally conceived) is a blunt instrument, because it is highly likely – even in Ireland, where the prosecution has the benefit of an evidential burden in its favour – that the person would not be found to have the requisite *mens rea* (that is, crudely, wrongful intent).[49] They might well be diverted down (through a plea of insanity) into the forensic psychiatric system, but it is equally – if despairingly – likely that the criminal investigation would stall at an early stage, given the complexity of taking forward investigations and prosecution in the face of cognitive impairment. And the use of the criminal law collapses into near incoherence in circumstances where both participants have cognitive impairments and appeared to be willing.

So much for the criminal law, looking at matters, in general, through the rear-view mirror. But JB's case, as we have demonstrated, shows: (1) how recourse to the law *in advance* of sexual activity becomes even thornier; and (2) that such recourse will almost inevitably to lead to conclusions that restrict sexual expression by those with cognitive impairments. Where such expression has the potential to cause harm to others, and assuming that there is a proper basis for asserting that risk, that restriction is understandable.[50] For example, in England and Wales, section 39 SOA 2003 makes it an offence (in effect) for a person involved in the care of an individual with a mental disorder impeding choice to engage in sexual activity to cause or incite them to engage in such activity.

Restrictions on sexual expression are also understandable where the expression has the potential to cause harm to the person themselves which they are (by reason of their cognitive impairment) incapable of protecting themselves from, again assuming that there is a proper basis for asserting that risk. However, it feels much less comfortable where it cannot properly be asserted that there is any risk of harm, but it is clear that any sexual activity that will take place will be non-consensual in the eyes of the criminal law on the part of the person themselves (or indeed, if both have cognitive impairments, on the part of both participants). It becomes even more complex given the provisions of the criminal law which might well, even if inadvertently, catch those concerned with the care of the person or people involved, if they turn a blind eye. In *Secretary of State for Justice v A Local Authority & Ors* [2021] EWCA Civ 1527, [2021] 3 WLR 1425, Baker and King LJJ sought (obiter) to explain how the provisions of section 39 SOA 2003 would not necessarily impact upon 'a care worker arranging private

[49] There has been no English case definitively determining this point, but see in this regard *R v B (MA)* [2013] EWCA Crim 3; [2013] 1 Cr App R 36, and *JB* at para 115.

[50] Note, we deliberately use the term 'understandable' here, rather than a more narrowly legal one such as 'justified', as we are seeking to capture a broad concept.

time for a long-married couple which she knows is likely to include sexual activity in those circumstances' (paragraph 71). However, the legal ice might be thought to remain perilously thin in such circumstances.

Some of these complexities can be avoided by following the law as it stands. That law does not just include the MCA 2005, and much emotional harm in England and Wales could be avoided, we suggest, if local authorities interpreted their obligations under the Equality Act 2010 to 'improv[e] the delivery to disabled pupils of information which is readily accessible to pupils who are not disabled'[51] so as to include information about sexual relations rather than, as all too often appears to be the case, simply seeking to avoid the problem.[52]

Even within the four walls of the MCA 2005, and as emphasised by the Supreme Court in *JB*,[53] no conclusion that a person lacks capacity to make a decision can or should be reached unless all practicable steps to support them to do so have been taken without avail: section 1(3) MCA 2005 (and, in Ireland, section 8(3) of the Assisted Decision-Making (Capacity) Act 2015). However, this can go only so far, as there will remain some people who, even with appropriate support, are unable to make the relevant decisions.

It would be possible to reform the statutory law. For instance, and as developed further in Chapter 6 by Sorinmade and Peisah in this volume, it might be possible to adopt the model of advance decisions to refuse treatment to develop an 'advance decision as to intimacy', to allow consent to survive the onset of cognitive impairment.[54] Advance decisions to refuse treatment are not unproblematic in both theoretical and practical terms.[55] It is possible to envisage equal, if not more serious, difficulties in translating such a model to the sexual sphere,[56] but at least they start from a clear foundation of the decision, in principle, being one made by the person. Even more radically, the statutory law could be reformed so as to recognise a path for substitute consent to be given by another at the time of potential sexual activity (whether or not the person ever had had the capacity to give such a consent).[57] It is possible to anticipate some (though surely not all) of the unintended consequences to which such a course of action could give

---

[51] Para 1(2)(c) of Schedule 10 to the Equality Act 2010. Alex is grateful to participants at the 2023 Mental Diversity Law Network Law conference, where a version of this work was presented for stimulating this line of inquiry.

[52] The work of Jodie Rawles in the related field of information about contraception is illuminating and challenging. See the interview with her available at Ruck Keene (2022).

[53] *JB* at para 118.

[54] See work of Boni-Saenz, for instance (2021).

[55] See Auckland (2018) with reference to the specific issues that arise in the context of dementia.

[56] See also here Sorinmade, Ruck Keene and Peisah (2021).

[57] See, in the American context, the work of Boni-Saenz (2021).

rise. Among these would be the fact that, unless both the criminal and civil law were amended, substitute consent could be lawful for purposes of the civil law but at the same time give rise to the authorisation of what would otherwise be a criminal offence. And, more broadly, it is easy to imagine the scope for problematic judgements being made about 'good' and 'bad' sexual activity by those charged with giving consent.

Some of these proposals may well fall to be considered in due course, and JB's case has certainly brought to the fore issues which have been lurking for many years and which, as we have seen, were largely ducked when the SOA 2003 was passed. In the interim, however, we make a suggestion that is at once more modest and more radical: namely, that we should recognise that while professionals and the courts *can* ask and answer the question as to whether or not a person can make a decision to engage in sexual relations, in most cases, they *should not* ask the question.

It is striking that despite many judges identifying the issue as a particularly challenging one, none has asked *why* they need to address it. Rather, it is simply assumed to be something which can be legitimately considered and, consequently, something which should be considered in the context of care planning for those with cognitive impairments. The Supreme Court equally made this assumption in *JB*. Had judges asked why they needed to address the question – in advance – of a person's capacity to make decisions relating to sexual relations, it might perhaps have been possible to identify that this is the paradigm example of a question which needs to be located in its context. In other words, simply answering the question in the abstract is likely to lead those working with the person down one of two difficult routes: (1) thinking that they have to take steps to restrict all sexual expression by the person or situations where the person may be 'exposed' to others initiating sexual activity; or (2) thinking that if they do not take steps to facilitate sexual expression by the person, they will in some way be acting unlawfully. Neither of these chains of reasoning is necessarily correct. In relation to the first, this is because – as the Supreme Court made clear in *JB* – there is no necessary identity between the civil and criminal law conceptions of consent. In relation to the second, this is because the law is concerned with inappropriate restriction of sexual activity between consenting individuals, not the unilateral expression of sexual desire.

Rather, we suggest, the real focus should be upon the person's ability to make decisions about contact with others. If they lack that functional capacity, which is to be considered (depending upon the situation) either by reference to decisions about contact with the world at large, to specific categories of people, or to specific individuals,[58] it is legitimate to consider

[58] See *City of York Council v C* [2013] EWCA Civ 478, [2014] Fam 10 at para 35, and, for amplification on the facts of a specific case involving different categories, *Re EOA* [2021] EWCOP 20 at para 50.

questions of contact through the prism of the person's best interests. If there is the potential that the person will engage in sexual activity when they have contact with either the specific individuals or categories of people identified, then it will be necessary to consider the potential for that activity to cause harm and/or distress to either the person or someone else. Then, but only then, will it be necessary to consider whether the person has capacity to decide to engage in sexual relations. At that point it is then possible to ask a focused, rather than abstract question.

Such an approach would bring clarity to the position and would also provide a rather more coherent explanation as to whether and why the (necessarily intrusive) exploration of a person's capacity in this domain is being considered than the present situation, where consideration is essentially ad hoc. It would also allow more attention to be paid to the fact that the MCA 2005 requires focus on the person's ability to make the decision at the material time, rather than – as can all too often happen at the moment – for it to be considered and 'written off' on a one-off basis. It would not replace the use of the criminal law but would provide a clearer delineation of the respective places of questions of capacity in civil and criminal law. We do not suggest that this approach can resolve all the dilemmas in this area, but it may help in terms of identifying the 'least worst' answer until and unless either (1) a way is found for the law to tip-toe discretely away from asking at least some of the questions that are posed; or (2) statutory law reform creates an entirely new framework.

## Conclusion

As already noted, it seems difficult to find any way in which to identify that another decision could have been reached in the *JB* case, given the questions posed of the Supreme Court. We have further noted that this would be the case even with a greater reference to the provisions of the ECHR and/or CRPD than was made by the Supreme Court. However, the iron logic of the decision is one that may well leave many uncomfortable (as, indeed, it seems to have left Lord Stephens, given his determined attempts to use the 'relevant information' to personalise the capacity test). We have, therefore, explored in the immediately preceding section whether one way in which to think about this is to ask whether the question about sexual decision-making capacity really needs to be asked, and have posed an approach which may mean that it is asked in the right way and in the right circumstances.

It is undoubtedly the case that this is an area ripe for law reform, not least so as to be able to give sustained – democratic – consideration to the question of whether and how the law should include a workaround for the fact that a person cannot give the form of contemporaneous consent that is currently (and we say rightly) understood to be necessary to avoid sexual activity being, prima facie, criminal. Whether such reform could ever produce a truly satisfactory resolution to the clash of principles exposed by JB's case is, however, a question that we find difficult to be entirely optimistic about.

## References

Arstein-Kerslake, A. (2015) 'Understanding sex: the right to legal capacity to consent to sex', *Disability & Society*, 10, 1459–1473.

Auckland, C. (2018) 'Protecting me from my directive: ensuring appropriate safeguards for advance directives in dementia', *Medical Law Review*, 26(1), 73–97.

Boni-Saenz, A. (2021) 'Advance consent and network consent', in R. Shuttleworth and L. Mona (eds), *The Routledge handbook of disability and sexuality*. Oxford: Routledge, pp 221–230.

Cusack, A. (2015) 'The right to love: over- and under-criminalisation in the sexual autonomy of persons with intellectual disabilities', *Human Welfare*, 4(8), 8–10.

Department of Justice (2014) *Discussion paper on sexual offences against vulnerable persons*. Dublin: Department of Justice.

Filala-Butora, J. (2018) 'Article 23: respect for the home and the family', in I. Banketas, M. Ashley Stein and D. Anastasiou (eds) *The UN Convention on the Rights of Persons with Disabilities: A commentary*. Oxford: Oxford University Press, pp 628–655.

Flynn, E. (2017) '*The final countdown: Ireland's ratification of the UN Convention on the Rights of Persons with Disabilities*' (Human Rights in Ireland, 31 January 2017). Available at: http://humanrights.ie/mental-health-law-and-disability-law/the-final-countdown-irelands-ratification-of-the-un-convention-on-the-rights-of-persons-with-disabilities/ (Accessed 30 March 2023).

Habermas, J. (1987) *The theory of communicative action, lifeworld and system Volume 2: A critique of functionalist reason*. Boston, MA: Beacon Books.

Heri, C. (2020) 'Shaping coercive obligations through vulnerability: the example of the ECtHR', in L. Lavrysendan and N. Mavronicola (eds), *Coercive human rights: Positive duties to mobilise the criminal law under the ECHR*. London: Hart, pp 93–140.

Home Office (2000) *Setting the boundaries: Reforming the law on sex offences. Vol. 1*. London: HMSO.

Kilcommins, S., Edwards, C. and O'Sullivan, T. (2014) 'An international review of legal provisions and supports for people with disabilities as victims of crime', *Irish Council for Civil Liberties*, 26.

Law Commission (2000) *Consent in sex offences: A report to the Home Office Sex Offences Review*. London: HMSO.

Law Reform Commission (2013) *Sexual offences and capacity to consent*. Dublin: Law Reform Commission.

McCormack, B., Kavanagh, D., Caffery, S. and Power, A. (2005) 'Investigating sexual abuse: findings of a 15-year longitudinal study', *Journal of Applied Research in Intellectual Disabilities*, 18, 217–227.

Ruck Keene, A. and Price, A. (forthcoming) '*Age-related dementia and the law: the challenges of mental capacity and equality*' , in Westwood, S. and Knauer, *Research Handbook on Law, Society and Ageing*. Cheltenham: Elgar.

Ruck Keene, A. (2022) *Contraception, support and intellectual disability – in conversation with Jodie Rawles.* Available at: https://www.mentalcapacitylawandpolicy.org.uk/contraception-support-and-intellectual-disability-in-conversation-with-jodie-rawles/ (Accessed 26 September 2023).

Ruck Keene, A. and Enefer, A. (2022) 'What place has "capacity" in the criminal law relating to sex post JB?', *International Journal of Law and Psychiatry*, 85, 101843.

Ruck Keene, A., Kane, N., Kim, S.Y. and Owen, G. (2019) 'Taking capacity seriously? Ten years of mental capacity disputes before England's Court of Protection', *International Journal of Law and Psychiatry*, 65, 56–76.

Series, L. (2019) 'Disability and human rights', in N. Watson, A. Roulstone and C. Thomas (eds) *Routledge Handbook of disability studies*. Abingdon: Taylor & Francis, pp 72–84.

Series, L. and Nilsson, A. (2018) 'Article 12 CRPD: equal recognition before the law', in I. Banketas, M. Ashley Stein and D. Anastasiou (eds), *The UN Convention on the Rights of Persons with Disabilities: A commentary.* Oxford: Oxford University Press, pp 339–382.

Sorinmade, O., Ruck Keene, A. and Peisah, C. (2021) 'Dementia, sexuality, and the law: the case for advance decisions on intimacy', *The Gerontologist*, 61(7), 1001–1007.

3

# Capacity to Consent to Sex in the Civil and Criminal Law: Blurring the Boundaries

*Jaime Lindsey and Karen Brennan*

## Introduction

This chapter considers the legal test for capacity to consent to (or engage in) sexual activity at the boundary of the civil and criminal law. This is an area that has been under-explored, with focus tending to be in the respective silos of each jurisdiction. Instead, we combine our expertise as a mental capacity law scholar and a criminal law scholar, to consider the relationship between these two distinct branches of the law. We argue, drawing on new materialist theories (Barad, 2003; Barad, 2007; Garland-Thomson, 2011; Conaghan, 2013), that the boundary between the civil and criminal law on capacity to consent to sex is permeable and, moreover, that the underpinning justifications for the civil and criminal law regarding capacity to consent to sex[1] are fundamentally the same, with divergence primarily in relation to the procedural safeguards in the respective jurisdictions. We suggest that strengthening the procedural safeguards of the civil law, specifically the Court of Protection (CoP), is a more productive way forward than reinforcing the perceived boundary.

This tension between the civil and criminal law came to the fore following the Supreme Court decision in *A Local Authority v JB* (*JB*),[2] one of the few

[1] While the terminology used in *A Local Authority v JB* [2001] UKSC 52 is 'engage in' sexual relations, we still use the term 'consent to', given its importance in the criminal context, and the issue of consent is therefore central to our argument here.

[2] [2021] UKSC 52.

appellate decisions concerning the operation of the Mental Capacity Act 2005 (MCA), and the catalyst for the discussion in this edited volume. By way of background, we first see an attempt at defining capacity to consent to sex by Munby J in *X City Council v MB, NB and MAB*;[3] with subsequent interpretation under the MCA, consent to sex jurisprudence soon became a minefield. As decisions about consent to sex are excluded from the best interests approach of the MCA,[4] where the CoP is called upon to assess capacity to consent to sex it is concerned with whether or not an individual has the general capacity to consent, rather than capacity in relation to a specific individual.

In *JB* the Supreme Court affirmed the principle that it is necessary for the decision maker to understand that both they and the other person involved must give consent to the sexual activity in question, thereby recentring the role of consent in mental capacity law. Several responses to the *JB* decision and wider commentary about sexual capacity have raised concerns about the law representing a high threshold above that reasonably required of the non-disabled decision maker, with some even arguing that it is discriminatory (Arstein-Kerslake and Flynn, 2016; Pritchard-Jones, 2020; Ruck Keene and Enefer, 2022). What this critique means is that, in the absence of a mental impairment under section 2 of the MCA, many individuals may disregard the need for the consent of others, but they are not prevented from engaging in sexual relationships. This can be seen as a form of indirect discrimination against mentally disabled people. Criticism has also been levied by those who think the decision imposes too high a threshold and does not recognise the differences in the developments of the civil and criminal law (Ruck Keene and Enefer, 2022). While we acknowledge these wider critiques, we base our argument on the application of the law in England and Wales; arguments about abolition of a mental capacity threshold in its entirety have merit, but they are not the focus of this chapter, which considers what the role of consent should be in mental capacity law as it stands today. If we are to have a legal test for capacity to engage in sex at all, which is required under any ordinary interpretation of the MCA, then we think it is right as a matter of principle that it includes understanding consent. To fail to include consent as part of the test is to fail to account for an essential aspect of sexual relations, which is that it should always be consensual; if it is not, it is a sexual offence. This inevitably brings the criminal and civil law into closer alignment, which then raises questions about what opportunities arise from this to further bridge the gap between the two jurisdictions in ways which offer benefits for those impacted upon by mental capacity law.

3 [2006] 2 FLR 968.

4 S 27 MCA.

In this chapter we commence our argument from the starting point that it was right for the Supreme Court to place consent at the heart of the test for sexual capacity. Some of these arguments have been made elsewhere (Lindsey and Harding, 2021). Here, we focus on how the decision in *JB* represents a closer alignment of the civil and criminal law on capacity to consent to sexual activity. Although there remain important distinctions between the two jurisdictions,[5] we argue that the two areas of law have much more in common than might appear on first glance, justifying their alignment post-*JB*. Finally, we consider how hybrid orders might apply in this context, enabling more effective cross-working for difficult cases, moving beyond the apparent silos of the civil and criminal law.

## Consent, capacity and the law

### *The meaning of consent*

Consent is a foundational concept when thinking about sexual activity between adults, and it is of fundamental importance in the area of sexual offences, delineating lawful sexual activity from serious criminal offending. Consent has been extensively theorised and justified as a framework through which to understand sexual relationships (Lacey, 1998; Clough, 2014; Arstein-Kerslake and Flynn, 2016; Carline, Gunby and Murray, 2020), notwithstanding some critiques of consent as representing the correct approach to sexual relations, particularly from feminists (Lacey, 1998, pp 112–124; Cowan, 2007, p 51). At its core, consent is a mutual concept, whereby all parties involved in the sexual activity provide agreement to taking part in it. On the face of it, consent has a relatively simple definition in section 74 of the Sexual Offences Act 2003 (SOA): 'A person consents if he agrees by choice, and has the freedom and capacity to make that choice.' Lack of consent does not have to be communicated; the fact that the complainant did not resist or protest should not be taken to mean that they consented, as consent should not be assumed from the complainant's passivity.[6] Whether or not the complainant of a sexual offence consented, however, gives rise to complex issues. For example, difficulties arise in cases where the complainant on the face of it consented, giving what Wallerstein terms as 'factual consent', but where this was legally invalid due to the fact that she had no freedom or capacity to choose (Wallerstein, 2009). Aside from the circumstances included in the list of evidential and conclusive presumptions found in sections 75 and 76 of the SOA, the legislation left undefined the important concepts of capacity and freedom which the section

5 *JB* (n2) [99–116].

6 *Malone* [1998] 2 Cr App R 447.

74 definition embraces as essential to consent (Temkin and Ashworth, 2004; Elliott and de Than, 2007; Cowan, 2007; Elvin, 2008).

To some extent, the complexity of consent can, however, be overemphasised. It is a relatively simple concept that asks; does the other person(s) voluntarily agree to engage in the activity in question? The reasons for their agreement may vary and voluntariness may be disputed in specific instances, and this is where the difficulties arise, particularly in determining the meaning of the criminal law and its application on particular facts. However, we suggest that it is not difficult to understand the need for consent at a conceptual level; that is, it requires an understanding that there must be agreement to do the sexual activity proposed. Furthermore, it is a relatively low threshold to require an understanding that an absence of consent at all makes the sexual activity a form of criminal conduct.

### *Capacity to consent in the civil and criminal law*

The concept of capacity to consent is relevant to sexual offences in the criminal law in a number of ways, depending on whether the person with impaired capacity is the complainant or the defendant. Capacity is relevant to wider issues where the person with impaired capacity is the alleged perpetrator. For example, capacity can arise as a focus in relation to plea, sentencing and defences (Ruck Keene and Enefer, 2022). More specifically, at trial a defendant's capacity may arise as an issue in determining whether they had the *mens rea*, or mental fault, for the offence or whether they could rely on the insanity defence. In cases where the person lacking capacity is the victim of a sexual offence, their capacity is crucial to the issue of whether they consented for the non-consensual sexual offences found in sections 1–4 of the SOA. Their capacity is also relevant to the special offences found in sections 30–31 of the SOA which offer additional protection to persons with a mental disorder – which includes a disability or disorder of mind – against sexual exploitation. These offences criminalise sexual offences[7] against persons who due to a mental disorder were 'unable to refuse' either because (a) he lacks capacity to choose whether to agree (whether because he lacks sufficient understanding of the nature or reasonably foreseeable consequences of what is being done or for any other reason) or (b) he is unable to communicate such choice. These provisions make no reference to 'consent', and so a lack of consent does not need to be proven. However, there is some degree of overlap between these provisions, especially the concept of inability to refuse, and the concept of consent found in section 74.[8]

7 Including sexual touching; causing or inciting to engage in sexual activity; engaging in sexual activity in their presence; causing to watch a sexual act: SOA ss 30–33.

8 See later discussion on *R v C*.

Capacity is crucial to the question of whether the complainant consented for the purposes of the non-consensual offences because the definition *incorporates* the requirement that the complainant had the capacity to choose.[9] Like in the civil law, capacity may be lost due to various causes, including mental impairment, being drugged, intoxicated, unconscious, or extreme youth. However, there is also surprisingly little case law on the meaning of capacity for the purposes of section 74, despite the statute being now 20 years old. The House of Lords in *R v C*[10] addressed the meaning of capacity in the context of the concept of being 'unable to refuse' found in the section 30–33 offences, and therefore offers guidance on the meaning of capacity more generally, and its interaction with the civil law. The House of Lords held that the assessment of whether a complainant was unable to refuse due to lacking capacity to understand or for any other reasons is an individualised assessment, based on the situation in which the complainant was in at the time of the alleged offence. Therefore, the focus was not on their 'status' as a disabled person, nor was the question about whether they had capacity in general, but it was focused on the particular circumstances at hand, recognising that persons with mental disorders may have fluctuating abilities depending on the context. The core issue, according to the House of Lords, was autonomy, namely their ability to make a free choice, which meant that the ability of the complainant to understand the relevant information was only part of the assessment. Therefore, 'or for any other reason', according to Baroness Hale, was 'clearly capable of encompassing a wide range of circumstances in which a person's mental disorder may rob them of the ability to make an autonomous choice, even though they may have sufficient understanding of the information relevant to making it'.[11]

In addition to whether the complainant understood the information relevant to the decision, it was also necessary to show that she had the ability to process that information – to weigh it – so as to arrive at a choice.[12] Although the judgment did not address the meaning of capacity outside of the sections 30–33 provisions, the emphasis on autonomy, choice and freedom of choice very much reflects the core definition of consent given in section 74 and the meaning of capacity under the MCA: the criminal test for capacity, like that under the MCA, is one which involves understanding of the relevant information as well as the ability to process/weigh that information to arrive at a choice. Indeed, in *R v A(G)* the Court of Appeal,

---

9 s 74 SOA (definition of consent).

10 *R v C* [2009] 1 WLR 27.

11 (n10) [25].

12 *Ibid.* [24–25].

agreeing with the 'obvious desirability' of having similar tests, held that the approach to capacity in the criminal law should be 'necessarily informed by the definition and guidance contained in sections 2 and 3 of the Mental Capacity Act 2005', though it recognised that a jury would 'not need to be directed in strict accordance' with the MCA provisions.[13]

What this analysis of the criminal law shows is that the meaning of capacity in relation to consent to sex is already very closely aligned with the civil law; it is focused on choice, which may be undermined by a range of circumstances, including mental disorder. As identified earlier, and elsewhere in this collection, in *JB* the Supreme Court affirmed the pivotal role of consent in understanding information relevant to sexual relationships, bringing it in line with the criminal law. It is, in some ways, obvious why consent was a central feature of that case, given the expert evidence and pattern of behaviour by JB. In fact, had the Supreme Court sidestepped the issue by focusing on risks of pregnancy, disease and the mechanics of the sexual act, they would likely have attracted significant criticism. For example, when asked by Dr Thrift about the other person withdrawing consent during a sexual act JB said, at paragraph 34:

> 'That's a tricky one … If the person gives consent then she's already given consent and you have to go through with it to the end. Once you're half way through she can't say "I don't give you consent" 'cos you're already doing what you need to do. She cannot change her mind if you are already doing it. Cos it's her fault in the first place for saying yes. She can't say yes and then say no. Already said yes and you've got your chance.'

Dr Thrift recounted how JB did not shift in this view across all her assessment sessions, and how JB was visibly shaken at the idea that a partner would be able to withdraw consent. A defendant who may well lack capacity under the MCA due to their inability to understand whether the other person was consenting may be convicted of rape. This was recognised in *JB* by the Supreme Court considering the issue of protection – although he was risky to others, he was also in need of protection due to the risk of conviction which would have a particularly negative impact on him in light of his vulnerabilities.[14]

At a criminal trial, there is no specific question about whether the defendant had 'capacity'. Rather, evidence of a mental disorder/disability

[13] [2014] EWCA Crim 299 [19]. The SC in *JB* (n2) agreed that, if the tests were the same, strict adherence to the MCA guidance would not be needed in a criminal case [103].

[14] [40, 74].

falls to be considered in a different way – either on the question of whether he had the *mens rea* for the offence (specifically, in the case of non-consensual offences, a reasonable belief in consent) or whether he could rely on insanity as a defence. There is little case law on the issue of what mental disabilities may be relevant in assessing the question of whether 'having regard to all the circumstances' the defendant had a reasonable belief in consent in the case of non-consensual offences such as sexual assault and rape.[15] In *R v B* a delusional belief arising from a psychotic illness or a personality disorder could not be considered as a reasonable belief in consent, but the Court of Appeal left open the question about whether there may be other situations where a defendant's mental disability could be considered as contributing to a reasonable belief such as where they had an impaired ability to read subtle social signals.[16]

It is also important to emphasise that *JB* is not an unusual case, thereby refuting the argument that it distorts the wider application of the law to provide unjustified intrusion into people's lives. As one of the authors has argued elsewhere, cases concerning allegations of abuse either by the person or against the person are already the most typical application of capacity to consent to sex jurisprudence in the CoP (Lindsey, 2020; Lindsey and Harding 2021). Therefore, the consent requirement is almost always a central aspect of the cases that reach the CoP anyway; the *JB* case merely affirms that practice. Furthermore, the capacity question is much more likely to be an issue where the person is the alleged victim of sexual exploitation in the CoP, rather than the perpetrator (Lindsey, 2020; Lindsey and Harding, 2021). This is, perhaps, unsurprising given what we know about sexual abuse of women with disabilities (Lindsey, 2016; see also Hollomotz, Chapter 7 in this collection).

Ralph Sandland (see further in this collection at Chapter 1) has articulated that concerns about sex and disabled adults are not new, linking the civil case law on capacity to consent to sex with the historical development of the management of sexual activity by those with mental impairments (Sandland, 2013a; Sandland, 2013b). While Sandland argues that, historically, the focus was on controlling female sexuality in this regard, in more recent times we see the focus on protecting vulnerable females and restricting the risky behaviour of dangerous males.[17] It is within this context that the debate surrounding the application of the civil law on capacity to consent to sex has emerged and its relationship with the criminal law has been considered. However, although there have been advances in recent decades in rules of

15 SOA, ss 1(2) (rape) and 3(2) (sexual assault).

16 [2013] EWCA Crim 3.

17 *Ibid.*

evidence and court procedures,[18] as well as in criminal law doctrine, with the aim of improving access to justice for these vulnerable victims of sexual violence, the conviction rate for sexual crimes is notoriously low, and it is often said that these crimes have effectively been decriminalised (Imkaan and Rape Crisis England and Wales, 2020). Thus, when we think about the meaning of consent/capacity – and the respective roles of the criminal and civil jurisdictions – it is important to put this in the context of the wider criminal justice system's failure to prosecute and convict the vast majority of incidents of sexual violence, and the wider social context in which these crimes are understood and minimised. Recourse to an alternative form of protection, the MCA, is therefore understandable against this backdrop (Herring and Wall, 2014).

However, where the criminal law declines to prosecute those who are suspected of perpetrating sexual violence due to, for example, difficulties in the evidence – something which poses particular issues in cases involving persons with mental disabilities[19] – it may be problematic for the civil law to step in to fill this gap in terms of seeking to fulfil individual or public protection, as the consequences for individuals who are the subject of CoP proceedings can be quite draconian.[20] This may be particularly so in instances where the person is the victim/potential victim of sexual offending, as in this situation it is the *victim* who bears the burden of the court order, not the person who may be seeking to exploit their vulnerability and commit a sexual offence against them. In addition, irrespective of whether the person is the potential victim or offender in the criminal context, an order under the CoP may mean that the person is not permitted to engage in *any* sexual activity, meaning they are prevented from engaging in consensual as well as non-consensual sex. Further, such orders may be imposed for lengthy periods with infrequent reviews. The fact that the CoP lacks the procedural safeguards that apply in the criminal law is particularly troubling in this context. Recognition in *JB* of the function of the CoP in relation to public protection may have the impact of enhancing the role of the CoP in this respect, thus potentially further diminishing the criminal law's position in addressing sexual offending against/by persons with disabilities.

---

[18] For example, special measures directions (Youth Justice and Criminal Evidence Act 1999, ss 16–30); preventing a defendant from cross-examining the complainant in person (Youth Justice and Criminal Evidence Act 1999, s 34); rules on hearsay evidence/previous consistent statements (Criminal Justice Act 2003 s 120) and sexual history evidence (Youth Justice and Criminal Evidence Act 1999, ss 41–43).

[19] The evidence of the complainant (victim) and defendant is crucial in sexual offence cases where consent is the issue. Other evidence of lack of consent may be lacking, and the credibility of the complainant and defendant as witnesses is especially important.

[20] For further discussion of the consequences of criminal and civil proceedings, see later.

It is true that there may be situations where the more appropriate jurisdiction to deal with the case is the CoP, such as where there is limited public interest in prosecuting, given the circumstances as a whole. However, it is also crucial that, in instances where the criminal law does not prosecute, whether this is for evidential or public interest reasons, both victims and offenders are not in effect 'punished' by the civil law without the safeguards available in the criminal system. This is one area where space opens for greater interaction between the two jurisdictions, and we outline one suggestion later in relation to the use of hybrid orders. Other possibilities may also emerge, particularly when considering what constitutes 'justice' for victims of sexual offending, and which may mean finding alternative and more effective ways to address sexual violence either within the criminal justice system or outside it, such as, for example, through the use of restorative justice practices or alternatives to criminal justice which draw on or are based in the civil law (McGlynn, 2011; McGlynn, Westmarland and Godden, 2012).

## Blurred lines between the criminal and civil law

In this section we explore the issue of the boundaries between the civil and criminal law, arguing, in line with Clough's analysis of the binaries of mental capacity law (Clough, 2021), that the civil and criminal law is another binary which operates in this field, to the exclusion of considering the complexities, links and boundedness between the jurisdictions of the civil and criminal law. In doing this we draw on new materialist theories (Barad, 2003; Barad, 2007; Garland-Thomson, 2011; Conaghan, 2013) to consider how these boundaries might operate in the approaches to sexual capacity. We show how the justifications underpinning the civil and criminal law already have several similarities and the differences that remain would benefit from further erosion of the boundaries between them.

Materialism means recognising that the world is made up of matter; that physicality and cause and effect apply to human behaviour as much as to any other phenomena (Murphy and Margolis, 1995). New materialist theories are developed from a foundation of materialism, but which was departed from in the mid-20th century towards social constructionist understandings of the world and a focus on language. Karen Barad, a leading advocate of new materialism, explains that there is a strong relationship between the material world and our linguistic world, where matter is an active agent in the process of phenomena, rather than a neutral result of other practices (Barad, 2003; Barad, 2007). This means that the way we perceive phenomena, talk about, embody and experience them impacts upon them – any reliable understanding of the world must be based on an '*intra-action*' between the material and discursive world (Barad, 2007, p 815). The importance of feminist interpretations of new materialism is that they are based in the social world, analysing the ways in which our material conditions impact upon our social, emotional and psychological lives, often placing the concept of embodiment as central to an understanding of the world (Fletcher, Fox and McCandless, 2008; Garland-Thomson, 2011; Fox and Thomson, 2017; Clough, 2021). Social norms and relationality shape our behaviours in a material sense as much as through our linguistic characterisations of ourselves (Nedelsky, 2011).

As Clough has argued regarding the MCA, it is essential to begin to break down binaries and to think more creatively about how to deal with the most challenging scenarios. We suggest that the civil and criminal law is one more *perceived* boundary in the world of mental capacity law, building on Clough's description and critique of the bounded nature of this field. As she explains about the MCA, 'The Act itself is premised upon particular ideals of subjectivity … It sets up a framework of legal and spatial relations, drawing boundaries around and within those relations as it does so. These boundaries are inflected with an interwoven network of binaries which help to shape and form the logics of the legislation as well as broader legal frameworks' (Clough, 2021, p 40). Having some sort of boundary between the criminal law and civil law is inevitable in that they are separate jurisdictions, but that boundary is not impenetrable. As Clough explains, 'the binary construction here is historically framed and contingent, and – of course – could be otherwise' (Clough, 2021, p 56). We suggest this analysis can be applied to the civil/criminal law binary too. In fact, Clough herself criticises the approach taken in the line of cases pre-*JB* to capacity to consent to sex in similar terms, particularly focusing on the problematic capacity/incapacity binary (Clough, 2021, pp 68–69). Yet similar reasoning can be applied to the perceived civil/criminal binary. For example, in *JB* the Supreme Court closely considered the case law emanating from the criminal sphere and appeared to be influenced by it in coming to the conclusions they did regarding the role of consent in the civil law. Their reading shows a willingness to turn to the criminal law for help while also attempting to maintain a distinct and delineated boundary between the two jurisdictions. Despite some differences remaining, we show that the civil and criminal law here are already closely aligned. As a result, we should move away from trying to reinforce the boundary and, instead, think about how the civil and criminal law can continue to operate together in productive ways for those impacted upon by both jurisdictions.

As we outline later, we acknowledge that there remain some differences between the civil and criminal jurisdictions, but it is when either jurisdiction is operationalised that these differences perhaps become most apparent, as each system will operate within its own silo in the pursuit of its own purposes until a particular case is concluded. Broadly speaking, at a general level, the criminal law's focus on retrospective condemnation and punishment of a crime that has already been committed, as well as on future public protection, marks it out as different to the civil law. However, as we explain later, this does not mean there is no scope for increasing interaction between the two spheres, notably outside of the courtroom context, particularly in working towards the shared aim of public protection.

The already existing similarities between the two in respect of public protection may be further harnessed at points where spaces appear to allow for beneficial interactions. What these interactions may be, and the benefits involved, will undoubtedly depend on the situation and, in particular, whether the person is the victim/potential victim or offender/potential offender. It may require shifts from both the civil and criminal law in terms of how they approach these cases. For example, there may be opportunities to address the issue of disabled victims suffering the burdens of a CoP order which protects them from abusive individuals who seek to exploit their vulnerability, but which leave open the possibility of them having a consensual sexual relationship with others. At present the failure to criminalise the conduct of the abuser means that it is the victim who has restrictions placed on them for their own protection, something which fails to respect their right to a consensual sex life with an appropriate (non-abusive) partner. However, criminalisation may not be possible due to difficulties with the evidence, and the criminal process itself may harm the victim. In this sense, neither the civil nor the criminal system works well for the benefit of persons with disabilities, particularly in terms of addressing the (often) competing objectives of protection and autonomy. There may be scope to consider alternatives at the boundary of the two which can bridge these difficulties and provide for a just and effective outcome, such as with the use of hybrid orders, which we discuss in the final substantive section of this chapter. The overlap between the two in terms of the importance of consent, and the shared aim of public protection, makes it easier to consider innovative ways of approaching these cases.

Specifically, with regard to how the concept of consent is *applied* in either context, there remain some potential differences between the two areas, set out in *JB*.[21] These distinctions start from the basis of the criminal law being retrospective and the MCA being prospective in nature and, relatedly, the differing standards of proof – balance of probabilities in the civil courts versus beyond reasonable doubt in the criminal courts. The application of the test for capacity/consent in the criminal context is situation or person specific. As Baroness Hale stated in *R v C*: '[i]t is difficult to think of an activity which is more person and situation-specific than sexual relations. One does not consent to sex in general. One consents to this act of sex with

[21] *JB* (n2), particularly paras 97–116.

this person in this particular time and place.'[22] However, while the criminal law must look at the capacity of the individual in a particular set of historical circumstances and in relation to a specific sexual act with a specific person, the role of mental capacity law is broader and requires a general assessment of the person's understanding and abilities.

This means that capacity is assessed differently in the civil context, where the test is said to be issue specific in how it is applied, meaning that it asks whether the person understood the nature of the sexual act in a general or 'abstract' sense, without consideration of the specific circumstances of the potential sexual act, such as the proposed sexual partner (Herring and Wall, 2014; Clough, 2014). This may mean that, although the test for capacity is similar in both jurisdictions, it may apply differently based on whether it is conceptualised on assessment as issue or situation specific. While this is the doctrinal position, the reality of most mental capacity jurisprudence is that the courts here do also look to past behaviour and focus on sexual capacity in respect of specific relationships or specific concerns about an individual's sexual behaviour. This is evident in the JB case itself, where he had a history of risky sexual behaviour and there were concerns about his treatment of individuals. While JB did not have a regular partner, as we see in many CoP sexual capacity cases,[23] he did have a history of sexually dangerous and risky behaviour which suggests the situation-specific elements of his circumstances were also relevant factors, if only in contextualising his understanding. So, in practice, there may not be a significant difference in how capacity is assessed in both contexts, even more so post-*JB*.

The material dimension of the JB case is also in the consequences the approach has for JB and those around him, as well as for mental capacity law's future subjects. The decision has shaped how his circumstances ought to be responded to, including by professionals and the judiciary, when faced with similar cases. Practitioners such as social workers and carers who work closely with sexually risky individuals on a daily basis are always operating at the intersection of the civil and criminal law, merely looking for ways to harness the tools at their disposal to provide protection for potential victims and break down the legal binaries. That is not to make a positive normative judgement about that way of working, but it does reflect the reality for professionals on the ground who seek the tools available to them irrespective of whether they fall within the criminal or civil law. Moreover, the resources allocated to a case such as JB are impacted upon by the direction the law

---

22 (n10).

23 See, for example, *Local Authority X v MM* [2007] EWHC 2003, *D Borough Council v AB* [2011] EWHC 101, *The London Borough of Tower Hamlets v TB and SA* [2014] EWCOP 53, *IM v (1) LM (2) AB (3) Liverpool City Council* [2014] EWCA Civ 37.

takes. For example, including the consent element across the criminal and civil law approaches means that resources are more likely to be directed at facilitating individuals to understand consent rather than simply preventing sexual relationships. We have even seen in *Re CH v A Metropolitan Council*[24] that parties can be awarded damages by the court for failures to provide timely sex education. Conversely, if consent were to remain in the bounds of the criminal law alone, then there would be less impetus on professionals to direct resources to facilitating capacity and understanding consent as an essential element of that. There is, therefore, an important relationship between how the civil and criminal systems operate through social work with risky individuals such as JB. If we can move away from the embedded notion that the civil and criminal law are two dichotomous legal regimes which ought not to be blurred, then we can deal with the material reality of how they operate together in a beneficial way for those impacted by and working at their intersection. Below, we explore the various claimed divergences between the civil and criminal law and show that in respect of substantive law, theory/justification and consequences, the civil and criminal law are already closely aligned.

### *Substantive differences*

In this first section, we build on the analysis of the doctrinal position already stated to analyse the apparent substantive legal differences. In doing this, we can see that the differences that do remain post-*JB* are not as strong, on closer inspection, as they might first appear. This is exemplified earlier, where we have shown the close doctrinal relationship between the two jurisdictions. The Supreme Court in *JB* agreed with earlier authorities that 'it is in principle desirable, though not necessary, that there should be the same test for capacity' in the two jurisdictions. However, it disagreed with the conclusion of the Court of Appeal in *A(G)* that the difference between the criminal and civil tests was 'without distinction'.[25] Although it made some obiter observations on this, it held that the issue was best left to be determined on the basis of the facts of individual cases.[26]

Although the tests may not be precisely equivalent, in substance there are important similarities: both the civil and criminal tests focus on understanding and processing information, with consent being a central feature of this assessment. While some discussion has suggested that the focus of the test in the civil law is now capacity to 'engage in' sexual relations, and that this does

[24] [2017] EWCOP 12.

[25] [25].

[26] [108–116].

distinguish the two areas, we think this distinction is trivial (Ruck Keene and Enefer, 2022, p 8). It is, of course, the case that the consent issue is most pertinent in the criminal law when it is a potential perpetrator 'proposing' sex, and that nobody would seriously ask the question as to whether the victim understood the perpetrator's consent. However, that does not create a stark difference in the civil and criminal law, it is an application of the law to the factual circumstances of the case and with regard to the issues at stake. It is still right to say that consent is a central feature of both the civil and criminal law regarding capacity, but it may apply differently in different circumstances in both domains.

### *Theory/justificatory differences*

Moving next to the underpinning theoretical bases for each area, we consider the extent to which they converge. This is important because, we argue, there are now several justificatory similarities between the civil and criminal law which indicate increased convergence of the underlying basis for the law's role. Of course, the criminal law is different from other forms of legal regulation because it involves the coercive power of the state to publicly censure and punish wrongdoing and it plays a declaratory or communicative function in this respect (Husak, 2004; Lamond, 2007; Ashworth, 2008). The civil law does not have this public aspect to it in terms of communicating anything about the wrongness of certain conduct, or censuring individuals for engaging in it. Nonetheless, it is evident that there is marked overlap between the two systems: the civil and criminal law are both concerned with respecting sexual autonomy and with protecting people. This may be the wider public or an individual victim in a criminal case and, under the MCA, may include protecting the disabled victim from abuse or the potential perpetrator from potentially committing an offence. Furthermore, we now have Supreme Court authority that it is legitimately one of the functions of the MCA to protect the public.[27] Lord Stephens explained:

> The information relevant to the decision includes information about the 'reasonably foreseeable consequences' of a decision, or of failing to make a decision, which consequences are not limited to the consequences for P … The consequences for other persons or for members of the public are therefore a part of the information relevant to the decision … In this way the court as a public authority, in determining what information is relevant to the decision, must include reasonably foreseeable adverse consequences for P and for

[27] Para 92.

> members of the public. In practice, by doing so, the court under the MCA protects members of the public.[28]

The idea, then, that the MCA was set up to empower and protect the individual subject of its jurisdiction alone is no longer a justifiable premise, at least not in its doctrinal and practical application post-*JB*. We do have some concerns with the approach of the Supreme Court in this regard, in particular with the potential risks of using the MCA as a tool primarily aimed at public protection, given its potentially severe consequences for those to whom it applies which are not mirrored by the procedural safeguards of the criminal process. Yet even if one objects to the public protection narrative at a conceptual level, it remains highly persuasive to incorporate the concept of consent as part of the information relevant to a decision to engage in sex. That, in our view, is not justified by protection of the public, but as a matter of realistic analysis of what a person must understand about the fundamentals of sexual activity. Therefore, while the tools may be seen to be used 'on the ground' by practitioners to protect the wider public, that does not undermine the principled justification for centring consent in the legal test, which aligns the criminal and civil law. The test for capacity in relation to sex in both areas of law is justified by the importance of consent in sexual relations, highlighting their close relationship.

### *Consequential differences*

Next we look at the consequences of the civil and criminal law and argue that, in practice, these will often be similar in nature for adults who face a finding of incapacity in relation to sexual relationships and for adults who engage in criminal sexual conduct. On the face of it, most people would consider that the criminal and civil law have quite different consequences for those involved. To start with, because the criminal law operates as a form of public censure to sanction individuals for what are considered public wrongs, the use of the criminal law is considered particularly oppressive, and something which should be a 'last resort' (Husak, 2004; Ashworth 2008). The burdensome consequences of a criminal conviction, particularly for a serious offence, include stigma and punishment. In the case of sexual offences, both are likely to be significant, with the sanction likely to include imprisonment, thereby imposing restrictions on the individual's liberty.[29] Yet on any detailed analysis of mental capacity law, it is quite clear that it also operates in an oppressive way by authorising extensive restrictions on

[28] *Ibid*.

[29] For example, the punishment for rape is a maximum of life imprisonment (s 1(4) SOA 2003), and for sexual assault is a maximum of ten years' imprisonment (s 3(4) SOA 2003).

the liberty of the person – perpetrator or victim. Findings of incapacity in these domains can lead to highly restrictive care and supervision regimes which amount to a deprivation of liberty, hence the application of the Deprivation of Liberty Safeguards (DoLS) framework (Series, 2022). It is therefore not such a leap to compare the consequences of criminalisation, including punishment, with restrictions on liberty under mental capacity law. The level of supervision, sometimes lifelong, that can be associated with findings of incapacity in respect of sex can be in some circumstances just as, if not more, onerous than in the criminal law. Individuals may not have their capacity reassessed in any prompt manner and so they may be subject to continuous supervision to prevent them from engaging in incapacitous sex. Thus, although there are differences between the two, both systems can result in burdensome consequences, including restrictions on liberty. It is therefore important to ensure that there are limits to who/what is subject to the jurisdiction of each and that procedural safeguards are in place to protect individuals from these oppressive aspects, which leads us to the next point.

### *Procedural differences*

Our final point of analysis of difference relates to the procedural aspects of the civil and criminal law. We argue that the differences between the procedural protections are more stark than in any of the aforementioned areas. This is one area in which the criminal and civil law have not converged in relation to consent to sex, which we suggest is a potential problem for the CoP in how it deals with incapacity. This is particularly so given the consequences of a finding of incapacity in this regard. As we have already highlighted, due to the close overlap with the criminal law's consequences, civil law interventions ought to have stronger procedural protections. For example, we argue that the person ought to have direct legal representation, including representation which represents the person's own views and not just an application of what is in the person's best interests (Ruck Keene, Bartlett and Allen, 2016; Lindsey, 2022a). We also argue, drawing on work by one of the authors published elsewhere, that the person must be able to call their own expert evidence in mental capacity disputes rather than relying on a single joint expert (Lindsey, 2022a). This would be important in sexual capacity cases because it is essential for the person to be able to be on an equal evidential footing to challenge a finding of incapacity. While legal aid is currently available to Ps in some instances, including for DoLS challenges,[30] there is wider availability of legal aid in the criminal

[30] Civil Legal Aid (Financial Resources and Payment for Services) Regulations 2013, regulation 5(1)(g).

sphere as compared to civil justice, for reasons related to issues of loss of liberty, albeit even in relation to criminal justice legal aid has been severely impacted in recent years (Dehaghani and Newman, undated; Moorhead, 2004; Dehaghani and Newman, 2022).[31] We think that expansion of legal aid in mental capacity disputes is also necessary, given the similar potential impacts on those affected by findings of incapacity. As a result, we suggest that procedural justice protections ought to be much stronger in the CoP. This is something that one of the authors has argued for elsewhere (Lindsey, 2022a) and, if enacted, we could make the argument that civil and criminal law are even more closely aligned, which justifies further the hybrid approach.

In the foregoing sections we have highlighted that the essence of the issues is fundamentally the same under the MCA as under the criminal law; that is, whether or not a person is or has been exploited in some manner because of their impaired mental functioning which prevents them from understanding that sexual relations are a mutual, consensual, intimate act. Furthermore, we have shown the already present similarities across theory, consequences and substantive law. In light of the strong similarities in the underpinnings of the civil and criminal law on the issue of capacity to consent to sex, this perceived hard boundary is not immovable and practitioners should be willing to use the two jurisdictions more interchangeably and creatively to work together. For the CoP, though, we would also recommend greater procedural safeguards being adopted to avoid the risks of criminalisation of sexual behaviour without due process.

## Hybrid orders and responding to risky sexual behaviour

The analysis already provided points towards greater use of a hybrid approach to dealing with the problem of capacity to consent to sex, and specifically its application to cases of sexual violence where the person is the perpetrator. We consider how a hybrid approach might be developed for use in the intersection between the criminal law and civil law, drawing on analysis of other types of hybrid order, including the sexual risk order under section 122A of the SOA 2003 and those in the adult safeguarding context.[32] We consider some of the conceptual criticisms of these orders, arguing for modifications of how they are currently formulated to provide an effective way of dealing with those individuals at the intersection of the civil and criminal law.

[31] See Legal Aid, Sentencing and Punishment of Offenders Act 2012.

[32] One of the authors has argued for the implementation of a safeguarding adults order with specific recommendations for a support-based approach, see Lindsey (2020; 2022b).

The orders subject to analysis here are a form of civil/criminal hybrid procedure, which operate within the civil jurisdiction but can provide for criminal sanctions in the event of a breach. Different orders have different consequences for breach, but typically will require proof on the civil standard of the balance of probabilities. This means that criminal consequences can result from a civil standard of proof. Despite this distinctiveness, hybrid orders have taken hold in the politics of law making over the past two to three decades, perhaps most notably with the advent of anti-social behaviour orders which were introduced in the Crime and Disorder Act 1998 (Ashworth et al, 1998) but also with some wider support and success in the domestic abuse context (Wing-Cheong, 2017; Lindsey, 2020). A particular benefit of protection orders in the domestic abuse context is that they are targeted against the perpetrator of abuse. While this may seem obvious, it is important to note, because women (and it is disproportionately women who suffer domestic abuse) have often had to flee their home, friends, jobs and support networks to escape abuse. Therefore, placing consequences and restrictions on the perpetrator is essential if women are not to suffer double victimisation. The point is also relevant to the application of mental capacity law. As one of the authors has written elsewhere, too often in safeguarding investigations concerning disabled women, mental capacity law is used to remove a woman from an abusive partner by restricting and coercing her rather than through restrictions against the perpetrator (Lindsey, 2020; Lindsey, 2022b). If hybrid orders are to be enacted in this context, it is essential that they are focused on perpetrators of abuse rather than, again, operating as ways of restricting disabled women.

Turning next to the role of hybrid orders as they presently exist in the criminal law, Sexual Risk Orders (SROs) are a specific type of hybrid order under section 122A of the SOA.[33] A chief of police can apply for an SRO to apply to an individual who is believed to pose a risk of sexual harm against the public, but that person need not have been convicted of a criminal offence.[34] SROs are a civil order and are therefore controversial, given their potential for intrusion into the lives of adults who have not been convicted, or even

[33] There are other types of criminal orders that can be made for sexual conduct of this nature, such as Sexual Harm Prevention Orders (SHPOs) under s 103A(2) SOA. This article focuses on SROs rather than SHPOs as SROs have potentially broader scope, not requiring criminal proceedings in relation to the alleged perpetrator. However, SHPOs are worthy of further analysis as they apply where a person is found not guilty by reason of insanity or under a disability, thereby making them potentially relevant for some of the individuals who fall within the CoP's jurisdiction too.

[34] *Chief Constable of Kent Police v Carter* [2022] EWHC 1972 (Admin): confirmed that it is not necessary that the respondent committed a criminal offence.

tried, for a criminal offence.[35] The requirements for an SRO to be imposed are that they have done an act of a sexual nature; and, as a result of which, there is reasonable cause to believe that it is necessary to make an order to protect the public from harm.[36] Despite being a civil order, SROs are hybrid in nature because they act at the intersection of the civil and criminal law. For example, it must be proved to the criminal standard, beyond reasonable doubt, that the person has done an act of a sexual nature. However, the civil standard of proof applies to the second part of the test – that there is reasonable cause to believe that it is necessary to make an order to protect the public from harm – meaning this only needs to be established on the balance of probabilities. What this might mean depends on the individual case, and there is relatively little case law on this. However, *R v Mayne (Phean)*[37] suggests that it may be sufficient that a prosecution of the criminal conduct was not possible, for whatever reason that may be, but there is still a perceived need to protect the public due to the nature of the alleged offences, in that case accessing child sexual abuse material. Consequences for breach of SROs are also criminal in nature and can lead to a maximum term of imprisonment of six months or five years, depending on the indictment.[38]

While SROs may appear to encroach on the freedom of adults who have not been convicted of a criminal offence, two important features stand out to us as justifying their use. Firstly, the requirement to establish that the person has done an act of a sexual nature must be proven beyond reasonable doubt. This imports a criminal threshold into the analysis, which we think is important to show that the person has a degree of risk in their behavioural profile. Secondly, there is a proportionality requirement for the court to consider when making an SRO, which brings the law in line with the requirements of the European Convention on Human Rights.[39] These two elements together appear to balance the needs of the wider public to be protected against the need for the individual to not have their rights interfered with without due process.

While SROs are, of course, not within the remit of the CoP's powers, we raise them here for two reasons. Firstly, those working with individuals such as JB ought to consider the use of SROs as an alternative to CoP proceedings

---

[35] For example, see *R v Mayne (Phean)* [2021] EWCA Crim 737; [2022] 1 Cr App R (S) 9, where an SRO was made following arrest (but not prosecution) for accessing child sexual exploitation pornography online.

[36] S122A(6) SOA.

[37] See footnote 35.

[38] S122H SOA.

[39] For example, see the judicial review of interim SROs where discussion of vulnerability of victims was a key part of the proportionality analysis, *R (on the application of Anderson Pinheiro) v North Tyneside Magistrates Court and anor* [2022] EWHC 1176 (Admin).

in relevant cases. For example, where the primary concern is about sexual harm and sexual risk, rather than mental incapacity. We think that by arguing for a blurring of the boundaries of the criminal and civil law this ought to encourage professionals working with risky adults in this context to consider the full range of legal interventions that might be available to them. Where the adult has a disability there may be a tendency to resort to the MCA framework, due to its relative simplicity and accessibility. However, it is not the only legal framework that is relevant here and greater cross-agency working between social work, criminal justice and healthcare is warranted, albeit inter-agency working has long been desired but not always successfully achieved (Klevens et al, 2008; Davies, Barlow and Fish, 2023). Secondly, we argue that there may be scope to incorporate an order, similar in nature to SROs, but for application to individuals who may, by reason of their mental impairment, be unable to understand the consent of the other party in a sexual relationship. At present, the CoP has the power to grant injunctions under section 16(5) of the MCA, and the MCA's jurisdiction also intersects with that of the inherent jurisdiction of the High Court, which has been used somewhat interchangeably with the MCA in some instances.[40] Both of these forms of injunctive relief could be applied where the person is at risk of sexual abuse. However, it is less clear that an injunction could be granted against a person in the name of his or her own protection. Instead, expansion of safeguarding powers could be a way forward for use in cases of abuse where the person is believed to be the perpetrator and has care and support needs, which is the requirement that triggers the safeguarding duties under the Care Act 2014 (Lindsey, 2022b) or the Social Services and Well-being (Wales) Act 2014. This approach may provide a clearer route for professionals working with individuals such as JB to tailor any intervention in the ways in which it is most needed, without needing to engage the criminal justice system as is required for SROs. One of the authors has argued elsewhere for the use of targeted orders in the safeguarding context, which in principle could deal with cases such as that of JB, including that local authorities should be given 'the power to apply for protection orders in the safeguarding context, but in ways that focus on perpetrators rather than coercing the vulnerable adult' (Lindsey, 2020, p 159).

Hybrid orders have been extensively criticised, most acutely by Hendry and others, whose criticisms centre on the preventive turn of criminal law, 'othering' and instrumentalisation of the subjects of these orders (Green and Hendry, 2021; Hendry, 2022). We do not find these concerns persuasive as an objection, in absolute terms, to the use of hybrid orders. This is because we would suggest that their application itself is not a harm,

[40] *Southend on Sea v Meyers* [2019] EWHC 399.

rather, the harmful consequences only crystallise for the individuals subject to them at the point at which those individuals breach them. Provided the prohibited conduct in question is fundamentally criminal in nature (that is, meets the criminal threshold for a specific offence), we think this justifies the consequences that flow, as a prohibition on criminal conduct is not unreasonable. However, a more persuasive criticism of hybrid orders has been articulated, which we think does merit careful consideration here. This is the criticism that hybrid orders circumvent the procedural safeguards of the criminal law (Hendry and King, 2017; Hendry, 2022) and permit criminal sanctions on the basis of a civil law burden of proof.[41] We are alive to this criticism, and so a hybrid approach which seeks to operate across the boundaries of the civil and criminal law on capacity to consent to sex would need to ensure strong procedural justice protections. We have not sketched out in detail in this chapter what this hybrid order might look like in practice, as that is beyond our scope. However, if a hybrid order were to be incorporated into safeguarding legislation, we think it would be essential to strengthen the procedural safeguards before implementation. Specifically, this would require that the subject of the order must have direct representation, including representation which represents their own views and not just an application of what is believed to be in their best interests if they lack capacity, they must be able to call their own expert evidence (Lindsey, 2022a) and must have legal aid to bring any challenge against the imposition of the order.

## Conclusion

This chapter has argued that the Supreme Court's focus on consent in the test for mental capacity to engage in sexual relations was the right approach. This is not only because it places greater emphasis on an important substantive element to sexual relations, but also because it shows the alignment between the civil and criminal law. We have argued that the perceived civil/criminal law binary regarding consent to sex is illusory, highlighting the ways in which the two areas are underpinned by similar justifications. Differences do remain, but there are more similarities than might first appear. We think that there is diffusion across the boundary between the civil and criminal law and that this allows closer overlap between the two jurisdictions, which

[41] In *Mayne (Phean)* (footnote 35), for example, he had not attended or been compelled to attend the Magistrate's Court hearing. The Court of Appeal was critical of this, stating: '[i]f such drastic orders are to be made it seems to us that this should be at a hearing at which the defendant is present and legally represented, so that the court can consider submissions about the wording and proportionality of the order proposed' [9].

could be harnessed to provide a hybrid solution in the form of a civil order, with criminal sanctions, for criminal sexual behaviour which is otherwise difficult to pursue through the criminal courts. We acknowledge there are procedural safeguards needed for such an approach to be expanded, but we think this is possible within the wider project of rethinking how to approach capacity in the realm of consent to sex.

## References

Arstein-Kerslake, A. and Flynn, E. (2016) 'Legislating consent: creating an empowering definition of consent to sex that is inclusive of people with cognitive disabilities', *Social & Legal Studies*, 25(2), 225–248.

Ashworth, A. (2008) 'Conceptions of overcriminalization', *Ohio State Journal of Criminal Law*, 5, 407–425.

Ashworth, A. et al (1998) 'Neighbouring on the oppressive: the government's "anti-social behaviour order" proposals', *Criminal Justice*, 16(1), 7–14.

Barad, K. (2003) 'Posthumanist performativity: toward an understanding of how matter comes to matter', *Signs: Journal of Women in Culture and Society*, 28(31), 801–831.

Barad, K. (2007) *Meeting the universe halfway: Quantum physics and the entanglement of matter and meaning*. Durham, NC: Duke University Press.

Carline, A, Gunby, C and Murray, J. (2020) *Rape and the criminal trial: Reconceptualising the courtroom as an affective assemblage*. Basingstoke: Palgrave Macmillan.

Centre for Women's Justice, End Violence Against Women coalition, Imkaan, and Rape Crisis England and Wales (2020) 'The decriminalisation of rape: why the justice system is failing rape survivors and what needs to change' (Nov 2020), available at: https://www.endviolenceagainstwomen.org.uk/wp-content/uploads/C-Decriminalisation-of-Rape-Report-CWJ-EVAW-IMKAAN-RCEW-NOV-2020.pdf (Accessed 22 September 2023).

Clough, B. (2021) *The spaces of mental capacity law: Moving beyond binaries*. Oxford: Routledge.

Conaghan, J. (2013) 'Feminism, law and materialism: reclaiming the 'tainted' realm' in V.E. Munro and M. Davies (eds), *Ashgate research companion to feminist legal theory*. Farnham: Ashgate.

Clough, B. (2014) 'Vulnerability and capacity to consent to sex – asking the right questions?', *Child and Family Law Quarterly*, 26(4), 371–397.

Cowan, S. (2007) 'Freedom and the capacity to make a choice', in V. Munro and C. Stychin (eds), *Sexuality and the law – feminist engagements*. Oxford: Routledge-Cavendish.

Davies, P., Barlow, C. and Fish, R. (2023) 'The hard and complex work of implementing new multi-agency risk assessment approaches to policing domestic abuse', *Crime Prevention and Community Safety*, 25, 148–165.

Dehaghani, R. and Newman, D. (undated) *Legal aid and criminal defence in Wales and England: Evidence submitted to UK Parliament: future of legal aid.* [Technical Report]. Cardiff University available at: https://orca.cardiff.ac.uk/id/eprint/135682/4/Parliament%2Bsubmission%2BRD%2BDN%2BFInal.pdf (Accessed 9 April 2024).

Dehaghani, R and Newman, D. (2022) 'Criminal legal aid and access to justice: an empirical account of a reduction in resilience', *International Journal of the Legal Profession*, 29(1), 33–52.

Elliot, C and deThan, C. (2007) 'The case for rational reconstruction of consent in criminal law', *Modern Law Review*, 70(2), 225–249.

Elvin, J (2008) 'The concept of consent under the Sexual Offences Act 2003', *Journal of Criminal Law*, 72(6), 519.

Fletcher, R, Fox, M and McCandless, J. (2008) 'Legal embodiment: analysing the body of healthcare law', *Medical Law Review*, 16(3), 321–345.

Fox, M and Thomson, M. (2017) 'Bodily integrity, embodiment, and the regulation of parental choice', *Journal of Law and Society*, 44(4), 501–531.

Garland-Thomson, R. (2011) 'Misfits: a feminist materialist disability concept', *Hypatia*, 26(3), 591–609.

Green, A and Hendry, J. (2021) 'Ad hominem criminalisation and the rule of law: the egalitarian case against knife crime prevention orders', *Oxford Journal of Legal Studies*, 42(2), 634–660.

Hendry, J. (2022) '"The usual suspects": knife crime prevention orders and the "difficult" regulatory subject', *The British Journal of Criminology*, 62(2), 378–395.

Hendry, J. and King, C. (2017) 'Expediency, legitimacy, and the rule of law: a systems perspective on civil/criminal procedural hybrids', *Criminal Law, Philosophy*, 11, 733–757.

Herring, J. and Wall, J. (2014) 'Capacity to consent to sex', *Medical Law Review*, 22(4), 620–630.

Husak, D. (2004) 'The criminal law as last resort', *Oxford Journal of Legal Studies*, 24(2), 207–235.

Klevens, J., Baker, C.J., Shelley, G.A. and Ingram, E.M. (2008) 'Exploring the links between components of coordinated community responses and their impact on contact with intimate partner violence services', *Violence Against Women*, 14(3), 346–358.

Lacey, N. (1998) *Unspeakable subjects: Feminist essays in legal and social theory.* Oxford: Hart.

Lamond, G. (2007) 'What is a crime?', *Oxford Journal of Legal Studies*, 27(4), 609–632.

Lindsey, J. (2016) 'Developing vulnerability: a situational response to the abuse of women with mental disabilities', *Feminist Legal Studies*, 24(3), 295–314.

Lindsey, J. (2020) 'Protecting vulnerable adults from abuse: under-protection and over-protection in adult safeguarding and mental capacity law', *Child and Family Law Quarterly*, 32(2), 157–176.

Lindsey, J. (2022a) *Reimagining the Court of Protection: Access to justice in mental capacity law*. Cambridge: Cambridge University Press.

Lindsey, J. (2022b) 'Law's legitimacy and social work support in safeguarding adults at risk of abuse in England', in M. Donnelly, R. Harding and E. Tascioglu (eds), *Supporting legal capacity in socio-legal context*. Oxford: Hart.

Lindsey, J. and Harding, R. (2021) 'Capabilities, capacity and consent: sexual intimacy in the Court of Protection', *Journal of Law and Society*, 48(1), 60–83.

McGlynn, C. (2011) 'Feminism, rape and the search for justice', *Oxford Journal of Legal Studies*, 31(4), 825–842.

McGlynn, C., Westmarland, N. and Godden, N. (2012) '"I just wanted him to hear me": sexual violence and the possibilities of restorative justice', *Journal of Law and Society*, 39(2), 213.

Moorhead, R. (2004) 'Legal aid and the decline of private practice: blue murder or toxic job?', *International Journal of the Legal Profession*, 11(3), 159–190.

Murphy, M.F. and Margolis, M.L. (1995) 'An introduction to cultural materialism', in M.F. Murphy and M.L. Margolis (eds), *Science, materialism and the study of culture*. Gainesville, FL: University Press of Florida.

Nedelsky, J. (2011) *Law's relations: A relational theory of self, autonomy, and law*. Oxford: Oxford University Press.

Pritchard-Jones, L. (2020) 'A Local Authority v JB [2020] EWCA Civ 735 and A Local Authority v AW [2020] EWCOP 24: rethinking sexual capacity?', *Medical Law Review*, 29(1), 143–156.

Ruck Keene, A, Bartlett, P and Allen, N. (2016) 'Litigation friends or foes? Representation of "P" before the Court of Protection', *Medical Law Review*, 24(3), 333–359.

Ruck Keene, A and Enefer, A. (2022) 'What place has "capacity" in the criminal law relating to sex post JB?', *International Journal of Law and Psychiatry*, 85(Nov–Dec), 101843.

Sandland, R. (2013a) 'Concubitu prohibere vago: sex and the idiot girl', *Feminist Legal Studies*, 21(1), 81–108.

Sandland, R. (2013b) 'Sex and capacity: the management of monsters?', *Modern Law Review*, 76(6), 981–1009.

Series, L. (2022) *Deprivation of liberty in the shadows of the institution*. Bristol: Bristol University Press.

Temkin, J. and Ashworth, A. (2004) 'The Sexual Offences Act 2003: (1) Rape, Sexual Assaults and the Problems of Consent', *Criminal Law Review*, 328–346.

Wallerstein. (2009) '"A drunken consent is still consent – or is it?" A critical analysis of the law on a drunken consent to sex following Bree', *Journal of Criminal Law*, 73(4), 318.

Wing-Cheong, C. (2017) 'A review of civil protection orders in six jurisdictions', *Statute Law Review*, 38(1), 1–22.

4

# Reflections from Practice: The Practicalities of Assessing Sexual Mental Capacity

*Claire Bates*

Supported Loving is a nationwide network dedicated to advancing best practices in sexuality and intimate relationships, primarily for individuals with learning disabilities. The most common request we receive, as network leader, is for training and guidance related to sexual activity and mental capacity. We provide training to various professionals, including social workers, nurses and support staff. Attendees often express concerns about sexual activity or physical contact with the people they support right from the start.

Chapter 1 by Sandland, 'Historical Perspectives on Law, Sexual Intimacy and Capacity', offers insight into the evolution of the law concerning sexuality and mental capacity. Initially, legal developments aimed to protect women with cognitive or intellectual disabilities who could not provide consent to sexual acts, via the looming threat of prosecution. The Mental Deficiency Act 1913 marked a moral shift, underpinned by the eugenic ideology regulating the reproductive choices of individuals categorised as 'mental defectives', often depriving women of the right to a sexual relationship. It was not until the 2003 review of the Sexual Offence Act that the law refocused on an individual's ability to consent to sexual activity, rather than their diagnosis. The Mental Capacity Act 2005(MCA) was envisioned as a progressive piece of legislation, enshrining our rights to make decisions in law if we possess the requisite cognitive capacity. However, practitioners in training sessions do not uniformly view the MCA in this way. It is not uncommon to encounter the belief that all individuals with cognitive or intellectual disabilities must 'pass' a capacity assessment before being permitted to engage in a sexual relationship. This view of the MCA as a standard prerequisite suggests a prevailing adherence to the historical views described in Chapter 1, challenging their enduring influence on current practices.

Historical biases affecting the sexual autonomy of people with cognitive or intellectual disabilities still influence practice. Paternalistic attitudes, particularly towards women, persist, as seen in Bates et al (2020), McCarthy et al (2022) and practical experiences, like those shared by Supported Loving. Unfortunately, this group faces restrictions in developing and maintaining sexual relationships. Working with parents of adults with intellectual disabilities reveals concerns about sexual activity (Bates et al, 2021), and parents are often fearful of abuse, exploitation or pregnancy. Sadly, these concerns are not unfounded, given the higher rates of abuse and exploitation of adults (McCarthy et al, 2017; Dike et al, 20220). The ramifications and problems of identifying such abuse are clear to see in Hollomotz's Chapter 7 in this volume. Additionally, older women without disabilities living in residential care are also at a higher risk of sexual abuse (Care Quality Commission, 2020). Individuals with cognitive or intellectual disabilities encounter a scarcity of inclusive sexual education resources, highlighting their risk of falling victim to sexual exploitation (Roden et al, 2020; Douglas and Sedgewick, 2023), and a higher risk of unsafe, non-consensual encounters due to difficulty in understanding boundaries and consent (Bates and Matthews, 2024.

Chapter 1 sheds light on the development of the 'test' for capacity around sexual activity in criminal law. Before the case of *X City Council v MB*,[1] civil courts had no framework for assessing capacity to consent for sexual activity. Not taking responsibility (or fear) of making a judgement surrounding capacity can be seen in practice (if not referred to the Court of Protection). Practitioners can be reluctant to act as decision maker. Social workers or learning disability nurses frequently take on this role and seek guidance from Supported Loving. Willner et al (2011) found gaps in knowledge among community teams for adults with cognitive and intellectual disabilities regarding capacity assessments for sexual activity and that they can be 'rushed into' in this area. This prompts us to consider whether the civil law adequately addresses this issue or, in some instances, has gone too far in its approach.

In Chapter 2, Ruck Keene, Enefer and Cusack questioned whether the law should intervene in this area and provide recourse for resolving the dilemmas that arise. While the intrusion of the law into our sexual decisions can be invasive, for individuals with cognitive or intellectual disabilities, their lives often face restrictions most of us could not imagine. When others are involved in making significant decisions on their behalf, such as managing

[1] [2006] EWHC 168 (Fam).

their finances and determining their living arrangements, many individuals in this situation often face scrutiny regarding their capacity to engage in sexual activity and frequently encounter restrictions in this regard. The use of a mental capacity assessment for sexual activity has been critiqued as ableist by some. Imagine if our own sexual and relationship choices faced similar scrutiny: 'Most people faced with the decision whether or not to have sex do not embark on a process of weighing up complex, abstract or hypothetical information. There is a danger that the imposition of a higher standard for capacity may discriminate against people with a mental impairment.'[2]

Ruck Keene, Enefer and Cusack highlight a discrepancy in the current system: despite the MCA's placing a strong emphasis on the presumption of capacity as its first principle, the practical assessment of people's capacity concerning sex has become standard practice. Supported Loving offers training to practitioners, who often believe that both sexual and non-sexual relationships are expected to undergo a formal capacity assessment, gaining authoritative approval from figures like social workers. High-profile abuse scandals have fostered a climate of protectionism surrounding people with intellectual or cognitive disabilities. This has led to risk-averse practices surrounding intimate relationships and sex, including widespread evaluations of sexual capacity. This is not solely a critique of the social care system, but, as emphasised in Chapter 2, is supported by a legal system prioritising protection over empowerment. Current case law has increased the complexity and number of criteria individuals must understand in order to be deemed to have the capacity for sexual activity without a corresponding increase in training, fuelling the anxiety and uncertainty among assessors.

Ruck Keene, Enefer and Cusack illustrate the balancing act, within the legal framework, between promoting autonomy and protecting people and the public. This challenge is most evident among frontline staff who deal with complex individuals, but often lack adequate training in sex and intimate relationships (Bates et al, 2020). Many practitioners lack knowledge about the standard capacity assessment for sexual activity, proper procedures to follow when a person lacks capacity and the scope of activities covered by this assessment. The case of JB faded complexity, as some assessors wrongly believed every sexual partner needed assessing, rather than focusing on the individual's understanding a partner's consent, including the inability to consent if unconscious and the possibility of withdrawing consent at any time. Some assessors struggle to grasp the abstract nature of assessing a partner's consent.

Ruck Keene, Enefer and Cusack's argument centres on a person's ability to decide on contact with others. From a practice perspective, this is an

---

2 *A Local Authority v TZ* [2013] EWCOP 2322 at [55].

interesting proposition. Capacity for contact with a specific person or categories of people is seldom discussed, and the legal test is less well known than that for sexual activity. They argue that if there is potential for harm or distress in contact with a specific individual or category of people, it should be necessary to explore their capacity surrounding sexual relations. This approach allows for specific, rather than abstract, questions, which can benefit individuals who struggle with abstract concepts and who may understand the questions better if linked to familiar people and situations. Relevant information for contact assessments is included in our training, however, it appears to be rarely known or utilised by the practitioners. Assessing contact so as to protect individuals in specific contexts (for example, strangers who make contact via social media) could still enable them to engage sexually with individuals who posed no risk (for example, people in their social circle) and be supportive of their right to engage in sexual activity.

Supported Loving is passionate about upholding people's sexual rights. It could be argued that the case of JB demonstrated a progressive change with regard to how people with cognitive and intellectual disabilities are viewed in legal terms, emphasising their sexual desires. The omission of a partner's consent from the sexual capacity assessment appeared illogical, potentially leaving people vulnerable to committing sexual assault. While recognising the added complexity (especially for assessors) and the expanded reach of the Court of Protection to others (not just the person being assessed), it could protect people from prosecution. We agree with Ruck Keene, Enefer and Cusack that, in practice, consent can be over-complicated; for example, assessors are often unsure what to include. We know people are held to a higher standard, for example, by using the ASK (Assessment of Sexual Knowledge) to assess capacity instead of the standard test which is primarily used in education, research or clinical settings to evaluate sexual knowledge – likely driven by a lack of confidence, blame culture and an overemphasis on safeguarding. There can be a fear that an incident will occur, and the assessor wants assurance that the person can consent, leading to unnecessarily lengthy assessments.

Ruck Keene, Enefer and Cusack emphasise how JB's case recentred the role of consent in mental capacity and better aligned the civil and criminal law. In practical terms, a positive is the hope that educational resources will be produced with an increased focus on understanding consent. Resources in this area are increasing, but there is considerable scope for improvement. Supported Loving is frequently asked to provide training surrounding relationship education, including consent. This is vital, as many adults with cognitive or intellectual disabilities have had limited access to relationships and sex education (Baines et al, 2018), leaving them vulnerable to accusations of sexual abuse and/or becoming a perpetrator of abuse through a lack of understanding of consent. This is important, considering that criminal law has sought to improve justice for victims of sexual violence with limited success, with women with disabilities experiencing an increased risk of sexual assault (McCarthy et al, 2017; Dike et al, 2022).

As Lindsey and Brennan state in Chapter 3, protecting individuals via the MCA is beneficial without requiring a legal conviction and preventing abuse. We welcome this development but share their concerns about the rights of individuals regarding sex, given the fewer procedural safeguards as compared to criminal trials. If someone lacks capacity, supervision may be lifelong, unless they regain capacity. We support the authors' argument for strengthening procedural safeguards in civil law, as well as increased training and monitoring to ensure necessary reviews of best interest decisions.

A frequently underutilised legal mechanism is the Sexual Risk Order (SRO), which may be imposed when an individual poses a risk related to their sexual activities. Lindsey and Brennan share how this tool is seldom applied, due to a preference to apply the MCA framework on account of its simplicity and accessibility. SROs are often overlooked outside of the legal profession, who rarely receive training on sexual matters (Bates et al, 2020). Inadequate knowledge extends to available procedures, encompassing more than just the SROs. Training sessions on mental capacity rarely include attendees with experience of referring a case to the Court of Protection. Course attendees may not realise the importance of promoting education to help individuals gain capacity or the right to appeal decisions through the Court of Protection. It is crucial that all those involved in the life of the person are aware of the process for making a challenge, if necessary.

In summary, the changing legal landscape around sexual capacity reflects progress and ongoing challenges influenced by historical paternalistic laws. The evaluation of mental capacity for sexual relations bridges civil and criminal laws, potentially leading to a hybrid solution involving civil orders and criminal penalties for sexual misconduct, indicating a shift in how we address this issue. JB's case highlighted alternative ways to handle concerns about sexual capacity, yet a perfect legal solution remains challenging. We hope the legal framework continues to evolve, embracing principles of autonomy and safeguarding. We advocate for the provision of vital training and comprehensive guidance to everyone engaged in the lives of individuals with cognitive and intellectual disabilities. We stress the significance of empowering individuals themselves with knowledge about their rights and avenues for legal redress.

## References

Baines, S., Emerson, E., Robertson, J. and Hatton, C. (2018) 'Sexual activity and sexual health among young adults with and without mild/moderate intellectual disability', *BMC Public Health*, 18, 667.

Bates, C. and Matthews, R. (2024) 'No "cookie cutter rules": best practice for social care staff in supporting autistic adults with relationships and sexuality', *Advances in Autism*. Available at: https://doi.org/10.1108/AIA-05-2023-0027.

Bates, C., McCarthy, M., Milne Skillman, K., Elson, N., Forrester-Jones, R. and Hunt, S. (2020) 'Always trying to walk a bit of a tightrope: The role of social care staff in supporting adults with intellectual and developmental disabilities to develop and maintain loving relationships', *British Journal of Learning Disabilities*, 48(4), 261–268.

Bates, C., McCarthy, M., Milne Skillman, K., Elson, N., Hunt, S. and Forrester-Jones, R. (2021) '"She misses the subtleties and I have to help – help to make the invisible visible": parents' role in supporting adults with intellectual and developmental disabilities with intimate relationships', *International Journal of Care and Caring*, 5(3), 489–507.

Care Quality Commission (2020) *Promoting sexual safety through empowerment*. [Online] Available at: https://www.cqc.org.uk/publications/major-report/promoting-sexual-safety-through-empowerment (Accessed 2 November 2023).

Dike, J.E., DeLucia, E.A. and Semones, O. (2022) 'A systematic review of sexual violence among autistic individuals', *Review Journal of Autism and Developmental Disorders*, 10, 576–594.

Douglas, S. and Sedgewick, F. (2023) 'Experiences of interpersonal victimization and abuse among autistic people', *Autism*, 0(0). https://doi.org/10.1177/13623613231205630 (Accessed 9 April 2024).

McCarthy, M., Hunt, S. and Milne-Skillman, K. (2017) '"I know it was every week, but I can't be sure if it was every day": domestic violence and women with learning disabilities', *Journal of Applied Research in Intellectual Disabilities*, 30, 269–282.

McCarthy, M., Bates, C., Elson, N., Hunt, S., Milne-Skillman, K. and Forrester-Jones, R. (2022) '"Love makes me feel good inside and my heart is fixed": what adults with intellectual disabilities have to say about love and relationships', *Journal of Applied Research in Intellectual Disabilities*, 35(4), 955–965.

Roden, R.C., Schmidt, E.K. and Holland-Hall, C. (2020) 'Sexual health education for adolescents and young adults with intellectual and developmental disabilities: recommendations for accessible sexual and reproductive health information', *Lancet Child Adolescent Health*, 4(9), 699–708.

Willner, P., Jenkins, R., Rees, P., Griffiths, V.J. and John, E. (2011) 'Knowledge of mental capacity issues in community teams for adults with learning disabilities', *Journal of Applied Research in Intellectual Disabilities*, 24, 159–171.

# PART II

# The Law in Practice

5

# Where Is the Love? Promoting a Rights-based, Person-centred and Relational Approach to Social Work Practice

*Becky Squires and Hannah Morgan*

## Introduction

Social work practice has been rightly criticised for failing to adequately promote and protect the sexual rights and wellbeing of disabled people globally, and specifically of those who draw upon adult social care (Ballen, 2008, Lee et al, 2018; James et al, 2020; Goulden, 2021). In this chapter we examine the practice context in England, and suggest that our findings and recommendations have urgent, broader relevance. Too frequently, social work practice in relation to intimacy and sexual relations has been risk averse, and deficit rather than strengths based. It has focused on regulating, not enabling, the intimate lives of disabled and older people supported by services, and has adopted a reductionist understanding of what constitutes sex and intimacy. This has particularly been the case in the lives of people who are assessed as lacking capacity to consent to sexual and intimate activities and where concerns about capacity are framed within the context of safeguarding someone from abuse. Despite some progress, social work has yet to fully embrace the potential of person-centred and relational practice in order to make good the promises created by the United Nations Convention on the Rights of Persons with Disabilities (UNCRPD) and in England and Wales by the Mental Capacity Act 2005, the Care Act 2014 (England) and Social Services and Well-being (Wales) Act 2014.

In this chapter we advocate an approach that draws on a blend of legal, ethical and relational literacies for social work education and practice that enable knowing and doing the right thing in real-world situations (Braye and Preston-Shoot, 2016). Grounded in the claims of the disabled people's movement for equal treatment and full citizenship, the chapter advocates the need for pedagogical and relational practice to realise the rights and capabilities of older and disabled people for sexual agency. Such rights-based practice keeps the principles of social justice and equality at the heart of what we do, and provides a passionate challenge to accepting anything less.

Social work's deep roots in promoting social justice (IFSW, 2014) both enable and require it to reframe practice by challenging medicalised and individualised models of disability and ageing (Turner and Crane, 2016a) and technical, rather than relational, assessment of mental capacity (Herring and Wall, 2014). Seeing the whole person, and sexuality as an indivisible part of that whole, requires a shift in power and a 'humbling of the professional position' (Foster, 2007, p 366) to enable the value and rights-based, empowering practice that makes a positive difference to people.

In this chapter we examine the literature on the sexual wellbeing and agency of older and disabled people and critically reflect on the challenge for social work of talking about love and relationships alongside outcomes and risk in transactional and austere times. We use vignettes from our practice to explore the lived realities of this context, with the emphasis on the practicable steps social workers can take to challenge assumptions, create change and promote the right to love and relationships. We conclude by calling for social work practice that sees the whole person and their rights and needs and draws upon its own potential to make the critical difference in life-enhancing outcomes.

## An awful lot of social work

Societal shifts since the creation of the welfare state have contributed to a drifting of social work's focus away from meeting need to a neoliberal preoccupation with managing risk (Webb, 2006). A key element of such a risk-averse society is to regard safety as the primary value, an essentially defensive and negative position (Beck, 1992). In the face of political, organisational and psychological challenges to social work in a 'risk society' (Beck, 1992), practice can too easily become defensive and 'morally timid' (Stanford, 2010), withdrawing from the sort of positive risk taking that enables flourishing lives (James et al, 2020). Such defensive social work practice has been described as the profession's 'open secret' (Whittaker and Havard, 2015, p 1160), manifesting through a broad spectrum of responses (Harris, 2003). In relation to social work concerned with matters of intimacy and mental capacity, these range from over-intervention, which could mean seeking to prevent or restrict intimate contact, or under-intervention through failure to discuss or support intimacy. Local authorities, anxious about the ever-growing list of potential legal, reputational and financial consequences that might befall them, may adopt defensive, standardised and risk-averse practices as a way of managing not only risk but the complexity of human experience (Aymer and Okitikpi, 2000).

Human relationships are the source of great joy, satisfaction and pleasure, but they can also be messy, unpredictable, and run the risk of disappointment and rejection. There remains a strong tendency in social work practice, exacerbated in austere times, to focus on meeting only basic practical needs, ruling out the potential for positive outcomes and for personal growth and learning. This is at odds with the great value placed on romantic relationships by those who use adult social care, even if this means the risk of falling in love and ending up heart-broken (McCarthy et al, 2019).

Disabled and older people's private lives are subjected to invasive restriction and legal enquiry, very often without enabling social work practice to explore what is possible, what is needed and what would make a difference. The implementation of the Mental Capacity Act has shone a light on the extent to which local authority actions wrap those who may lack capacity in 'forensic cotton wool' rather than allowing them 'as far as possible to make the same mistakes that all other human beings are at liberty to make and not infrequently do', as Justice Hedley concluded in *A NHS Trust v P.*[1] There are numerous examples of judgments where risk-averse forensic cotton wool has been used to restrict the intimate relationships of those deemed to lack capacity to consent to them. An illustrative example is *CH v a Metropolitan Council*,[2] where the local authority did not contest the challenge that their practice violated CH's right to a private and family life guaranteed by Article 8 of the European Convention on Human Rights (ECHR), apologising and paying damages to CH. As James et al noted, for CH and his wife there had been 'three years of enforced abstinence, confusion, anxiety, distress', and they ask the stark question 'where was the social work?' (James et al, 2020, p 96). Or, as our local authority lawyer colleague put it, 'There needs to be an awful lot of social work before we go to court'.

This chapter is about that social work; that is, the work undertaken by people using the legally protected title of social worker as defined in England under The Social Worker Regulations 2018 and requiring registration with the professional regulator Social Work England. However, we also adopt a more expansive understanding and application of social work, in keeping with the International Federation of Social Workers (IFSW) Global Definition of Social Work (IFSW, 2014) and the Professional Capabilities Framework refreshed by the British Association of Social Workers (BASW), described

1 *A NHS Trust v P* [2013] EWHC 50 (COP).

2 CH v A Metropolitan Council [2017] EWCOP 12.

as the 'profession-led backbone' of all social work education and continued professional development (BASW, 2018). We also draw upon the Disabled Adults and Social Workers Charter co-produced by BASW and Shaping our Lives, an organisation of people who use services (BASW, 2016a, b), which, alongside describing the need to work together to 'help people stay safe and not be at risk of abuse or neglect', also commits to looking at 'all choices to help someone have a good life' and 'different ideas as well as regular care services'. This provides a roadmap for what social work should and can be.

We explore the learning for social work practice from disability studies (Morgan and Roulstone, 2012) and legal and feminist scholarship that challenges conventional and deficit-based models of incapacity (Series, 2015). We present a number of composite vignettes drawn from our practice experience to highlight common issues and situations. They describe real-world responses that take positive steps to enable sexual expression, identity and agency in people's lives in ways that are individualised, person centred and which seek to empower rather than limit. Throughout this chapter, the vignettes illustrate the powerful impact of everyday social work. We argue that for social work to embody a commitment to the enjoyment of human rights for all people, it must presume the existence of intimacy in the lives of disabled and older people, to ask, and to find ways of answering, the question 'where is the love?' by responding positively – joyfully – in respecting and promoting intimacy and love in people's lives.

## Person-centred approaches: where is the love in disabled and older people's lives?

Sexual expression and wellbeing is a basic human right, but for many older and disabled people there is a lacuna between the standards set out in law and their experiences. The World Health Organization (WHO) asserts that sexuality 'is a central aspect of being human throughout life' and that it 'encompasses sex, gender identities and roles, sexual orientation, eroticism, pleasure, intimacy and reproduction', with good sexual health comprising of 'a state of physical, emotional, mental and social well-being in relation to sexuality' (WHO, 2021). The right to respect for a private and family life is enshrined in Article 8 of the ECHR, and the UNCRPD (2006) sets out that discrimination against disabled people in all matters related to marriage, family, parenthood and relationships should be eliminated. The UNCRPD applies to all disabled people, including those to whom the Convention refers as having intellectual and mental, or psycho-social, disabilities (UN, 2006; Mental Health Europe, 2017).

For many people with either lifelong impairments and/or impairments acquired through circumstance or ageing processes, the vision of the UNCRPD is not yet reflected in their reality. Liddiard argues that disabled people 'have a sexual history marked by oppression, suppression and violence' and that they are 'assumed to lack the capabilities and capacities to embody sexuality, sensuality, expression and desire' (Liddiard, 2017, p 1). Beyond her own work, Liddiard notes that while there are 'notable exceptions' (see Gillespie-Sells et al, 1998), there are few explorations of disabled people's intimate relationships, and often work focuses on accessing sex workers or forms of sexual support rather than on enabling intimate relationships to start, continue and flourish.

Sexual pleasure can act as an antidote to physical and emotional pain, strengthen social connection, deepen intimate relationships and alleviate feelings of isolation (Tepper, 2000). Evidence from the lived experience of disabled and older people consistently underlines the value and importance of intimate relationships (see, for example, Siebelink et al, 2006; Dunk-West and Hafford-Letchfield, 2018; Luong et al, 2011). Despite this, scholarship in relation to disability and intimacy continues to show that for significant numbers of disabled and older people, sexual and intimate relationships remain an aspiration rather than a reality. The proportion of adults with learning disabilities who have a partner is extremely low (Emerson et al, 2005), and issues of intimacy, social inclusion and citizenship are not prioritised in social work with disabled and older adults (Hafford-Letchfield, 2018; Linton et al, 2017; Lee et al, 2018). Turner and Crane's (2016b) research with adults with intellectual disability around sensuality and intimacy suggests that many people experience profound loneliness rather than close and fulfilling relationships.

### Andrew

Andrew is 59 and lives alone, following the death of his mother a year ago. He was given a diagnosis of bi-polar disorder following a 'breakdown' at university when he was 19. This coincided with the break-up of his relationship with Jenny, who had been his girlfriend since they were 14. He has undertaken some voluntary work in the local museum and latterly provided some care to his mother when she became terminally ill, but has not been in paid employment. Since his mother died, Andrew has become increasingly low in mood, withdrawn and is neglecting his self-care. He tells his social worker that no one will want to go out with someone who is 'mental'.

Andrew's story illustrates the experience of many people who live with mental ill health in relation to intimacy. Strong relationships are key to mental health recovery, and intimate relationships are key to mental wellbeing. Social work alongside Andrew will resist a focus solely on risk and vulnerability factors, and seek to build his capacity for sexual agency and wellbeing (Forrester-Jones et al, 2023). In practical terms, the social worker will need to work alongside Andrew and build a plan that takes account of Andrew's past experiences, current feelings and future hopes. Rather than just 'signposting' him to services, the social worker may need to build some practical and emotional bridges that enable him to take steps towards meeting and spending time with other people. If Andrew doesn't feel confident or able to do this by himself, the social worker can work relationally with him on a gradual approach, going together, considering environments with additional support, putting into practice positive and affirming experiences.

Andrew's comment to the social worker reveals an internalised adoption of the stigma that many people experiencing mental distress experience (Mental Health Foundation, 2021). Poor self-esteem is a critical factor in the wearing away of optimism and hope for the future, which are themselves foundational for good mental health and wellbeing (Crittenden, 2014).

Taking a rights-based and person-centred approach, social work with Andrew will actively seek to challenge the discrimination and low expectations he is reflecting in his words and actions. Social work has a facilitative role to play here, in being the belief in Andrew's worth while seeking out opportunities for activities and connections to build self-esteem and positive experiences as the prerequisite for exploring deeper relationships. A person's mental capacity for decision making around personal and intimate relationships would of course be assessed on their ability to understand, retain, use and weigh the relevant information, as well as being able to communicate their decisions. There is nothing in the information presented here to suggest to the social worker that Andrew may lack mental capacity for decision making around relationships. Social work practice has a key role in challenging assumptions and discrimination, and there should be no assessment of capacity based solely on the presence of a medical diagnosis of mental disorder. Equally, in recognising the external and internal factors that impact on the ability of Andrew and many other people to engage with personal growth and learning, confidence and self-belief, focused and supportive social work to enable Andrew's emotional strengths and capabilities to grow will be as essential as providing him with information on dating apps, or arranging for him to have some assistance with his personal care, alongside therapeutic and/or clinical support around his diagnosed mental disorder.

---

Disabled people may experience complex and multifaceted barriers in relation to developing intimate and sexual relationships, including physical conditions which can adversely affect sexual functioning (Esmail et al, 2007, Rembis, 2010), resulting in a reduction in sexual activity and lower levels of self-esteem (McCabe and Taleporos, 2003; Higgins et al, 2012). Wider social barriers include a lack of access to sexual and relationship education (Bywater and Jones, 2007), social isolation (Higgins et al, 2012) and public transport that is non-existent or inaccessible (Rembis, 2010). In the context of direct care provision, a lack of private time and space can be a significant barrier to intimacy (McCabe and Taleporos, 2003;

Kulick and Rydström, 2015), and the strain on sexual relationships when a partner is involved in providing intimate care (Marks, 2008). Reeve (2012) described these effects as 'psycho-emotional disablism' which acts as a barrier to the doing *and* the being of intimacy. Social work practice has a critical role in recognising and challenging not only the physical barriers that disabled and older people face in developing intimate relationships, but also the hidden negative impact on self-esteem and expectations. Resisting an individualised pathologising of mental distress is a core component of a social model approach to disability within social work practice. At the same time, there is a key role for social work to recognise and challenge less tangible but very real barriers to participation in society. Just as 'not all disabilities are visible', so too is the case for some of the impacts of discrimination.

There are also significant challenges for social work in relation to sexuality and mental capacity that arise from innate assumptions within society and a relatively small, although growing, body of research and other evidence in this field. Hollomotz (2011) suggests that a spectrum of vulnerability and violence characterises the portrayal of sexuality of adults with learning disabilities. Ward et al (2005) highlight the dearth of research on the sexual and gender identity of older people, particularly those who have dementia. They argue that older people living in care homes have their sexual expression subjected to a 'gendered dichotomy' (Ward et al, 2005, p 68), whereby male residents are punished for behaviour deemed to be sexually deviant, and female residents are protected from any experience of sexual relations. Limited research with older care home residents indicates that intimate relationships are highly valued (Ballard-Poe et al, 1994), and that where opportunities for physical proximity are facilitated, older people with dementia derive enjoyment and comfort in holding hands and stroking another person, for example (Ward et al, 2005).

**Robert**

Robert is 86 and has recently moved into Ferny Lodge care home. He was widowed many years ago and has an adult daughter, Jane. Robert has a diagnosis of Alzheimer's type dementia. Safeguarding concerns have been raised by the home after Robert has been found in the bedrooms of female residents. These women also have dementia and while they have not been able to provide an account of anything that happened, there is no evidence of any harm.

A number of personal items and clothing belonging to these women are reported as missing, and are found in Robert's room. When he is asked about this, Robert demonstrates through his behaviour that he is familiar and comfortable dressing and identifying as a woman.

Robert's story illustrates the often hidden sexuality and gender identity of older people who have lived through times of great fear of the consequences of expressing themselves. Changes in Robert's cognitive functioning may have altered his perception of risk and stigma and created an opportunity for him to express himself more freely. Ageing may be empowering for gay men (Simpson, 2018) and for older trans people (Willis et al, 2021). Sensitive, person-centred support alongside Robert is required to enable him to express his gender identity in ways that promote his dignity and respect. Creating a safe, private space with meaningful objects around him immediately negates the 'safeguarding' concerns. Robert's social worker can work with the care home to ensure that his support plan is inclusive of his needs around gender identity and sexuality and that staff and the home environment actively promote and support self-expression across all identities, drawing on appropriate person-centred resources.

Heteronormative approaches in social care with adults can easily mask the experience of people identifying as LGBTQ+. For older people, personal histories of the need to conceal sexual identity, a lack of support and resources and a fear of stigma all compound issues in expressing sexuality and intimate relationships in later life (Hughes, 2009). People with a learning disability 'label' are likely to experience this as defining their personhood, obscuring any questioning of their sexual identity (Abbott, 2015). In the video *Doug's story*, part of a series produced by the Social Care Institute for Excellence (SCIE, undated) on the experiences of LGBT people who use adult social care services, Doug, a young gay, physically disabled man living in residential care, highlights the strain of having to *come out* multiple times given the turnover of care staff, or of being asked to 'keep quiet [about his sexuality] around other residents'.

The social construction(s) of disability and ableist assumptions about who should and should not be sexual and intimate remain powerful forces in the experience of older and disabled people. For example, ageing bodies are so pathologised in media and advertising that ageing processes are presented as 'unwatchable' (Coupland, 2003), a conclusion equally applied to disabled bodies and minds. That these disabled and ageing bodies are constructed through a 'deviance paradigm' (Thomas, 2007) where conceptions of a 'normal' body, from which impairment or ageing creates 'deviations', has been well mapped and subject to sustained critique by feminist and disability studies scholarship and activism.

## The social model of disability and social work practice

The social interpretation of disability, commonly known as the social model of disability (Oliver, 1996), was articulated through action and scholarship by the disabled people's movement focusing attention on socially constructed barriers and restrictions. For many this has had a profound effect in transforming their self-identity from one of individual deficiency to one shaped by a wider structural and material exclusion (see Crow, 1996). Early criticism of the social model suggested that it failed to include the diversity of disabled people's experience (Corker, 1999), and its focus on material barriers to social participation resulted in the neglect of the personal, including the impact of impairment. There has been much work within disability studies to broaden its attention to the private sphere and to the particular concerns of, for example, disabled women (Morris, 1991; Crow, 1996) and LGBTQ people (Abbott and Howard, 2005). Thomas (1999) extended the model by coining the phrase 'impairment effects' to enable discussion of the impact of pain, fatigue and other restrictions caused by impairment.

Watson (2004) suggests that social model analysis needs to embrace 'interpersonal relations' as well as material factors, in order to fully reflect the diversity and social context of disabled people's lives. From the perspective of asserting the rights of older and disabled people to sexual identity and intimate relationships, this is critical; Roulstone (2012) argues that, to be effective, professional understanding of disability must include psycho-emotional disablism, the forms of exclusion and oppression that 'work along psychological and emotional pathways' (Thomas, 2004, p 37). Such disablism 'operates at both the personal and public levels, affecting what people can *do* as well as what they can be' (Reeve, 2004, p 83). While the development of positive initiatives such as personal budgets and direct payments undoubtedly has the potential to promote inclusion and elements of wellbeing, addressing emotional, sexual and psychological wellbeing is equally critical and requires skilled, direct work.

Social work has had a long but 'chequered' engagement with the social model of disability and the ideas and claims of the disabled people's movement (Morgan and Roulstone, 2012, p 137). The *Disabled Adults and Social Workers Position Statement* and *Charter* published by the British Association of Social Workers and Shaping Our Lives (2016), a national organisation of service users, sets out a clear aim of 'All disabled adults and social work [working] together to improve wellbeing, using the social model of disability to overcome barriers, and using a human rights approach to ensure equal and full citizenship for everyone' (Turner and Crane, 2016a, p 7). While the charter sets out guiding principles that include using the social model of disability, taking a rights-based approach, promoting independent living and 'not be[ing] satisfied until everyone has full and equal citizenship' (Turner and Crane, 2016b, p 1), it is noteworthy that there is no explicit mention of sexual wellbeing or relational intimacy. The charter refers specifically to *money*, *benefits*, access to *mainstream provision*, highlights *barriers that prevent disabled adults from living full lives* and specifically mentions *barriers to work*.

The UK Government-sponsored Disability Survey (2021) similarly focuses on issues such as employment and benefits. The only mention it makes in relation to sexuality is to ask respondents whether they agree or disagree that they would feel comfortable in an intimate relationship with a disabled person (Disability Unit, 2021). It is difficult to conceive of this question being asked if we were to replace 'disabled' with another protected characteristic under the Equality Act 2010. Disability and sexuality in this context, however, are presented as though they were light years apart, despite the voices of disabled people challenging discrimination and calling for equality (National Institute for Health and Social Care Research, 2021). Considerable work is still needed to firmly establish disabled and older people's right to intimacy as a crucial element of their wellbeing that must be considered within the purview of social work practice.

### *Sexual wellbeing in practice*

There is international consensus regarding the part that sexual wellbeing plays in quality of life. Sex, and good sexual health, are key components of wellbeing (Myers and Milner, 2007), creating pleasure, connection and enhancing self-identity and self-worth. In contrast, poor sexual health and reduced wellbeing lead to poor health outcomes (Sloane, 2014). While the Care Act 2014 in England provides a broad framework for personalised meaning and definitions of wellbeing, it is silent on issues of the rights of people to full participation in life in terms of sexual expression and relationships. The definition of wellbeing includes 'domestic, family and personal' relationships, and while it sets out that wellbeing should reflect the individual's 'views, wishes, feeling and beliefs' and that any action should be the 'least restrictive', again there is no specific mention of sexual or intimate relationships.

In England, the Care Act incorporated the development and maintenance of personal relationships into English law through its inclusion as an eligible need under the wellbeing principle (Bates et al, 2017). The duty on local authorities to promote the wellbeing of individuals creates a space in which people and practitioners can discuss sexual wellbeing, but the absence of language and direct reference to intimacy reflects a discomfort and a lacuna in these conversations. Scholarship and research indicate that sexuality in relation to people with intellectual or learning disability is 'shamed, segregated and silenced' (Turner, 2012, p 5). As Lee et al (2018) contend, practitioners, including social workers, must be confident and capable of discussing and working with issues relating to intimate relationships, without which sexual wellbeing can 'remain hidden as a social justice issue' (Turner and Crane, 2016a).

A social model approach challenges accepted notions of professional power within social work practice, arguing that the potential for agency lies within people and communities rather than through external intervention (Morgan and Roulstone, 2012). The 'gloriously ordinary life' envisioned by disability rights organisation Social Care Future and adopted by the Adult Social Care Committee of the House of Lords (2022, para 201) sets out that as disabled people: 'We all want to live in the place we call home with the people and things we love, in communities where we look out for one another, doing things that matter to us. That's the social care future we seek.'

---

**Salli**

Salli is 23. She lives in supported accommodation for people with learning disabilities and works in a social enterprise. Salli is very close to her family. She is the youngest of five siblings, all of whom have long-term partners or are married, and have children. Salli loves spending time with her nieces and nephews and wants to have a husband and her own family. Her parents are very worried that she is vulnerable to sexual abuse and would not be able to care for a baby.

Salli's story describes the hopes and aspirations of many people. The fact that she also has a learning disability reframes her story with assumptions of sexual vulnerability and the risk of violence (Hollomotz, 2011). A social work relationship that builds trust and creates the space and opportunity to think about sex and relationships will also enable the exploration of Salli's mental capacity and her capability for understanding the social, psychological and emotional elements of sexual wellbeing (Bywater and Jones, 2007). Social work that supports people with a learning disability to find their 'sexual voice' in terms of language, self-expression and experiences is supporting social justice (Turner and Crane, 2016b). Many adults with learning disabilities actively welcome support, resources and specialised dating agencies that facilitate opportunities for meeting other people in a safe space (McCarthy et al, 2019, and Salli's social worker has a key role in working alongside Salli's parents to acknowledge their concerns and build relationships that will enable Salli to explore her own sexuality and agency.

---

Balancing empowerment with risk management is a key social work role and an essential aspect of enabling people to live full lives (The College of Social Work, 2013). The Making Safeguarding Personal approach (Local Government Association, 2014) introduced a framework for person-centred and enabling social work practice that promotes wellbeing alongside the prevention of abuse and neglect. The Statutory Guidance to the Care Act (Department of Health and Social Care, 2023), 14:83 refers to sex solely in the context of abuse, and not wellbeing, including the case study of 'Miss Y', a young woman with learning disabilities who lacks capacity to consent to sex and is being abused by a number of men. The response is to 'safeguard' Miss Y through a multi-agency response including the police investigation of the perpetrators and the use of the Deprivation of Liberty Safeguards. The only reference to intimacy within the Guidance (beyond the provision of intimate personal care) relates to abuse from intimate partners. For us to truly realise and embed conversations and action in social work practice in relation to sexual relationships, we must see a commitment through statutory guidance and policy from the highest level.

Miss Y's case study describes a protective and reactive response to sexual abuse. While such an approach may be required in some circumstances, social work that is grounded in the notion of sexual wellbeing as a human right must practise in ways not limited by protectionism. Person-centred social work practice that presumes and supports the capacity for sexual agency of older and disabled people must embrace risk enablement (Bywaters and Jones, 2007). Social work practice, both in relationship-based support, assessment and support planning, must include the exploration of what personal and intimate relationships mean to the person. This should take account of the different aspects of relationships, practical, psychological and emotional, all of which matter deeply in contexts of intimacy. There is growing concern not only that the narrow objectivity of mental capacity assessments fails to positively address sexuality as a human right, but that the Mental Capacity Act may in fact contravene Article 12 UNCRPD, which states that disabled people should 'enjoy legal capacity on an equal basis with others in all aspects of life' (Series, 2015). Disabled and older people have an equal right to be protected from abuse, coercion and control. If we assume a negative inevitability about older and disabled people's relationships, however, we will deny people the opportunity to learn from experience and develop their capacity for decision making around relationships. 'Practicable steps' (principle 2 of the Mental Capacity Act) in this sense is about more than the provision of information in appropriate formats. Social work around sex and intimacy has to recognise the emotional dimension of sexual relationships. For a person to develop and maintain mental capacity for decision making in relation to matters of intimacy, they are likely to need the language, opportunity and safe space in which to talk about their feelings (as the CH case discussed earlier made clear). A social worker with confidence in their ability to listen and discuss intimacy, while staying curious and alert to the potential for harm or exploitation, will actively promote and enable the finding of an individual and independent 'sexual voice' (Turner and Crane, 2016a).

Section 27 Mental Capacity Act excludes sexual relations from decision making on behalf of another. In *A Local Authority v JB*,[3] the Supreme Court

---

[3] [2021] UKSC 52.

held that the relevant information a person must be able to understand, retain and use or weigh in order to have mental capacity to engage in sexual relations includes understanding the mechanics of sexual intercourse; that there are health risks involved; the risk of pregnancy; that sex is a choice; and that the other person must have the ability to consent to engage in sex and must in fact consent. Herring and Wall liken this approach to 'reducing capacity to consent to sex to an understanding of brute facts' (Herring and Wall, 2012, p 630). Lindsey and Harding (2021) suggest that a medicalised approach dominates within the Court of Protection, avoiding the social and contextual dimensions of sex, especially in regard to choice and consent, while Doyle (2010) argues that the reality for many women with intellectual disabilities is an absence of the knowledge, language and experience in relation to sexual activity that would enable their capacity for decision making.

The law and social work do not exist in isolation from each other, and effective and empowering social work practice will draw on emotional and relational literacies to reframe assumptions, challenge oppression and create the conditions for change, just as it draws on legal literacy. Person-centred social work provides a challenge to the dominant discourse, in relation to sexuality and intimacy, on a person's intellectual ability to consent. Perhaps what matters alongside understanding some of the facts about sex is also that consent 'is about values such as tenderness; respect; mutuality; sensitivity. It is about having time; feeling safe; and being free to say no. These are what are central to a capacity to engage in sex *for everyone*' (Herring and Wall, 2014, pp 629–630, emphasis added). In short, what is required is social work that actively seeks to promote a person's capability to protect their bodily health and integrity, understand and develop emotional connections, develop an understanding of intimacy and manage all these capabilities in different contexts (Lindsey and Harding, 2021). Social work in relation to matters of emotion and intimacy may (and perhaps should) look and feel very different to an assessment and commissioning pathway. As Jenkinson and Chamberlain (2019) remind us in a guidance note commissioned by the Principal Social Worker Network, there are commonly held misconceptions about social work: 'The first is that carrying out an assessment is the same as doing social work. The second is that social work does not include counselling' (Fenton, 2019, p 4). While an assessment is an intervention in its own right, it is not the only or the most appropriate response to human need and distress. Where assessments of mental capacity are concerned, the assessment should be part of a significant process of working with a person in person-centred ways that engage and explore their emotions and their sense of self in relation to others, as well as their cognition.

**Mats and Sara**

Mats and Sara are married and in their late 30s. Two years ago, Mats was involved in a climbing accident in which he sustained significant physical injury and cognitive impairment. He has limited verbal communication. Sara has told their social worker that she and Mats are having sex, as she intends to get pregnant and have the family they had always planned. Sara says it is 'obvious' that Mats is enjoying this aspect of their relationship and it is no one else's business.

Mats and Sara's intimate life together has become the 'business' of professionals by virtue of concerns that he may lack capacity to consent to sex as a result of his head injury. Sara's reluctance to make her private life more public is understandable but could be a real barrier in achieving an outcome that maintains her and Mats's self-respect and dignity. Establishing a supportive professional relationship that acknowledges the profoundly human aspect of this situation will provide the space for exploring emotions that can be extremely painful. There are potentially complex emotional issues of love, hope and change for the social worker to work through with Sara.

The tasks for the social worker – potentially alongside other specialist professionals – will include considering how best to communicate with Mats in order to establish a relationship, understand his wishes and feelings and any information relevant to the decision to have a sexual relationship with his wife, available from the period prior to his climbing accident. Mats's reported physical response to sexual activity with Sara may be relevant evidence of his feelings, but it does not equate to the requirements of an assessment of mental capacity as the law stands. The social worker will need to take all practicable steps to support Mats's capacity to understand and consent to sex with his wife, before any declaration of capacity is sought from the court. Given Sara's stated intention to become pregnant, Mats becoming a father is a consequence relevant to the decision making and an issue to which his capacity to consent also would need to be determined.

## The vital role of relational practice in supporting intimacy

As one of us has argued elsewhere, our experience is that students apply to study social work 'with the professed aim of "helping" and so to be confronted by an approach (the social model of disability) and a body of research and theorising (disability studies) that challenges their taken-for-granted assumption that social work practice is "helpful" is unsettling and can lead to resistance' (Morgan, 2012, p 215). It can indeed be highly unsettling to hear that your chosen profession has been seen by many disabled people as part of the problem rather than as an advocate or ally. While social work is a practice-based profession, founded on the principles of social justice, human rights and respect for diversities (IFSW, 2014), it has a history and legacy that is paternalistic (see, for example, Simcock and Castle, 2016). There are tensions between the expectations of professional organisations (the IFSW and BASW) and the confines of statutory practice, which is subject to political priorities as well as increasing professional regulation. However, as the case for rights-based social work set out in *Social Work, Cats and Rocket Science* argues: 'Social work is a profession which positively embraces ambiguity and all the associated emotional complexity which other professions avoid. Social workers are agents of social justice, charged with upholding values of human dignity, equality, democracy, and freedom. We make no apologies that we do not believe social work to be neutral or to operate in a neutral environment' (James et al, 2020, p 19).

Relationships are at the heart of social work practice (Trevithick, 2012). The literature on the qualities that people most value in their social worker consistently reveals the importance of being able to connect and relate in human and receptive ways (De Boer and Coady, 2007; Manthorpe et al, 2008; Beresford et al, 2008; Centre for Mental Health, 2023). Social work grounded in relational practice is also the greatest source of successful outcomes for people who have care and support needs (Ingram and Smith, 2018). Leece and Leece (2010) highlighted that many disabled people positively welcomed the opportunity for longer-term supportive social work relationships. A supportive professional relationship is an essential condition of enabling open discussion and exploration of issues relating to sexual, psychological and emotional wellbeing (Bywater and Jones, 2007).

Social work is characterised by the complexity and uncertainty of human experience and emotion (Ruch et al, 2018), and good social workers by their capacity for curiosity, courage and skill in working purposefully with relationships (Trevithick, 2012). Fenton suggests that 'getting close to a person provides protection against distant, bureaucratic and oppressive practice … A real relationship fills the space which might otherwise be occupied by prejudice, stereotyping and assumption' (Fenton, 2019, p 79). Being able to practise relationship-based social work is therefore not simply a professional matter, but a political one (Cooper, 2018).

In conventional social work settings, relational values are not always clearly articulated and 'alive in practice' (Charfe and Gardner, 2020). And yet, rights-based, empowering social work with adults needs to be so much more than a technical/rational approach to market-framed transactions (Lorenz, 2005). Alongside the *what* social workers do, exists the *how* we do it, and the *why*. Social workers are not lawyers. Social work practice must be legally literate, and it must also ensure the equal importance of ethical and emotional literacy to work alongside adults, in the context of discrimination and unequal outcomes. Social work has a critical role in challenging discrimination in all its forms and, while social workers must work within the law, they should also challenge situations where the law provides only a partial or insufficient response. It may be legally correct, for example, that a person is deprived of their liberty in a care home. The social work role extends beyond this to require consideration and action around that person's rights in relation to maintaining and developing personal relationships and expressing their sexual identity. The law, society and social work are all subject to continued evolution, and all will benefit from learning from the others.

The critical challenge that managerialist and transactional approaches pose for social workers (Garrett, 2010) is being able to do 'proper social work' (Fenton, 2019, p 9) that is founded on human rights and social justice and made possible through meaningful relationships. Relationships that are valued and nurtured have transformative, sustainable potential for the creation of hope and self-belief (Trevithick, 2012), and optimism, a critical component of mental wellbeing (Crittenden, 2014). A rights- and strengths-based social work approach sees people not through a lens of individual deficit and dysfunction but, rather, 'In the light of their capacities, talents, competencies, possibilities, visions, values, and hopes, however dashed and distorted these may have become through circumstance, oppression and trauma' (Saleebey, 1996, p 297).

'Technical-rational' responses (Schon, 1987) are insufficient for complex, personal issues. Relationships and sex, in most areas of life for most people, are messy, not straightforward, prone to disaster, and also where we are most likely to find profound joy and happiness. Social work with disabled and older people in matters of relationships, intimacy and sex must be technically and legally literate, but will make a real difference to the full enjoyment of human rights only through skilled relational practice that recognises what disabled people say they need:

1. non-judgemental attitudes about sex;
2. knowledge about sexual wellbeing and disability;
3. openness and a willingness to talk about sensitive issues, including sex;
4. trust – and being trustworthy. (Lee et al, 2018)

Sexuality and intimacy must have a central place in everyday social work conversations, assessments and support planning, for 'the sexual needs of disabled people are more likely to be met if things are discussed in an open and frank manner' (Bywater and Jones, 2007, p 86). 'Normalising' sexual issues and creating the conditions in which people feel safe to discuss them is essential (Higgins et al, 2012). Adult social care has a positive role to play in working alongside people in ways that facilitate their sexual expression and equality in relationships (BASW, 2018; 2019). Anti-discriminatory and anti-oppressive practice attends to 'oppression and the discrimination that gives rise to it' (Thompson, 2020, p 10) and must therefore be as much concerned with promoting and safeguarding the sexual rights of people with care and support needs as it should be with employment, housing or community engagement. Social workers who are supported both by their organisations and politically, to bring humour, creativity and something of their own humanity and self to practice are more likely to be able to create the conditions for positive outcomes for people.

Our interpretation of critically reflective, rights-based social work practice with adults is more than a simplistic repositioning of ideas of risk management. Social work practice should not only take a holistic view of the person's life but work in allyship with the disabled people's movement towards the dismantling of barriers to equity (Marks, 2008). A focus on individualised personal deficits rather than on the structural inequalities in society that perpetuate inequality and oppression (Fenton, 2019) has parallels with a model of individual adjustment to disability that has drawn critique from disability activists and scholars (Oliver, 1996). Relational, creative and empowering practice is a 'defence against the dark art' of managerialism, whereby a focus on managerial control and the efficiency of process has marginalised professional autonomy and judgement (see Lambley, 2010).

As Swango-Wilson notes, 'determination of what can be achieved by the individual with a disability is in large part a function of systems expectations and values' (Swango-Wilson, 2010, p 161). In their review of social work scholarship on sexuality, described as 'the expression of intimacy between individuals, but … mediated and "scripted" through the social world', Schaub et al identify four streams: LGB populations, lived experience of everyday sexuality, critical discussions around the construction of social work knowledge and sexuality as a 'source of risk, vulnerability and harm' (Schaub, Willis and Dunk-West, 2017, p 429), highlighting the need for broader and more reflexive exploration of sexuality within social work education and practice. Kattari et al (2017) argue that social work education treats older age and disability as two separate population groups, despite commonalities in the experience of oppression, and that disabled people age and older people can become disabled (whether or not they recognise this label). Thus, they suggest that 'applying a social model of disability across the lifespan … can promote intersectional and inclusive social work related to ageing and disability' (Kattari et al, 2017, p 865).

## Conclusion

We have set out the evidence that the intimate and sexual lives of very many older and disabled people have not yet fulfilled their potential, or the vision and promise of the UNCRPD. We contend that social work, as a profession grounded in social justice and the protection of human rights, has a critical role to play in challenging and redressing the marginalisation of disabled people's sexual rights and agency. Applying a social-model-of-disability lens to sexual relationships recognises the particular challenges for many older and disabled people in achieving mental capacity for decision making in relation to intimacy in a risk-averse social context. Social work must draw upon not just its value base but its skills in finding creative and persistent approaches to ensuring that principle 2 of the Mental Capacity Act is upheld – that a person is not to be treated as unable to make a decision unless all practicable steps to help him to do so have been taken without success.[4]

For social workers, recognising and prioritising intimacy in the lives of older and disabled people starts with questioning our own values and confidence in exploring intimacy. Social work education and continuing professional education have a critical role to play in ensuring that relationships play as a large a part in conversations and support planning as in other areas of our lives. Social work practice should, at all levels of an organisation, understand that intimate relationships and sexual agency are not just fundamental to a good quality of life but are also critical to preventing harm, abuse and loneliness. Intimate and sexual relations are at the heart of what it is to be human. Through relational, risk-enabling and empowering practice, social work can and must enable the possibility of joyful relationships as a human right for everyone, embracing the infinite possibilities and potential of humanity.

## References

Adult Social Care Committee of the House of Lords (2022) *'A gloriously ordinary life': Spotlight on adult social care.* Report of Session 2022–23 HL Paper 99. London: House of Lords.

Abbott, D. (2015) 'Love in a cold climate: changes in the fortunes of LGBT men and women with learning disabilities?', *British Journal of Learning Disabilities*, 43, 100–105.

Abbott, D. and Howarth, J. (2005) *Secret loves, hidden lives? Exploring issues for people with learning difficulties who are gay, lesbian or bisexual.* Bristol: Policy Press.

Aymer, C. and Okitikpi, T. (2000) 'Epistemology, ontology and methodology: what's that got to do with social work?', *Social Work Education*, 19(1), 67–75.

Ballan, M.S. (2008) 'Disability and sexuality within social work education in the USA and Canada: the social model of disability as a lens for practice', *Social Work Education*, 27(2), 194–202.

[4] Section 1(3) Mental Capacity Act 2005.

Ballard-Poe, L., Powell, C. and Mulligan, T. (1994) 'The importance of intimacy to men living in a nursing home', *Archives of Sexual Behavior*, 23(2), 231–236.

Bates, C., Terry, L.M. and Popple, K. (2017) 'Supporting people with learning disabilities to make and maintain intimate relationships', *Tizard Learning Disability Review*, 22(1), 16–23.

Beck, U. (1992) *Risk society: Towards a new modernity*. London: Sage.

Beresford, P., Croft, S. and Adshead, L. (2008) '"We don't see her as a social worker": a service user case study of the importance of social workers' relationship and humanity', *British Journal of Social Work*, 38, 1371–1388.

Braye, S. and Preston-Shoot, M. (2016) *Practising social work law* (4th edn). London: Palgrave Macmillan.

British Association of Social Workers (BASW) and Shaping Our Lives (2016a) *Disabled adults and social workers: Charter.* London: BASW.

British Association of Social Workers (BASW) and Shaping Our Lives (2016b) *Disabled adults and social workers: Position statement*. London: BASW.

British Association of Social Workers (BASW) (2018) *The 2018 Refresh of the Professional Capabilities Framework. Overview and a chance to have your say on the final version*. Birmingham: BASW.

British Association of Social Workers (BASW) (2019) *Capabilities statement for social workers working with adults with learning disability*. Birmingham: BASW.

Bywater, J. and Jones, R. (2007) *Sexuality and social work*. Exeter: Learning Matters.

Centre for Mental Health (2023) '*It feels like being seen': How can local authorities know if their mental health services are working well?* Available at: Briefing 60: 'It feels like being seen' | Centre for Mental Health.

Charfe, L. and Gardner, A. (2019) *Social pedagogy and social work*. London: Sage.

College of Social Work (2013) *College of Social Work (2013) Roles and functions of social workers in England: Advice note*. London: The College of Social Work. Available at: basw_115640-9_0.pdf

Cooper, A. (2018) 'What future? Organisational forms, relationship-based social work practice and the changing world order', in G. Ruch, D. Turney and A. Ward (eds), *Relationship-based social work: Getting to the heart of practice*. London: Jessica Kingsley.

Corker, M. (1999) 'Differences, conflations and foundations: the limits to "accurate" theoretical representation of disabled people's experiences', *Disability and Society*, 14(5), 627–42.

Coupland, J. (2003) 'Ageist ideology and discourses of control in skincare product marketing', in J. Coupland and R. Gwyn (eds), *Discourse, the body and identity*. Basingstoke: Palgrave Macmillan, pp 127–150.

Crittenden, P.M., Dallos, R., Landini, A. and Koslowska, A. (2014) *Attachment and family therapy*. London: McGraw-Hill Education.

Crow, J. (1996) 'Including all of our lives: renewing the social model of disability', in C. Barnes and G. Mercer (eds), *Exploring the divide: Illness and disability*. Leeds: Disability Press.

De Boer, C. and Coady, N. (2007) 'Good helping relationships in child welfare: learning from stories of success', *Child and Family Social Work*, 12, 32–42.

Department of Health and Social Care (2023) *Care and support statutory guidance*. London: Department of Health.

Disability Unit (2021) *UK Disability Survey research report, June 2021*, gov.uk, Available at: https://www.gov.uk/government/publications/uk-disability-survey-research-report-june-2021/uk-disability-survey-research-report-june-2021

Doyle, S. (2010) 'The notion of consent to sexual activity for persons with mental disabilities', *Liverpool Law Review*, 31(2), 111–135.

Dunk-West, P. and Hafford-Letchfield, T. (2018) *Sexuality, sexual and gender identities and intimacy research in social work and social care: A lifecourse epistemology*. London: Routledge.

Emerson, E., Malam, S., Davies, I. and Spencer, K. (2005) *Adults with learning disabilities in England 2003/4*. Leeds: Health & Social Care Information Centre.

Esmail, S., Munro, B. and Gibson, M. (2007) 'Couple's experience with multiple sclerosis in the context of their sexual relationship', *Sexuality and Disability*, 25, 163–177.

Fenton, J. (2019) *Social work for lazy radicals: Relationship building, critical thinking and courage in practice*. London: Macmillan.

Forrester-Jones, R., Dixon, J. and Jaynes, B. (2023) 'Exploring romantic need as part of mental health social care practice', *Disability & Society*, https://doi.org/10.1080/09687599.2023.2222900

Foster, V. (2007) 'Ways of knowing and showing: imagination and representation in feminist participatory social research', *Journal of Social Work Practice*, 21(3), 361–376.

Garrett, P.M. (2010) 'Examining the "conservative revolution": neoliberalism and social work education', *Social Work Education*, 29(4), 340–355.

Gillespie-Sells, K., Hill, M. and Robbins, B. (1998) *She dances to different drums: Research into disabled women's sexuality*. London: King's Fund.

Goulden, A. (2021) 'A critical review of social work interventions and programmes that support disabled youth with their sexual well-being', *Journal of Social Work Practice*, 35(4), 403–417.

Hafford-Letchfield, T. (2008) 'What's love got to do with it? Developing supportive practices for the expression of sexuality, sexual identity and the intimacy needs of older people', *Journal of Care Services Management*, 2(4), 389–405.

Harris, J. (2003) *The Social Work Business*. London: Routledge.

Herring, J. and Wall, J. (2012) 'Understanding capacity: "the heart may easily overrule the head"', 4 *Elder Law Journal*, 190.

Herring, J. and Wall, J. (2014) 'Capacity to consent to sex', *Medical Law Review*, 22(4), 620–630.

Higgins, A., Sharek, D., Nola, M., Sheerin, B., Flanagan, P., Slaicuinate, S., McDonnell, S. and Walsh, H. (2012) 'Mixed methods evaluation of an interdisciplinary sexuality programme for staff working with people who have an acquired physical disability', *Journal of Advanced Nursing*, 68(1), 2559–2569.

Hollomotz, A. (2011) *Learning difficulties and sexual vulnerability*. Philadelphia, PA: Jessica Kingsley.

Hughes, M. (2009) 'Lesbian and gay people's concerns about ageing and accessing services', *Australian Social Work*, 62(2), 186–201.

Ingram, R. and Smith, M. (2018) *Relationship-based practice: Emergent themes in social work literature*. IRISS Insight No 41. Glasgow: The Institute for Research and Innovation in Social Services.

International Federation of Social Workers (IFSW) (2014) *Global definition of social work*. https://www.ifsw.org/what-is-social-work/global-definition-of-social-work/ (Accessed 9 April 2024).

James, E., Mitchell, R. and Morgan, H. (2020) *Social work, cats and rocket science: Stories of making a difference in social work with adults*. London: Jessica Kingsley.

Jenkinson, A.J. and Chamberlain, J. (2019) *Social workers' knowledge and skills and the Care Act: Practice advice note*. NIHR Policy Research Unit in Health and Social Care Workforce, The Policy Institute, King's College London. https://doi.org/10.18742/pub01-008

Kattari, S., Lavery, A. and Hasche, L. (2017) 'Applying a social model of disability across the lifespan', *Journal of Human Behavior in the Social Environment*, 27(8), 865–880.

Kulick, D. and Rydström, J. (2015) *Loneliness and its opposite. Sex, disability and the ethics of engagement*. Durham, NC: Duke University Press.

Lambley, S. (2010) 'Managers: are they really to blame for what's happening to social work?', *Social Work and Social Science Review*, 14(2), 6–19.

Lee, S., Fenge, L. and Collins, B. (2018) 'Promoting sexual well-being in social work education and practice', *Social Work Education*, 37(3), 315–317.

Leece, J. and Leece, D. (2010) 'Personalisation: perceptions of the role of social work in a world of brokers and budgets', *British Journal of Social Work*, 41(2), 204–223.

Liddiard, K. (2017) *The intimate lives of disabled people: Sex and relationships*. London: Routledge.

Lindsey, J. and Harding, R. (2021) 'Capabilities, capacity and consent: sexual intimacy in the Court of Protection', *Journal of Law and Society*, 48(1), 60–83.

Linton, K.F., Adams Rueda, H. and Rankin Williams, L. (2017) *Disability, intimacy and sexual health. A social work perspective*. Washington, DC: NASW.

Local Government Association (2014) *Making safeguarding personal*. London: Local Government Association.

Lorenz, W. (2005) 'Social work and a new social order: challenging new liberalism's erosion of solidarity', *Social Work and Society*, 3(1), 93–101.

Luong, G., Charles, S.T. and Fingerman, K.L. (2011) 'Better with age: social relationships across adulthood', *Journal of Social and Personal Relationships*, 28(1), 9–23.

Manthorpe, J., Iliffe, S., Clough, R., Cornes, M., Bright, L. and Moriarty, J. and OPRSI (Older People Researching Social Issues) (2008) 'Older people's perspectives on health and well-being in rural communities in England: Findings from the evaluation of the National Service Framework for Older People', *Health & Social Care in the Community*, 16(5), 460–468.

Marks, D. (2008) 'Physical disability', in M. Davies (ed), *The Blackwell companion to social work* (3rd edn). Oxford: Blackwell.

McCabe, M. and Teleporos, G. (2003) 'Sexual esteem, sexual satisfaction, and sexual behaviour among people with physical disability', *Archives of Sexual Behaviour*, 32(4), 359–369.

McCarthy, M., Forrester-Jones, R. and Bates, C. (2019) 'Exploring support for people with intellectual and development disabilities', *National Institute of Health and Social Care Research*. Available at: https://www.sscr.nihr.ac.uk/projects/p122/

Mental Health Europe (2017) *Autonomy, choice and the importance of supported-decision making for persons with psychosocial disabilities*: MHE Position Paper on Article 12 UN CRPD on legal capacity. Available at: https://mhe-sme.org/wp-content/uploads/2017/11/Article_12_Position_paper.pdf

Mental Health Foundation (2021) *Stigma and discrimination*. Available at: https://www.mentalhealth.org.uk/explore-mental-health/a-z-topics/stigma-and-discrimination (Accessed 9 April 2024).

Morgan, H. (2012) 'The social model of disability as a threshold concept: troublesome knowledge and liminal spaces in social work education', *Social Work Education: The International Journal*, 31(2), 215–226.

Morgan, H. and Roulstone, R. (2012) 'Editorial. Special issue: Disability studies and social work education', *Social Work Education*, 31(2), 137–41.

Morris, J. (1991) *Pride against prejudice: Personal politics of disability*. London: Women's Press.

Myers. S. and Milner, J. (2007) *Sexual issues in social work*. Bristol: British Association of Social Work.

National Institute for Health and Social Care Research (2021) *Adults with learning disabilities need support to find love*. Available at: https://evidence.nihr.ac.uk/alert/romantic-relationships-adults-with-learning-disabilities/ (Accessed 9 April 2024).

Oliver, M. (1996) *Understanding disability: From theory to practice.* Basingstoke: Palgrave Macmillan.

Reeve, D. (2004) 'Psycho-emotional dimensions of disability and the social model', in C. Barnes and G. Mercer (eds), *Implementing the social model of disability: Theory and research.* Leeds: The Disability Press.

Reeve, D. (2012) 'Preparation for practice: can philosophy have a place in helping students incorporate the social model of disability within their praxis?', *Social Work Education: The International Journal*, 31(2), 227–234.

Rembis, M.A. (2010) 'Beyond the binary: rethinking the social model of disabled sexuality', *Sexuality and Disability*, 28, 51–60.

Roulstone, A. (2012) '"Stuck in the middle with you": towards enabling social work with disabled people', *Social Work Education: The International Journal*, 31(2), 142–154.

Ruch, G., Turney, D. and Ward, A. (eds) (2018) *Relationship-based practice: Getting to the heart of social work.* London: Jessica Kingsley.

Saleebey, D. (1996) 'The strengths perspective in social work practice: extensions and cautions', *Social Work*, 41(3), 296–305.

Schön, D.A. (1987) *Educating the reflective practitioner: Toward a new design for teaching and learning in the professions.* San Francisco, CA: Jossey-Bass.

Schaub, J. Willis, P. and Dunk-West, P. (2017) 'Accounting for self, sex and sexuality in UK social workers' knowledge base: findings from an exploratory study', *The British Journal of Social Work*, 47(2), 427–446.

SCIE (Social Care Institute for Excellence) (undated) *Social care TV: Working with lesbian, gay, bisexual and transgendered people – people with physical disabilities: Doug's story.* Available at https://www.youtube.com/watch?v=92cPuhePQwc

Series, L. (2015) 'Relationships, autonomy and legal capacity: Mental capacity and support', *International Journal of Law and Psychiatry*, 40, 80–91.

Siebelink, E.M., de Jong, M.D.T., Taal, E. and Roelvink, L. (2006) 'Sexuality and people with intellectual disabilities: assessment of knowledge, attitudes, experiences, and needs', *Mental Retardation*, 44(4), 283–294.

Simcock, P. and Castle, R. (2016) *Social work and disability.* Cambridge: Polity Press.

Simpson, P. (2018) 'Home and "hood": middle-aged gay man's stories of homes and neighbourhoods', in P. Dunk-West and T. Hafford-Letchfield (eds), *Sexuality, sexual and gender identities and intimacy research in social work and social care: A lifecourse epistemology.* London: Routledge, pp 69–85.

Sloane, H.M. (2014) 'Tales of a reluctant sex radical: barriers to teaching the importance of pleasure for wellbeing', *Sexuality and Disability*, 32(4), 453–467.

Stanford, S. (2010) '"Speaking back" to fear: responding to the moral dilemmas of risk in social work practice', *The British Journal of Social Work*, 40(4), 1065–1080.

Swango-Wilson, A. (2010) 'Systems theory and the development of sexual identity for individual with intellectual/developmental disability', *Sexuality and Disability*, 28, 157–164.

Tepper, M. (2000) 'Sexuality and disability: the missing discourse of pleasure', *Sexuality and Disability*, 18, 283–290.

Thomas, C. (1999) *Female forms: Experiencing and understanding disability*. Buckingham: Open University Press.

Thomas, C. (2004) 'Developing the social relational in the social model of disability: a theoretical agenda', in C. Barnes and G. Mercer (eds), *Implementing the social model of disability: Theory and research*. Leeds: The Disability Press.

Thomas, C. (2007) *Sociologies of disability and illness: Contested ideas in disability studies and medical sociology*. Basingstoke: Palgrave Macmillan.

Thompson, N. (2020) *Anti-discriminatory practice: Equality, diversity and social justice* (7th edn). Basingstoke: Palgrave Macmillan.

Trevithick, P. (2012) *Social work skills and knowledge: A practice handbook* (3rd edn). Maidenhead: McGraw-Hill/Open University Press.

Turner, G. (2012) 'The social-sexual voice of adults with mild intellectual disabilities: A qualitative case study'. Widener University, ProQuest Dissertations and Theses 355.

Turner, G. and Crane, B. (2016a) 'Sexually silenced no more, adults with learning disabilities speak up: a call to action for social work to frame sexual voice as a social justice issue', *British Journal of Social Work*, 46(8), 2300–2317.

Turner, G. and Crane, B. (2016b) 'Pleasure is paramount: adults with intellectual disabilities discuss sensuality and intimacy', *Sexualities Special Issue: Intellectual Disability and Sexuality: On the Agenda?* 19(5–6), 177–197.

United Nations (2006) *Convention on the rights of persons with disabilities*. New York: United Nations General Assembly.

Ward, R., Vass, A., Aggarwal, N., Garfield, C. and Cybyk, B. (2005) 'A kiss is still a kiss? The construction of sexuality in dementia care', *Dementia*, 4(1), 49–72.

Watson, N. (2004) 'The dialectics of disability: a social model for the 21st century?', in C. Barnes and G. Mercer (eds), *Implementing the social model of disability*. Leeds: Disability Press.

Webb, S.A. (2006) *Social work in a risk society: Social and political perspectives*. Basingstoke: Palgrave Macmillan.

Whittaker, A.J. and Havard, T. (2015) 'Defensive practice as "fear-based" practice: social work's open secret?', *British Journal of Social Work*, 46(5), 1158–1174. https://doi.org/10.1093/bjsw/BCV048

Willis, P., Raithby, M., Dobbs, C., Evans, E. and Bishop, J.-A. (2021) '"I'm going to live my life for me": trans ageing, care, and older trans and gender non-conforming adults' expectations of and concerns for later life', *Ageing and Society*, 41(12), 2792–2813.

World Health Organization (2021) *Sexual and Reproductive Health and Research (SRH)*. https://www.who.int/teams/sexual-and-reproductive-health-and-research/key-areas-of-work/sexual-health/defining-sexual-health (Accessed 9 April 2024).

6

# Promoting Human Rights around Intimacy for People Living with Dementia: A Psychiatric Perspective

*Oluwatoyin Sorinmade and Carmelle Peisah*

## Introduction

The global population of people aged 60 years and older will more than double, from 900 million in 2015 to about 2 billion in 2050 (World Health Organization, 2022) and the expectation is that this will be accompanied by an increase in the number of people living with dementia (PLWD), given the increased prevalence of dementia associated with ageing. Currently more than 55 million people live with dementia worldwide, and there are nearly 10 million new cases every year. Dementia is a syndrome characterised by deterioration in cognitive (intellectual) functions such as memory, orientation, language and judgement, causing functional impairment. Dementia has a range of physical, psychosocial and economic impacts, not only for the PLWD but also for their carers, families and society at large. Yet, there is often a lack of awareness and understanding of dementia and its impacts, resulting in stigmatisation and barriers to diagnosis and care (World Health Organization, 2023b). One of these impacts is on sexuality.

Older people, including PLWD, can continue to enjoy active sex lives. Regardless of dementia, the desire for intimacy may represent the expression of basic human instincts and needs, ranging from sexual needs to the need for companionship, physical contact and the relief of loneliness. In England and Wales and in Australia, as well as in many other jurisdictions arounds the world, the legal position is for individuals engaging in sexual activity (ranging from kissing, cuddling to sexual intercourse), to give 'here and now' consent to such activities. Herein lies the problem for PLWD who may have lost, or be wrongly presumed to have lost, mental capacity and on this basis may be precluded from engaging in sexual relations either in the interest of their safety or that of others. This is regardless of whether the intimacy desire is a basic human instinct or driven by changed behaviours arising as a result of dementia. As such, in the name of 'protection', clinical and legal practice in this area has become highly risk averse, usually to the detriment of PLWD. The current legal position dissuading sexual relations in PLWD (who have lost 'here and now' mental capacity for sexual relations) has been criticised as discriminatory, reflecting ageism and ableism, and a violation of their fundamental rights to privacy, private life and 'relational citizenship' (Kontos et al, 2016; Sorinmade, Ruck Keene and Peisah, 2021; Peisah et al, 2021). Notably, continued engagement in sexual relations has been associated with mental and physical wellbeing (Bach et al, 2013; Syme, 2014; Smith et al, 2019), and indeed, some behaviours described as 'difficult to manage' in some 'non-capacitous' PLWD are possibly manifestations of unmet sexual needs directly arising out of such prohibitions.

A range of international human rights are at stake here and articulated within the United Nations Convention on Rights of Persons with Disabilities (UNCRPD). These include rights to dignity (Article 1), legal capacity, support for decision making and respect for will and preferences (Article 12), equality and non-discrimination (Article 5), safeguarding and freedom from abuse and inhumane or degrading treatment as well as physical and mental integrity (Articles 16 and 17), privacy (Article 22), respect for the family (Article 23), access to the highest attainable standard of sexual health (Article 25) (Peisah et al, 2021).

Recognising the range of human rights at stake here, in this chapter we seek to explore normal sexuality and its expression in older adults including PLWD, and the benefits of such. We examine the consequences of thwarting its expression and the meeting of this basic need, particularly in care homes. We explore the current risk-averse, one-size-fits-all approach of the law and how its misapplication may interfere with the enjoyment of these basic human rights. We do so from the perspectives of two old age psychiatrists and human rights advocate-scholars from two jurisdictions: the United Kingdom (OS) and Australia (CP). This chapter is therefore grounded in clinical perspective and an approach framed by the importance of human rights norms, rather than in legal analysis. Our aim in this chapter is therefore to explore what more can and should be done to promote the right to intimacy and sexuality of PLWD. Despite the evidence – explored in this chapter – as to the benefits continued intimacy can have for PLWD, as well as the rights enshrined in the UNCRPD, it is surprising that such little attention is paid to something so integral to quality of life. In PLWD there is often a tendency to focus on the preservation of cognition and independence, with relative neglect of the need for physical and emotional intimacy (Kaplan, 1990; Rao, 2014). This chapter aims to go some way towards correcting this imbalance.

## Sexual health in older adults

The World Health Organization defines sexual health as a state of physical, emotional, mental and social wellbeing in relation to sexuality; it is not merely the absence of disease, dysfunction or infirmity. Sexual health requires a positive and respectful approach to sexuality and sexual relationships, as well as the possibility of having pleasurable and safe sexual experiences, free of coercion, discrimination and violence (World Health Organization, 2023a).

It is recognised that older adults still engage in sexual activity in different ways even after they consider themselves no longer sexually active (Colton, 2008). Older people, including people with dementia, continue to enjoy active sex lives (Manchester University, 2015), including 59% of men and 51% of women; and 41% of those are 80–91 years old (Lindau et al, 2018). Sexual expression in later life covers a wide spectrum of activities and experiences related to sexuality, romance and sexual identity, ranging from physical forms of intimacy to emotional and intellectual closeness and expressions of affection (Mahieu and Gastmans, 2015). Such sexual expression in later life has been linked with psychological and physiological benefits, including improved quality of life, lower rates of depressive symptoms and lower risk of certain cancers and fatal coronary events (Syme, 2014; Smith et al, 2019). Commentators have suggested that 'there's no less desire or need for camaraderie, intimacy and touch as we age' (AgingCare, 2023), and loneliness can have serious effects on an individual's health, including depression; more so in older adults who are especially vulnerable to loneliness and social isolation. Research suggests that up to one in five cases of depression in older adults could be prevented by reducing loneliness (National Institute for Health and Care Research, 2021). Notably, given the great variation in interest in sexual expression among older persons, it is important to recognise that individuals have the right not to be sexually active in later life too, which should be equally supported, as should their right to continue with sexual relations (Yon et al, 2017) if they so desire.

Part of this variation in interest in sexuality can be attributable to the constraints on its expression as one ages. Older men and women alike are confronted by a vast array of psychological, social and environmental changes, potentially impacting upon their sexuality and its expression (Chung, 2019). For example, sexual dysfunction including loss of libido and sexual desire, erectile dysfunction, ejaculatory and orgasmic dysfunction, are well recognised in older men. This may be due to many factors including declining physical health (specifically vascular changes) and medication side-effects as well as psychologically and physically driven decline in sex drive (Chung, 2019). Constraints on older women are similarly driven by psychological and physical factors. Socially, older women's sexuality may be limited by comparatively less availability of spousal or intimate partners as well as greater likelihood of having partners with their own sexual difficulties. In addition, up to half of sexually active older women report a distressing sexual problem, with low desire and problems related to genitourinary syndrome (vulvovaginal atrophy) being most common (Granville and Pregler, 2018). Sexually transmitted diseases (STDs) are reported among older persons, although at lower rates than among younger persons (Byers, 1983). At the same time, the ageing process is accompanied by biologic age-related increases in susceptibility to STDs. STDs, including HIV infection, can affect anyone including individuals aged 50 years or older (Rogstad and Bignell, 1991; Cranston and Thin, 1998; Gott et al, 1998), although older persons underestimate their HIV risk factors and are often diagnosed with HIV infection later in the course of the disease (Centres for Disease Control and Prevention, 2017). In older women, the increased friability of the vaginal mucosa can result in tears and micro-abrasions during sexual intercourse, facilitating disease transmission (Peterman et al, 1988; Scura and Whipple, 1990).

Social constraints that hinder the expression and meeting of sexual desires of older people are driven by intersectionality and compounded discrimination based on age (ageism), the presence of disability (ableism) and mental disorder (mentalism) (Dementia in Europe Ethics Report, 2021). Apart from the ageist stereotypes of older people that the cessation of the reproductive period implies the end of sexual life in older adults (D'Cruz, Andrade and Rao, 2020), some younger carers/relatives believe that older people are sexless (Weeks, 2002). Finally, an important factor in understanding sexuality and ageing, particularly with respect to the current older cohort, is the perception of sexuality of older persons themselves. In addition to the phenomenon of self-ageism, whereby older person have internalised society's stigmatisation and shame, older generations have low expectations regarding their rights to continued sexual enjoyment and receive scarce information and education concerning sexual issues (Bouman, Arcelus and Benbow, 2006). Many older people from this cohort have grown up in a context where sex, and particularly non-reproductive sexual behaviour, was considered dirty or sinful, and inappropriate in later life (Gewirtz-Maydan et al, 2018). Such negative views of sexuality at times constrained the sexuality of older women, who were not expected to take the initiative and who, in later life, have been stereotyped as non-sexual beings (Syme and Cohn, 2016).

## Dementia and sexuality: sexual health in PLWD

Sexual health and the expression of sexuality is equally important to PLWD. Importantly, the onset or progression of dementia does not necessarily translate to loss of sexuality (Benbow and Beeston, 2012). Studies have shown that among PLWD, 9% of women and 39% of men thought about sex once a week or more, and 37% of women and 74% of men considered sex to be at least a somewhat important part of their life. Additionally, 46% of men and 18% of women living with dementia were sexually active. These percentages were higher among partnered PLWD, rising to 59% of men and 51% of women (Lindau et al, 2018). Notably, some commentators have suggested that PLWD and their partners value nonsexual physical intimacy such as kissing or cuddling highly, and that most couples with dementia report valuing nonsexual intimacy higher than sexual intimacy (Harris, 2009). Regardless of these individual preferences, these statistics do challenge the notion that older people, and particularly PLWD, are sexless or non-sexual (Villar and Faba, 2021).

As emphasised earlier, the desire for and interest in sex are part of the human experience (Syme et al, 2017) and are, as such, basic human needs owed to all, including PLWD and their intimate partners. Article 25 of the UNCRPD protects the right to the highest attainable standard of health, which includes sexual health (Peisah et al, 2021). This right persists despite some PLWD losing decisional capacity for intimacy due to dementia and it has been suggested that a rigid restriction of such intimacy, for example in care homes (a discussed later on in this chapter), may have an adverse effect on the relationship between PLWD and their loved ones (Bartlett, 2010). In addition, research has suggested that being lonely can increase the risk of developing dementia by one third and that having two or three close relationships decreased the risk of dementia by three-fifths (National Institute for Health and Care Research, 2021). Moreover, regardless of dementia, the expression of the desire for sexual relations such as cuddling, kissing and including having sex may represent the expression of basic instincts and needs, ranging from sexuality to the need for companionship, physical contact and the relief of loneliness, and such physical contact might calm the individual and show them care and that they are loved (Alagiakrishnan, 2005; Tenenbaum, 2009). Furthermore, the failure to meet intimacy needs is a known driver of distress and changed behaviours in PLWD (Grigorovich et al, 2022).

Dementia, however, is not experienced in isolation. The effects of dementia – particularly around sexual relationships and intimacy – are also experienced by intimate partners, who are often primary caregivers. For example, it has been suggested that 'loving someone with dementia can be extremely lonely, and even isolating, especially if the spouse is the primary caregiver' (Livewell, 2020). In addition, research has suggested that being lonely can increase the risk of developing dementia by one third and that having two or three close relationships decreased the risk of dementia by three-fifths (National Institute for Health and Care Research, 2021). Notably, research suggests that almost two in three carers of people with dementia are lonely (National Institute for Health and Care Research, 2021). Other challenges faced by partners of PLWD includes if the PLWD misidentifies or misperceives their partner as their parent, sibling or child (Davies et al, 2010) and does not initiate sexual contact with them (Hayes, Boylstein and Zimmerman, 2009). Further difficulties emerge with role conflicts associated with being both a carer and a lover (AgingCare, 2023). The role transition, loss of self-identity and balance of power/responsibility shift that often accompanies dementia can be traumatic for the PLWD and their partner alike, leading to new interpersonal difficulties or an exacerbation of pre-existing interpersonal difficulties. Conversely, intimacy and sexual relationships between PLWD and their partners can provide mutual satisfaction, support and reassurance for both PLWD and partner alike, promoting positive coping and relational health, including being a positive part of each other's lives. Sometimes, sex is one of the few things that partners feel they can still share with the PLWD (Simonelli et al, 2007).

## Sexuality and the care home setting

Studies show that 42% of adults over 65 will spend time in a care home during their lifetime (Murtaugh et al, 1997), and an even larger proportion will have a loved one in nursing home care. Contrary to societal beliefs, sexual and intimate behaviours are exhibited by older adults in care home settings (Frankowski and Clark, 2009; Doll, 2013). A Californian study of retirement homes showed that 62% of men and 30% of women continued to engage in sexual intercourse, and 87% of men and 68% of women engaged in physical intimacy (Kessel, 2001; Bartlett, 2010). Another observational study found that 70% of the sexual activity was between men and women, and it ranged from loving and caring to eroticism (Ehrenfeld et al, 1999). Sexual relations have also been described between same-sex couples in care homes (Peisah et al, 2018).

There is public support in favour of sexual expression for PLWD in care homes (Syme et al, 2017), but, notwithstanding this evidence around the expression of sexuality in care homes, the need for sexual expression remains largely ignored and responded to inconsistently. There are a myriad of reasons for this, although it is mostly driven by the aforementioned ageism, ableism and mentalism compounded by knowledge deficits among staff. This is manifested by discomfort or negative reactions of staff and relatives to expression of sexuality among residents, usually fuelled by lack of understanding of ageing, human rights, sexuality and dementia (Bentrott and Margarett, 2011).

There is also the added complication of family reactions being fuelled by intra-family dynamics, particularly in blended families. When previously (that is, prior to the onset of dementia) the PLWD would not have tolerated such intrusion, dementia – by virtue of associated passivity, disempowerment and the silencing of voice – provides a perfect play ground for such conflicts. For example, sometimes conflict with adult step-children is played out with attempts to disrupt relationships (including sexual relationships) between biological and step-parents. Alternatively, relatives of the PLWD may not approve of the individual with whom the PLWD chooses to form a relationship. This often feeds right into safeguarding initiatives, including policy in care homes to inform relatives of sexual activities by the PLWD (Frankowski and Clark, 2009). Significantly, this information sharing is frequently independent of the choice or even consent of the PLWD, as family and staff are often perceived to hold the right to make such decisions, though their motives may or may not be in the person's interest (Syme et al, 2017). Moreover, while adult children may object to 'new' relationships formed after the onset of dementia, it is possible for the spouse of a PLWD to accept the forming of a new relationship by the PLWD in a care home, at a time when they no longer recognise their spouse, provided the relationship makes the PLWD happy (CBS News, 2007). Care homes are understandably wary of litigation and loss of revenue if family members were to remove their ageing relatives if sexual expression were permitted, which culminates in the care home interfering with the PLWD's sexual expression (Abellard, Rogers and Bales, 2017).

Perhaps the most important constraint to the expression of sexuality for people living with dementia in care homes is the issue of privacy and the associated shame of expressing one's sexuality in a public setting. This is particularly relevant to the current cohort of older persons, as discussed earlier. Notably, there is evidence to suggest that older people in care homes are conscious of the impression their sexuality and its expression makes on other residents, especially as some residents react negatively to other fellow residents engaging in such. The expression/experience of sexual relations is often a private matter, and considered as such by older people (Bauer et al, 2012), but this is often open to scrutiny for institutionalised older persons, and it can be inhibited by environmental constraints as well as active discouragement of sexual expression by PLWD, by staff and family (Lichtenberg and Strzepek, 1990; Roelofs, Luijkx and Embregts, 2021). For example, where environments are not discrete, many older people may refrain from sexual activity (Bauer et al, 2012). Physical barriers that can inhibit sexual relationships include lack of privacy conferred by shared rooms, and open doors with intrusion without permission (Davies et al, 2010; Dementia in Europe Ethics Report, 2021).

Older persons also face psychological barriers, such as disempowerment, diminished self-confidence and feelings of shame, embarrassment or stoicism (Harris, 2009). On a practical level, the dependence of some older adults – especially those in care homes – on others for their basic activities of daily living hinders their ability to engage in sexual relations independent of support from others (Frankowski and Clark, 2009). Other issues include that medications and associated side-effects also impact sexual desire and the ability of older adults to engage in sexual activities (Villar and Faba, 2021). There are also gender-based biases whereby relatives, and perhaps carers, readily take steps to preclude women in care settings from being erotically active (Ehrenfeld et al, 1999).

Accordingly, the continuation of sexual relationships and meeting intimacy needs among older people living in care homes is likely to be lower than for their counterparts living independently in their own homes (Villar and Faba, 2021). As a result, there is an abundance of loneliness in these settings and a yearning desire to be loved reported by some residents (Roach, 2004). More specifically, despite the equally important need of PLWD to engage in sexual activity, and the sexual and intimate behaviours exhibited by PLWD (Kamel and Hajjar, 2003), these needs are rarely acknowledged in residential care, despite having extensive public support (68.3%) for such (Syme et al, 2017). Unfortunately, there is usually limited explicit institutional and legal guidance on how to respond to sexual and intimate expression in a way that both supports and protects nursing home residents and staff (Lindsay, 2010). Studies show that most care homes do not have any policies on any aspect of resident sexuality (Syme et al, 2017) and, of the facilities that had policies, only 58.6% had written policies, with 11.2% of those requiring a physician's order to allow sexual activity (Lester et al, 2016). The Lester study demonstrated how concepts such as 'allowing', 'approving' or 'governing' sexual activity are now so integrated into policy, procedure and practice. Medicalisation, legalisation and institutionalisation of the sexuality of PLWD are now normalised processes in care homes.

The consequence of this is that the right and need to engage in healthy, intimate or sexual relationships are curtailed in care home settings, given the increased likelihood of exposure to civil litigation and even criminal charges for intimate partners of PLWD. This was exemplified by a case in the United States in which a 78-year-old husband was charged with, and subsequently exonerated from, sexual assault in the third degree of his wife, who was living with dementia and who had been newly admitted to a care home. The responses of the care home and law enforcement agencies, causing emotional and reputational trauma for the husband, were criticised widely (New York Times, 2015).

Evidence also suggests that in these settings PLWD are rarely given the opportunity to speak for themselves (Van Gorp and Vercruysse, 2012), rendering approaches to sexual expression by PLWD in care homes often devoid of person-centred components, such as resident choice. In fact, little is known about residents' preferences for sexual and intimate expression across different situations (Syme, Johnson and Fager, 2020). Without adequate policy as already described, a resident's voice may be lost in decision making (Syme et al, 2017), though evidence suggests that sexual issues remain a concern for older people in care facilities (Frankowski and Clark, 2009).

Despite studies suggesting that many individuals in care homes are lonely (National Institute for Health and Care Research, 2021), there is a complexity rendered by the debate about the variable contributions of disease processes versus normative sexual and intimacy needs to sexual behaviours in PLWD. For example, some commentators have suggested that there are instances when intimacy-seeking behaviour in PLWD is perceived as disease-driven 'symptoms' or 'responsive behaviours' rather than meaningful attempts to communicate or to engage with others (Grigorovich and Kontos, 2018). While some intimacy-seeking behaviours in PLWD are driven by biological disease processes causing disinhibition or even agitation, in this context known as 'inappropriate sexual behaviours', some commentators have suggested that this occurs in a minority of patients (28%) (D'cruz, Andrade and Rao, 2020), and some studies have even suggested that this might be lower than 2% (Algiakrishnan et al, 2005). Regardless, this confusion about aetiology of behaviours has led to restriction of sexual and intimate expression among residents, especially PLWD, based on discriminatory and ageist assumptions that PLWD are both incapable of purposeful and meaningful communication and the pursuit of life-enhancing relationships and are incapable, globally, of giving consent (Grigorovich et al, 2022). Moreover, the need to understand whether behaviours are driven by disease progression or because of a desire for intimacy serves to reinforce the need for a person-centred approach to care within these settings.

Notwithstanding our concerns about barriers to meeting intimacy and sexuality needs in care homes, equally important is the need for safeguarding against abuse. The actual prevalence of abuse in care remains unknown, because reporting is contaminated by a range of factors related to the victim, staff and the organisation (Burgess, Ramsey-Klawsnik and Gregorian 2008; Iverson, Kilvik and Malmedal, 2015). With regard to the victim, while factors such as expressive language and memory impairment may lead to under-reporting, paranoid ideation and paranoid delusions may lead to over-reporting. Notably, in one study of 119 alleged sexual perpetrators reported to state authorities for abusing older persons living in care, only 32 were confirmed as sexual perpetrators (Ramsey-Klawsnik et al, 2008). Regardless of the actual prevalence, if one older person is abused, then this is significant, but the important issue at stake is balancing safeguarding obligations against autonomy and privacy obligations, intruding on the lives of PLWD and infantilising them in the name of protection.

## What challenges does the law pose?

Recognising that older persons, as with all people, have a great diversity in both their interest in and expression of sexuality (Mahieu and Gastmans, 2015) is important in understanding why this very human experience does not lend itself to regulation by blanket, 'one-size fits-all' legal processes. Yet the law has been preoccupied with blanket approaches to safeguarding against abuse in this context, perhaps at the expense of other human rights to autonomy, privacy, expression of will and preferences, and meeting needs on account of disability (Sorinmade, Ruck Keene and Peisah, 2021; Peisah et al, 2021). To date, the concept of consent, its operation in law and real-world interpretation in clinical settings have been the means of achieving this safeguarding.

By illustration, in England and Wales the concept of consent has been operationalised domestically in legislation, with section 74 of the Sexual Offences Act 2003 defining consent as someone agreeing to something by choice, necessitating both freedom and capacity to make that choice. Under the Sexual Offences Act a person might commit an offence if they intentionally touch another person in a sexual way without the consent of the person being touched, and without any reasonable belief that the person is consenting to being touched sexually. In essence, the Sexual Offences Act 2003 prohibits sexual relations between individuals where one or both partners lack the relevant decisional capacity. Sexual relations in such situations are not lawful, including in the case of PLWD.

Likewise, section 3(1) of the English and Welsh Mental Capacity Act 2005 defines the process of ascertaining if an individual has the capacity to decide on an issue, that is, they must be able to understand the information relevant to the required decision, retain and use that information in weighing up their options and then communicate their decision in whatever way possible. Section 2(1) of the same Act states that a person lacks capacity in relation to a matter if at the material time he is unable to decide for himself in relation to the matter because of an impairment of, or a disturbance in the functioning of, the mind or brain. If a person lacks capacity to engage in sexual relationships, another individual cannot legally consent to sexual relations on behalf of another, as is enshrined by section 27 of the Mental Capacity Act 2005.

This legislation, in common with the majority of, if not all, jurisdictions around the world, is clear on the requirement for contemporaneous consent to sexual activity, as demonstrated in *A Local Authority v JB*[1] and as explored

[1] [2021] UKSC 52.

in more detail by both Ruck Keene, Enefer and Cusack (Chapter 2) and Lindsay and Brennan (Chapter 3) in this volume. In effect, consenting to sexual activity must happen before the sexual activity starts and must continue throughout the sexual activity. This is the approach taken by both civil and criminal laws, given that continued sexual relations with a person who has withdrawn consent during sex would also constitute a criminal offence.

This position of the law thus precludes PLWD who no longer have the capacity to consent to intimacy/express their sexuality from lawfully engaging in such activity. This inadvertently creates unmet needs for such individuals and places their relationships and sexual partners – sometimes long-standing relationships and partners which pre-date the onset of dementia – in precarious positions of potentially being criminalised (Sorinmade, Ruck Keene and Peisah, 2021). Such an approach is also evident in other jurisdictions beyond England and Wales. In Australia, for example, on 1 June 2022 the Crimes Legislation Amendment (Sexual Consent Reforms) Act 2021 came into force in New South Wales (NSW). This reformed the law of consent in NSW, Australia's most populous state, by amending the Crimes Act 1900 in relation to consent to certain sexual activities that, in the absence of consent, are sexual offences. The amendments introduced included new definitions of consent in Subdivision 1A Consent and Knowledge of Consent. Under the new section 61HI (1), 'A person consents to a sexual activity if, at the time of the sexual activity, the person freely and voluntarily agrees to the sexual activity'. Further, section 61HJ (1) outlines the circumstances in which there is no consent, if (a) the person does not say or do anything to communicate consent, or (b) the person does not have the capacity to consent to the sexual activity.

For professionals, complying with the law in relation to sexuality in the care of PLWD can be challenging. Some commentators have suggested that the curtailing of sexual interaction by PLWD who have lost the 'here and now' ability to consent is violating their basic human rights to dignity, autonomy and participation in everyday life and society and that such curtailing is discriminatory and based on age and disability (Peisah et al, 2021; Grigorovich et al, 2022). Some other commentators, in giving voice to the feminist charge of ownership of one's own body and actions, as well as preserving the rights of those in loving long-term relationships, have suggested that the approach taken by law is inhuman, or absurd (Bartlett, 2010).

It could be thus argued, that in the name of upholding the Article 16 right to safeguarding against abuse, the effect of the law in action is, at its worst, to subject PLWD to a violation of their rights to be safeguarded against cruel and inhumane treatment (Article 17), if not violation of other aforementioned rights to dignity, autonomy, expression of will and preferences, privacy and relationships.

Violation of dignity is at particular risk. 'Persons with advanced dementia should be cared for so they can keep their experiences of human dignity, dignity as merit, dignity as moral stature and dignity of identity. When persons with advanced dementia are seen as having lost their self (Millett, 2011), their human dignity is questioned and there is a risk that they become treated as objects' (Norberg, 2019, p 214). First-person accounts from PLWD show that what is most important to individuals with dementia is that they are valued, and are talked to and respected as they are real people (NYU Langone Health, 2003). They reported their major concern as being not so much a loss of cognition or identity, but the loss of value and the loss of relationship with others (Herring, 2008). Our legal system, with its emphasis on rationality and individuality, reinforces these concerns, rather than seeking to address them, by 'saving the person' and ignoring their relationships, often leaving them protected but lonely. This is despite the fact that people without disabilities such as dementia often take risks rendering them unsafe, merely for the sake of intimacy or feeling valued and loved. The inequity and injustice of this was identified in a recent qualitative study capturing the voice of older persons, including PLWD, with regard to sexuality and the law (Sorinmade et al, in review). As explored here, and elsewhere in this volume, the current legal position requires 'here and now' mental capacity to engage in sexual relations, and while the relevant laws were not explicitly implemented to restrict positive sexual expression of persons living with dementia, they pose a significant barrier to such expression by reinforcing ableism and ageism (Peisah et al, 2021; Grigorovich et al, 2022) by denying the normative needs of sexuality and intimacy afforded to younger or non-disabled populations. As such, the denial of needs for sexuality and intimacy is created and effected by this overreach of protectionism and safeguarding, despite these being valuable ideals.

The law rightfully expects us all to consent to sexual relations, and this is right and proper, as the law protects us all from abuse, exploitation and degrading treatment. Aside from the law, it is basic to self-respect/esteem for an individual to be able to have control of, and to consent to, what happens to their body and personal space. Herein lies the difficulty for individuals with dementia, where blanket laws are inappropriate, as are blanket presumptions about incapacity for sexual relations. Dementia has variable impact on capacity for sexual relations in different people, depending on the nature of the cognitive deficits relevant to sexual capacity, including memory, identification of partners, language and judgement. When capacity is lost, the law as it stands deems continued engagement in sexual relations unlawful. Such individuals who cannot consent to sexual relations (intimacy) are precluded from engaging in such, especially in care homes (CQC, 2019), often for fear of the associated liability and prosecution. In this way, PLWD are thereby consigned to 'celibacy', perhaps inadvertently so, by the current laws, even if their intended partner is fully capacitous.

There are also no provisions in law for the decision to engage in sexual relations to be made/ceded to a Lasting Power of Attorney or for the courts to make such decisions in order to circumnavigate the restrictions imposed by the Mental Capacity Act 2005. From a legal perspective this is perhaps understandable, given the parameters of the criminal law through the Sexual Offences Act 2003. Enacting such provisions would require reforms of the criminal law's approach to consent and capacity (Sorinmade, Ruck Keene and Peisah, 2021). This may also not be antithetical to liberty and autonomy, given the difficulty of proxy decision making and 'best interests guessing' in this space.

Even now, the subjective nature of interpretation of the legislation is problematic, with decisions about intrusion, action and safeguarding being influenced by normative judgements about the kind of relationships we see as 'acceptable' among older persons. For example, staff are more likely to walk past a married couple engaged in a long-term relationship but be alerted to a new relationship or one involving a change in sexuality, due to social norms about what is taboo or inappropriate. Given that we know that many partners still enjoy sex and intimacy in their relationship even if one of them develops dementia (Alzheimer's Society, 2023), the issue for the operation of the law and its effects on sexuality arises when others, mainly health professionals and care home management, become witness to the expression of sexuality and beholden to the law and its interpretation. Thus, the issue of sexuality comes to light only when there is healthcare professional scrutiny of sexuality in the private home, and assessments are often precipitated when the person's choice diverges from the advice of professionals (Kong and Ruck Keene, 2018) or when they move into a care home (NPR, 2012).

The invariable consequence is that PLWD lacking decisional capacity to engage in sexual relations are stopped from engaging in intimacy by different measures, including physical separation as well as the use of medication such as antipsychotics (NPR, 2012; International Psychogeriatric Association, 2015). Tort law, regulatory law and criminal law impose a duty on carers to ensure that vulnerable people are safe in their care. Accordingly, care staff and organisations might be liable for any range of civil, criminal or regulatory 'offences' if sexual relations occur between individuals where one or both participants lack/s the relevant decisional capacity to engage in such activity, and care home staff knew that such activity was occurring and failed to prevent it (Bartlett, 2010).[2]

[2] See also, *Secretary of State for Justice v A Local Authority & Ors* [2021] EWCA Civ 1527.

## The role of health and care professionals: an important linchpin

The role of the health professional is crucial in either inhibiting or facilitating sexual expression. Yet they are equally amenable to the aforementioned ageism, ableism and erotophobia, and to societal values and beliefs regarding sexuality, including sexophobic attitudes regarding sex in later life (Grigorovich et al, 2022; Villar and Faba, 2021). Embarrassment, dissatisfaction with treatment, negative attitudes and seeming disinterest by health professionals can all inhibit discussions in this area (Colton, 2008; Bauer, Haesler and Fetherstonhaugh, 2016). Some studies have found that conversations were rarely initiated by the older person due to the shame, embarrassment and discomfort they felt from being a sexually active human being with a sexual health problem (Colton, 2008; Slinkard and Kazer, 2011). Also, the healthcare professional's gender, age, speciality and history with the patient influence how comfortable an older adult is discussing sex (Colton, 2008). There is also evidence that people are far less likely to want to discuss their sexual relationships if they are homosexual or bisexual because they are worried about professional responses, resulting in them going back into the closet (Westwood, 2016).

There are also other healthcare professional-mediated factors that exclude PLWD from sexual relations. These include lack of knowledge, more restrictive or negative attitudes about older adult sexuality and lack of resources to develop policy and train staff (Hajjar and Kamel, 2003; Syme, Lichtenberg and Moye, 2016), and the need to safeguard the welfare of otherwise vulnerable individuals. Some studies have shown that some professionals respond to sexual expression by PLWD with expressions of disgust, denial and discouragement (Cornelison and Doll, 2013; Howard, Brassolotto and Manduca-Barone, 2019) and feel the urge to intervene (Villar et al, 2018). Heteronormative assumptions regarding gender roles and sexual conduct further influence professionals' perceptions of the sexual expression of PLWD. For example, the sexual expressions of men are more likely to be eroticised and perceived as dangerous to others, while the sexual expressions of women are more likely to prompt a protective response (Sandberg, Bertilsdotter Rosqvist and Grigorovich, 2020). There is also evidence that professionals lack cultural competency in sexual and gender diversity and that they may hold more negative perceptions of the sexual expressions of LGBTQ PLWD (Caceres et al, 2020). This can affect preparedness of LGBTQ patients to discuss their sexual relationships and their sexual needs (Westwood, 2016). Finally, many professionals do not understand obligations regarding consent, privacy and confidentiality, and autonomy. It is not unheard of for clinicians and administrators to accept and deal with third-party decision makers such as health providers or other attorneys, without consultation with the older person themselves, about aspects of care including sexuality and sexual relationships. This might lead to treatment, confinement or possible restrictions on the enjoyment of their human rights such as free movement, free association, privacy or family contact (Mitchell et al, 2021).

As doctors and psychiatrists, we have the 'luxury' of being beholden first and foremost to our ethical professional standards which define our primary duty of care to our patients and their families. Accordingly, notwithstanding our acknowledged duties to do so in a lawful manner compliant with any mandatory reporting obligations, we (the authors) approach the issue of sexuality in PLWD with primary ethical responsibilities (principlism) of promoting autonomy, acting with beneficence (doing good) and non-maleficence (doing no harm) and justice (Taylor, 2013). This is augmented by our roles as human rights advocates and experts in capacity assessment (O'Neill and Peisah, 2021). We are guided in our work by the World Health Organisation (World Health Organization, 2023c) definition of elder abuse, which emphasises harm: 'as an intentional act, or failure to act, by a caregiver or another person in a relationship involving an expectation of trust that causes harm to an adult 60 years and older'.

Our involvement in this area is usually precipitated when a PLWD's sexual expression is scrutinised by others, often when care homes need to discharge their duty of care, or when a complaint has been made by a family member. Our starting point is always a presumption of capacity, for which we require good reason to intrude and even assess capacity. We do not act as agents of care facilities and, while the context for referral is often risk management-driven, we intrude and assess only if the patient, the sexual partner or the family requests and requires our opinion and support (through a referral from a general practitioner) or there is a risk of harm to the patient or their sexual partner. Sometimes we choose not to proceed and assess the patient, and our approach is merely to educate about all the issues discussed in this chapter, including a more valid, nuanced assessment of sexual capacity and consent for PLWD (Hillman, 2017). It is important for care staff and care home management to understand that the diagnosis of dementia does not equate with loss of sexual capacity or loss of the ability to give consent. Many PLWD actually retain mental capacity to consent to sexual relations but are stopped from doing so, due to the inability of their carers or relatives to recognise their consenting capacity (Grigorovich et al, 2022).[3]

In approaching the assessment of capacity, we consider that in this setting, capacity is not categorical (all or nothing) and we favour a supported decision-making approach based on strengths and weaknesses

[3] See also, *A v AG and CI (No. 2) (Rev 1)* [2021] EWCOP 5; *Re SF* [2020] EWCOP 15.

of the person (Peisah et al, 2013). While surrogate, rather than supported, decision-making remains in legal force in England and Wales through the best interests requirement in the Mental Capacity Act, such an approach is consistent with both Article 12 of the UNCRPD and, indeed, sections 1(3) and 3(2) of the Mental Capacity Act. Part of our approach is based on the risk threshold approach, namely the more serious the decision, the greater capacity required.[4] As applied to sexual capacity, a person might be capable of consenting to some intimate acts such as kissing but not sexual penetration, or capable of consenting to contact with certain individuals but not with others (Testad et al, 2014; Wilkins, 2015). Implicit to this approach is a skill-based assessment (Peisah et al, 2013) of the person's understanding of the nature and consequences of the act, allowing the person to use whatever means they have available to them to indicate their understanding (Bartlett, 2010),[5] including observing their behaviour in relation to the act, this all being tailored to the specific sexual act in question, using a task-specific approach to capacity assessment.

## Recommendations for heath and legal policy reform

In making recommendations for legal and health policy reform, we draw on our combined academic and frontline clinical expertise in providing treatment and care of older patients and their families both at home and in care homes for over 30 years. We suggest that any true solution to this somewhat 'wicked problem' that cuts across health, social and legal services, as well as human rights, must lie in a multidisciplinary approach. We suggest further, that improved education and understanding at the coalface of care is required. Our recommendations are framed around a group of principles, as follows:

(i) *Adopt a human rights approach to sexuality* that is anchored in existing common and statutory law. This encompasses the common law presumption of capacity and a hierarchical risk-based approach to capacity determination. Common law references to best interests are paralleled in human rights framework references to the expression of will and preferences and supported decision making (for example, UNCRPD Article 12, and sections 1(3) and 3(2) of the Mental Capacity Act in England and Wales). In a practical sense from a policy point of view, there are guides on how to use supported decision making in this setting (Peisah et al, 2013; Wilkins, 2015).

[4] Lord Donaldson in *Re T* [1992] 4 All ER 649 at para 28.

[5] *KK vs STCC* [2012] EWHC 2136 (COP); *Re MAB* [2006] EWHC 168 (Fam).

(ii) Another approach could be for the law to be modified to allow for PLWD who have lost the decisional capacity to consent to sexual relations to be assessed by relevant professionals with a view to determining if it is in their best interests[6] to continue engaging in sexual relations and to determine the processes to enable them to do so safely, where their continued engagement in sexual relations is found to be appropriate and in their best interests.

(iii) *Capacity assessment requires expertise and training*, which must be made available to all professionals interfacing with PLWD. There needs to be understanding of the task-specific nature of capacity assessment, and rigid adherence to the basic principles of presumption of capacity. PLWD should be empowered to make decisions on sexual relations by providing them appropriate information that is relevant to the decision in question. Their decision-making ability should only be rebutted if it is determined that they are unable to use the information at their disposal to make such a decision, and only after they have been supported maximally in their decision-making process.

(iv) *Human rights literacy must be embedded within all aged care education*, with particular attention to addressing ageism, ableism and mentalism, and taught to all staff interfacing with PLWD.

(v) *Recognition that sexuality and intimacy needs can be integral to quality of life*; this requires integration of sexual health and intimacy needs into care plans as standard (Wilson, 2006).

(vi) *Care staff need education with regard to sexuality*. There is a recognised need to equip staff with confidence, skills and knowledge in supporting the expression of sexuality in care facilities (Ho and Goh, 2022).

(vii) *Care facilities need specific guidelines and policy to support and optimise the expression of sexuality* by their residents, such as the Sexual Assessment Tool SexAT, a self-audit scoring system developed to assist residential aged care facilities to audit their facilities with regard to discrete policies for residents, staff and relatives around sexuality (Bauer et al, 2013).

(viii) *Policy must enforce the provision of LGBTQ-friendly facilities* to ensure the safe expression of sexuality in all of its forms (Buczac-Stec et al, 2023).

(ix) *Safeguarding from sexual abuse must be maintained without descending into being overly protective or paternalistic.* Awareness raising and education of care staff is required to ensure that all residents are protected from, abuse given the complexities around reporting of elder abuse (World Health Organization, 2022), especially PLWD (Burgess and Phillips, 2006), and findings that suggest that elder abuse is hidden, often

[6] Mental Capacity Act 2004 section 4 and *Aintree University Hospital NHS Trust v James* [2013] UKSC 67 at [45].

ignored and a violation of human rights (House of Commons, 2003; House of Lords, 2007). Clear, well-defined and easy-to-understand/ apply criteria for raising safeguarding concerns on behalf of PLWD will also be pertinent, bearing in mind the high rates of elder abuse (Yon et al, 2017). At the same time there must be respect for privacy, a presumption of capacity and recognition that a person's room in a care home is their home.

(x) *Understand the link between unmet needs for intimacy, touch and sexuality, and many changed behaviours in dementia* such as sexual disinhibition and aggression. Identifying the 'cause' of the behaviour for what it is, for example, by functional analysis of the behaviour, and introducing appropriate psychosocial interventions (Testad et al, 2014) might lead to better outcomes for the PLWD, their partners, fellow residents and staff.

(xi) *Promotion of autonomy* through early discussion of sexuality and the impact of dementia on sexuality at diagnosis. Clinicians might initiate discussion with the PLWD about views on sexuality, their wishes and relationships, akin to suggested approaches with individuals with Motor Neurone Disease (Abellard, Rogers and Bales, 2017). This might be further strengthened by changing the law to allow for Advance Decisions on Intimacy (Sorinmade, Ruck Keene and Peisah, 2021), whereby the current self makes decisions for the future self with regard to sexuality if they lose the ability to give 'here and now' consent to sexual relations in future.

(xii) *An alternative to Advance Decision on Intimacy might be achieved* by amendment of section 9 of the MCA 2005 to enable the Health and Welfare Attorney to pursue the best interests process as defined by the Mental Capacity Act, and to decide whether an individual who has lost the capacity to consent in sexual relations should engage in such relations or not. This might involve a set of instructions by the donor of the Lasting Power of Attorney to the donee on how they would want to be treated on matters of sexual relations if they lost the decisional capacity on such matters. In both this and (ii) as well as (xi), amendments would also be needed to the criminal law to allow for both these measures (a full discussion of this, or the merits of either approach, is outside the scope of this chapter).

## Conclusion

In this chapter we have emphasised that 'pleasure and comfort are two things that people with dementia desperately need but often lack' (Agingcare, 2023) and that physical intimacy continues to be a source of comfort, support and pleasure for many years (Alzheimer's Society, 2023). The 'touch' that a

PLWD receives should be not only when receiving care, but 'touch' that is consistent with their will and preferences and touch that they find soothing and comforting and meets needs for intimacy and sexuality when they exist. In essence, the care of PLWD should extend beyond medication, personal care and nutrition, to enable them to engage fully with their basic human needs and fulfilment of their human rights.

Not all human experiences can be legislated for, although the question arises as to how the law could approach these difficulties better, given the relatively prohibitive approach to sex with the incapable adult mandated by current laws. It has been argued that reviewing the laws, to explore for allowances to be made for sexual relations in a PLWD who has lost the relevant decisional capacity, would be fraught with difficulties and that an improved guidance on prosecutorial discretion, or changes to the criminal law, might be one of the ways forward (Bartlett, 2010).

A possible option is for a reconsideration of where the bar is set for PLWD regarding whether they have 'here and now' capacity, and what factors are considered when determining if a PLWD is consenting to sexual relations. At minimum, what is needed is fundamental systemic change, promoting education and awareness raising among those who are vested with the power to either promote the enjoyment of sexuality and intimacy or thwart it. The consequences of not getting this right have the most impact, not on healthcare or legal professionals or care home managers, but on the most vulnerable, PLWD. This is not hyperbole or catastrophisation, given what we know about both the source of changed behaviours in dementia and the prevalence of depression and loneliness in care settings. As such, the views and expertise of older people, including PLWD, need to be incorporated into policy and law making, particularly where they will be most affected (United Nations, 2021). Research has shown that public opinion can have a significant effect on policy, with several examples of policy advancement driven by the public voice (Burstein, 2003). The anticipation is that policies and procedures will be developed that will capture public opinion, protect the human rights of PLWD while also protecting them from harm and support safe sexual expression for PLWD (Syme et al, 2017).

Despite the challenges, it is important to advocate for the rights of PLWD to have needs met with regard to sexuality, intimacy and relationships, needs that are often intrinsic to quality of life. In doing so it is essential that we pull down the barriers that prevent older people from full enjoyment of human rights to autonomy, dignity, privacy, supported decision making and expression of will and preferences. Equally important is the need to promote the enjoyment of life's experiences by PLWD in a safe manner, devoid of abuse and exploitation (United Nations, 2021). This might be a wicked problem, but it is still not an unsolvable one, perhaps solved by a combined approach of all healthcare, legal and social care stakeholders but, most importantly, integrating the voice of those with lived experience.

## References

Abellard, J., Rodgers, C. and Bales, A. (2017) 'Balancing sexual expression and risk of harm in elderly persons with dementia', *Journal of the American Academy of Psychiatry and the Law*, 45, 485–492.

Aging Care (2023) *Dementia poses unique intimacy challenges for spousal care givers*. Available at: https://www.agingcare.com/articles/dementia-intimacy-challenges-156319.htm (Accessed 25 August 2023).

Alagiakrishnan, K., Lim, D., Brahim, A., Wong, A., Wood, A., Senthilselvan, A., Chimich, W.T. and Kagan, L. (2005) 'Sexually inappropriate behaviour in demented elderly people', *Postgraduate Medical Journal*, 81(957), 463–466.

Alzheimer's Society (2023) *How does dementia affect sex and intimacy?* Available at: https://www.alzheimers.org.uk/get-support/daily-living/sex-intimacy-dementia (Accessed 26 August 2023).

Bach, L.E., Mortimer, J.A., VandeWeerd, C. and Corvin, J. (2013) 'The association of physical and mental health with sexual activity in older adults in a retirement community', *The Journal of Sexual Medicine*, 10(11), 2671–2678.

Bartlett, P. (2010) 'Sex, dementia, capacity and care homes', *Liverpool Law Review*, 31, 137–154.

Bauer, M., Haesler, E. and Fetherstonhaugh, D. (2016) 'Let's talk about sex: older people's views on the recognition of sexuality and sexual health in the health-care setting', *Health Expectations*, 19(6), 1237–1250.

Bauer, M., Fetherstonhaugh, D., Tarzia, A., Nay, R., Wellman, D. and Beattie, E. (2012) 'I always look under the bed for a man. Needs and barriers to the expression of sexuality in residential aged care: the views of residents with and without dementia', *Psychology and Sexuality*, 4, 296–309.

Bauer, M., Fetherstonhaugh, D., Nay, R., Tarzia, L. and Beattie, E. (2013) *Sexuality Assessment Tool (SexAT) for residential aged care facilities*. (Available from the Australian Centre for Evidence Based Aged Care, La Trobe University, Melbourne VIC 3086.)

Benbow, S.M. and Beeston, D. (2012) 'Sexuality, aging, and dementia', *International Psychogeriatrics*, 24(7), 1026–1033.

Bentrott, M.D. and Margrett, J.A. (2011) 'Taking a person-centered approach to understanding sexual expression among long-term care residents: theoretical perspectives and research challenges', *Ageing International*, 36, 401–417.

Bouman, W.P., Arcelus, J. and Benbow, S.M. (2006) 'Nottingham Study of Sexuality & Ageing (NoSSA I). Attitudes regarding sexuality and older people: a review of the literature', *Sexual and Relationship Therapy*, 21(2), 149–161.

Buczak-Stec, E., König, H.H., Feddern, L. and Hajek, A. (2023) 'Long-term care preferences and sexual orientation: a systematic review and meta-analysis', *Journal of the American Medical Directors Association*, 24(3), 331–342.

Burgess, A. and Phillips, S. (2006) 'Sexual abuse, trauma and dementia in the elderly: a retrospective study of 284 cases', *Victims and Offenders*, 2, 193–204.

Burgess, A.W., Ramsey-Klawsnik, H. and Gregorian, S.B. (2008) 'Comparing routes of reporting in elder sexual abuse cases', *Journal of Elder Abuse and Neglect*, 20(4), 336–52.

Burstein, P. (2003) 'The impact of public opinion on public policy: a review and an agenda', *Political Research Quarterly*, 56(1), 29–40.

Byers, J.P. (1983) 'Sexuality and the elderly', *Geriatric Nursing*, 4, 293–297.

Caceres, B.A., Travers, J., Primiano, J.E., Luscombe, R.E. and Dorsen, C. (2020) 'Provider and LGBT individuals' perspectives on LGBT issues in long-term care: a systematic review', *The Gerontologist*, 60(3), e169–e183.

CBS News (2007) *Justice O'Connor's Husband Finds New Love*. Available at: https://www.cbsnews.com/news/justice-oconnors-husband-finds-new-love/ (Accessed 26 August 2023).

Centers for Disease Control and Prevention (CDC) (2017) *HIV among people aged 50 and over*. Atlanta, GA: CDC. Available at: https://www.cdc.gov/hiv/group/age/olderamericans/ (Accessed 23 March 2023).

Colton, J. (2008) 'Sex and the elderly: What physicians should know about their older patients'. Yale Medicine Thesis Digital Library. Available at: http://elischolar.library.yale.edu/ymtdl/317 (Accessed 26 August 23).

Chung E. (2019) 'Sexuality in ageing male: review of pathophysiology and treatment strategies for various male sexual dysfunctions', *Medical Sciences*, 7(10), 98.

Cornelison, L.J. and Doll, G.M. (2013) 'Management of sexual expression in long-term care: ombudsmen's perspectives', *The Gerontologist*, 53(5), 780–789.

CQC (2019) *Relationships and sexuality in adult social care services. Guidance for CQC inspection staff and registered adult social care providers*. Available at: https://www.cqc.org.uk/sites/default/files/20190221-Relationships-and-sexuality-in-social-care-PUBLICATION.pdf (Accessed 26 August 2023).

Cranston, R.D. and Thin R.N. (1998) 'How common are sexually transmitted infections in the elderly?', *Sexually Transmitted Infections*, 74, 379.

Davies H.D., Newkirk, L.A., Pitts, C.B., Coughlin, C.A., Sridhar, S.B., Zeiss, L.M. and Zeiss, A.M. (2010) 'The impact of dementia and mild memory impairment (MMI) on intimacy and sexuality in spousal relationships', *International Psychogeriatrics*, 22(4), 618–628.

D'cruz, M., Andrade, C. and Rao, T.S.S. (2020) 'The expression of intimacy and sexuality in persons with dementia', *Journal of Psychosexual Health*, 2(3–4), 215–223.

Dementia in Europe Ethics Report (2021) *Sex, gender and sexuality in the context of dementia: A discussion paper.* Available at: https://www.alzheimer-europe.org/sites/default/files/2022-02/2022-02-25%20Alzheimer%20Europe%20ethics%20report%202021.pdf (Accessed 27 September 2023).

Doll, G. (2013) 'Sexuality in nursing homes: practice and policy', *Journal of Gerontological Nursing*, 39, 30–37.

Ehrenfeld, M., Bronner, G., Tabak, N., Alpert R. and Bergman, R. (1999) 'Sexuality among institutionalized elderly patients with dementia', *Nursing Ethics*, 6(2), 144.

Frankowski, A.C. and Clark, L.J. (2009) 'Sexuality and intimacy in assisted living: residents' perspectives and experiences', *Sexuality Research & Social Policy*, 6, 25–37.

Gewirtz-Meydan, A., Hafford-Letchfield, T., Benyamini, Y., Phelan, A., Jackson, J. and Ayalon, L. (2018) 'Ageism and sexuality', in L. Ayalon and C. Tesch-Römer (eds), *Contemporary perspectives on ageism*. Cham, Switzerland: Springer, pp 148–162.

Gott, C.M., Ahmed Jushuf, I., McKee, K., Morgan, K., Riley, V.C. and Rogstad, K.E. (1998) 'Characteristics of older patients attending genitourinary medicine clinics', *Health Care in Later Life*, 3, 252–257.

Grigorovich, A. and Kontos, P. (2018) 'Advancing an ethic of embodied relational sexuality to guide decision-making in dementia care', *The Gerontologist*, 58(2), 219–225.

Granville, L. and Pregler, J. (2018) 'Women's sexual health and aging', *Journal of American Geriatric Society*, 3, 595–601.

Grigorovich, A., Kontos, P., Heesters, A., Martin, L.S., Gray, J. and Tamblyn Watts, L. (2022) 'Dementia and sexuality in long-term care: incompatible bedfellows?', *Dementia*, 21(4), 1077–1097.

Hajjar, R.R. and Kamel, H.K. (2003) 'Sexuality in the nursing home, part 1: attitudes and barriers to sexual expression', *Journal of American Medical Directors Association*, 4, 152–156.

Harris, P.B. (2009) 'Intimacy, sexuality, and early-stage dementia. The changing marital relationship', *Alzheimer's Care Today*, 10(1), 63–77.

Hayes, J., Boylstein, C. and Zimmerman, M.K. (2009) 'Living and loving with dementia: negotiating spousal and caregiver identity through narrative', *Journal of Aging Studies*, 23(1), 48–59.

Herring, J. (2008) *Response to the Nuffield Council on Bioethics on Dementia: Ethical issues.* Available at: https://www.nuffieldbioethics.org/wp-content/uploads/Jonathan-Herring.pdf (Accessed 26 August 2023).

Hillman, J. (2017) 'Sexual consent capacity: ethical issues and challenges in long-term care', *Clinical Gerontologist*, 40(1), 43–50.

Ho, P.J. and Goh, Y.S. (2022) 'Health care professionals and care staff challenges and experiences of managing sexual expression among older adults ≥60 years in long-term care facilities: a qualitative review and meta-synthesis', *Age and Ageing*, 51(1), afab230.

House of Commons (2003) *Health – second report*. Available at: https://publications.parliament.uk/pa/cm200304/cmselect/cmhealth/111/11101.htm (Accessed 26 August 2023).

House of Lords (2007) *Health – the human rights of older people in healthcare*. Available at: https://publications.parliament.uk/pa/jt200607/jtselect/jtrights/156/156i.pdf (Accessed 26 August 2023).

Howard, L., Brassolotto, J. and Manduca-Barone, A. (2019) 'Navigating tensions about resident sexual expression in Alberta's continuing care homes: a qualitative study of leaders' experiences', *Sexuality Research and Social Policy*, 11(1), 632–642.

International Psychogeriatric Association (2015) *IPA complete guides to Behavioral and Psychological Symptoms of Dementia (BPSD)*. Available at: https://www.ipa-online.org/UserFiles/file/IPA_BPSD_Specialists_Complete_Guide_Online_2015_Final.pdf (Accessed 26 August 2023).

Iversen, M.H., Kilvik, A. and Malmedal, W. (2015) 'Sexual abuse of older residents in nursing homes: a focus group interview of nursing home staff', *Nursing Research and Practice*, 2015, 716407.

Kamel, H.K. and Hajjar, R.R. (2003) 'Sexuality in the nursing home, part 2: managing abnormal behavior: legal and ethical issues', *Journal of the American Medical Directors Association*, 4, 203–206.

Kaplan, H.S. (1990) 'Sex, intimacy, and aging process', *Journal of the American Academy of Psychoanalysis*, 18(2), 185–205.

Kessel, B. (2001) 'Sexuality in the older person', *Age and Ageing*, 30(2), 121–124.

Kong, C. and Ruck Keene, A. (2018) *Overcoming challenges in the Mental Capacity Act 2005: Practical guidance for working with complex issues*. London: Jessica Kingsley Publishers.

Kontos, P., Grigorovich, A., Kontos, A.P. and Miller, K.L. (2016) 'Citizenship, human rights, and dementia: towards a new embodied relational ethic of sexuality', *Dementia*, 15(3), 315–329.

Lester, P.E., Kohen, I., Stefanacci, R.G. and Feuerman, M. (2016) 'Sex in nursing homes: a survey of nursing home policies governing resident sexual activity', *Journal of the American Medical Directors Association*, 17, 71–74.

Lichtenberg, P. and Strzepek, D. (1990) 'Assessment of institutionalized dementia patients' competencies to participate in intimate relationships', *The Gerontologist*, 30, 117–120.

Lindau, S.T., Dale, W., Feldmeth, G., Gavrilova, N., Langa, K.M., Makelarski, J.A. and Wroblewski, K. (2018) 'Sexuality and cognitive status: a U.S. nationally representative study of home dwelling older adults', *Journal of the American Geriatrics Society*, 66(10), 1902–1910.

Lindsay, J.R. (2010) 'The need for more specific legislation in sexual consent capacity assessments for nursing home residents', *The Journal of Legal Medicine*, 31, 303–323.

Livewell (2020) *What are the moral issues when spouses of dementia patients seek outside relationships?* Available at: https://livewell.care/what-are-the-moral-issues-when-spouses-of-dementia-patients-seek-outside-relationships/ (Accessed 20 August 2023).

Mahieu, L. and Gastmans, C. (2015) 'Older residents' perspectives on aged sexuality in institutionalized elderly care: a systematic literature review', *International Journal of Nursing Studies*, 52(12), 1891–1905.

Manchester University (28 January 2015). *Love and intimacy in later life: Study reveals active sex lives of over-70s.* Available at: http://www.manchester.ac.uk/discover/news/love-and-intimacy-in-later-life-study-reveals-active-sex-lives-of-over-70s (Accessed 21 July 2023).

Millett, S. (2011) 'Self and embodiment: a bio-phenomenological approach to dementia', *Dementia*, 10(4), 509–522.

Mitchell, W., Byrnes, A., Bergman, A. and Peisah, C. (2021) 'The human right to justice for older persons with mental health conditions', *The American Journal of Geriatric Psychiatry*, 29(10), 1027–1032.

Murtaugh, C.M., Kemper, P., Spillman, B.C. and Carlson, B.L. (1997) 'The amount, distribution, and timing of lifetime nursing home use', *Medical Care*, 35, 204–218.

National Institute for Health and Care Research (2021) *How can we reduce the toll of loneliness in older adults?* Available at: https://evidence.nihr.ac.uk/collection/how-can-we-reduce-the-toll-of-loneliness-in-older-adults/ (Accessed 25 September 2023).

New York Times (2015) 'Sex, dementia and a husband on trial at age 78'. Available at: https://www.nytimes.com/2015/04/14/health/sex-dementia-and-a-husband-henry-rayhons-on-trial-at-age-78.html?r=0 (Accessed 25 September 2023).

Norberg, A. (2019) '*Sense* of self among persons with advanced dementia', in T. Wisniewski (ed), *Alzheimer's disease*. Brisbane, AU: Codon Publications (Chapter 13).

NPR (2012) *Dementia complicates romance in nursing homes.* Available at: https://www.npr.org/sections/health-shots/2012/06/26/155792238/dementia-complicates-romance-in-nursing-homes#:~:text=Dementia%20Complicates%20Romance%20In%20Nursing%20Homes%20:%20Shots%20-%20Health%20News%20Consensual,in%20the%20way%20of%20love (Accessed 26 August 2023).

NYU Langone Health (2003) *Partial view: An Alzheimer's journal.* Available at: https://medhum.med.nyu.edu/view/12083 (Accessed 26 August 2003).

O'Neill, N. and Peisah, C. (2021) *Capacity and the law* (4th edn). Australasian Legal Information Institute (AustLII) Communities. Available at: https://austlii.community/wiki/Books/CapacityAndTheLaw (Accessed 25 September 2023).

Peisah, C., Burns, K., Edmonds, S. and Brodaty, H. (2018) 'Rendering visible the previously invisible in health care: the ageing LGBTI communities', *The Medical Journal of Australia*, 209(3), 106–108.

Peisah, C., Sorinmade, O.A., Mitchell, L. and Hertogh, C.M. (2013) 'Decisional capacity: toward an inclusionary approach', *International Psychogeriatrics*, 25(10), 1571–1579.

Peisah, C., Ayalon, L., Verbeek, H., Benbow, S.M., Wiskerke, E., Rabheru, K. and Sorinmade, O. (2021) 'Sexuality and the human rights of persons with dementia', *The American Journal of Geriatric Psychiatry*, 29(10), 1021–1026.

Peterman, T.A., Stoneburner, R., Allen, J., Jaffe, H.W. and Curran, J.W (1988) 'Risk of HIV transmission from heterosexual adults with transfusion-associated infections', *Journal of the American Medical Association*, 259, 55–58.

Ramsey-Klawsnik, H., Teaster, P.B., Mendiondo, M.S., Marcum, J.L. and Abner, E.L. (2008) 'Sexual predators who target elders: findings from the first national study of sexual abuse in care facilities', *Journal of Elder Abuse and Neglect*, 20(4), 353–376.

Rao, T.S. (2014) 'Forbidden fruit in the golden years: elderly sexuality', *Journal of Geriatric Mental Health*, 1, 8–13.

Roach, S. (2004) 'Sexual behaviour of nursing home residents: staff perceptions and responses', *Journal of Advanced Nursing*, 48(4), 371–379.

Roelofs, T.S.M., Luijkx, K.G. and Embregts, P. (2021) 'Love, intimacy and sexuality in residential dementia care: a client perspective', *Clinical Gerontologist*, 44(3), 288–298.

Rogstad, K.E. and Bignell, C.J. (1991) 'Age is no bar to sexually acquired infection', *Age and Ageing*, 20, 377–378.

Sandberg, L.J., Bertilsdotter Rosqvist, H. and Grigorovich, A. (2020) 'Regulating, fostering and preserving: the production of sexual normates through cognitive ableism and cognitive othering', *Culture, Health & Sexuality*, 23(10), 1421–1434.

Scura, K.W. and Whipple, B. (1990) 'Older adults as an HIV-positive risk group', *Journal of Gerontological Nursing*, 16, 6–10.

Simonelli, C., Tripodi, F., Rossi, R., Fabrizi, A., Lembo, D., Cosmi, V. and Pierleoni, L. (2007) 'The influence of caregiver burden on sexual intimacy and marital satisfaction in couples with an Alzheimer spouse: caregiver burden on sexual intimacy and marital satisfaction', *International Journal of Clinical Practice*, 62(1), 47–52.

Slinkard, M.S. and Kazer, M.W. (2011) 'Older adults and HIV and STI screening: the patient perspective', *Geriatric Nursing*, 32, 341–349.

Smith, L., Yang, L., Veronese, N., Soysal, P., Stubbs, B. and Jackson, S.E. (2019) 'Sexual activity is associated with greater enjoyment of life in older adults', *Sexual Medicine*, 7(1), 11–18.

Sorinmade, O., Ruck Keene, A. and Peisah, C. (2021) 'Dementia, sexuality and the law: the case for advance decisions on intimacy', *The Gerontologist*, 61, 1001–1007.

Sorinmade, O., Ruck Keene, A. and Peisah, C. (in review) *The Law, Dementia, and Sexuality – is the law striking the right balance*? Unpublished data.

Syme, M.L. (2014) 'The evolving concept of older adult sexual behaviour and its benefits', *Generations*, 38(1), 35–41.

Syme, M.L. and Cohn, T.J. (2016) 'Examining aging sexual stigma attitudes among adults by gender, age, and generational status', *Aging & Mental Health*, 20(1), 36–45.

Syme, M., Johnson, P. and Fager, M. (2020) 'Person-centered sexual expression: determining preferences of future nursing home residents', *The Gerontologist*, 60(4), 725–734.

Syme, M.L., Lichtenberg, P. and Moye, J. (2016) 'Recommendations for sexual expression management in long-term care: a qualitative needs assessment', *Journal of Advanced Nursing*, 7, 2457–2467.

Syme, M., Yelland, E., Cornelison, L., Poey, J., Krajicek, R. and Doll, G. (2017) 'Content analysis of public opinion on sexual expression and dementia: Implications for nursing home policy development', *Health Expectations*, 20(4), 705–713.

Taylor, R.M. (2013) 'Ethical principles and concepts in medicine', *Handbook of Clinical Neurology*, 118, 1–9.

Tenenbaum, E. (2009) 'To be or to exist: standards for deciding whether dementia patients in nursing homes should engage in intimacy, sex, and adultery', *Indiana Law Review*, 42, 675.

Testad, I., Corbett, A., Aarsland, D., Lexow, K.O., Fossey, J., Woods, B. and Ballard, C. (2014) 'The value of personalized psychosocial interventions to address behavioral and psychological symptoms in people with dementia living in care home settings: a systematic review', *International Psychogeriatrics*, 26(7), 1083–1098.

United Nations (2021) *Protecting the human rights of older persons*. Available at: https://www.ohchr.org/en/statements/2021/11/protecting-human-rights-older-persons (Accessed 29 August 2023).

Van Gorp, B. and Vercruysse, T. (2012) 'Frames and counter-frames giving meaning to dementia: a framing analysis of media content', *Social Science & Medicine*, 74(8), 1274–1281.

Villar, F. and Faba, J. (2021) 'Older people living in long-term care: no place for old sex?' in P. Simpson, P. Reynolds and T. Hafford-Letchfield (eds), *Desexualisation in later life: The limits of sex and intimacy*. Bristol: Bristol University Press, pp 153–170.

Villar, F., Celdrán, M., Serrat, R., Fabá, J. and Martínez, T. (2018) 'Staff's reactions towards partnered sexual expressions involving people with dementia living in long-term care facilities', *Journal of Advanced Nursing*, 74(5), 1189–1198.

Weeks, D. (2002) 'Sex for the mature adult: health, self-esteem, and countering ageist stereotypes', *Sexual and Relationship Therapy*, 17, 231–240.

Westwood, S. (2016) 'Dementia, women and sexuality: how the intersection of ageing, gender and sexuality magnify dementia concerns among lesbian and bisexual women', *Dementia*, 15(6), 1494–1514.

Wilkins, J. (2015) 'More than capacity: alternatives for sexual decision making for individuals with dementia', *The Gerontologist*, 55, 716–723.

Wilson, M.M.G. (2006) 'Sexually transmitted diseases in older adults', *Current Infectious Disease Reports*, 8, 139–147.

World Health Organization (2022) *Abuse of older people*. Available at: http://www.who.int/mediacentre/factsheets/fs357/en/ (Accessed 26 August 2023).

World Health Organization (2023a) *Sexual health*. Available at: https://www.who.int/health-topics/sexual-health#tab=tab_1 (Accessed 22 September 2023).

World Health Organization (2023b) *Dementia*. Available at: https://www.who.int/news-room/fact-sheets/detail/dementia (Accessed 22 September 2023).

World Health Organization (2023c) *Abuse of older people*. Available at: www.who.int/health-topics/abuse-of-older-people#tab=tab_1 (Accessed 22 September 2023).

Yon, Y., Mikton, C.R., Gassoumis, Z.D. and Wilber, K.H. (2017) 'Elder abuse prevalence in community settings: a systematic review and meta-analysis', *Lancet Global Health*, 5(2), e147–e156.

7

# "I just felt that I was somebody who was there to be abused": A Sociological Analysis of Structural Causes for Delayed Naming of Sexual Violence at the Intersection of Disability and Gender

*Andrea Hollomotz*

## Introduction

One in five women experience sexual violence across their lifetime (Feder and Howarth, 2014). According to the Crime Survey England and Wales the risk for disabled women is twice as high (Office for National Statistics, 2019). This is likely an underestimate, due to considerable methodological and sampling challenges when it comes to including all disabled women (Hollomotz et al, 2023). Even within the restraints of the currently available statistical evidence, it follows that at least two in five disabled women experience sexual violence across their lifetime. Heightened risk occurs at the intersection of gender and disability: the risk for disabled women is more than five times that of disabled men (Office for National Statistics, 2019).

An under-explored related common occurrence is that many women do not realise they are experiencing sexual violence as the assault happens. Three decades ago Kelly and Radford (1990, p 39) reported that many women discounted and minimised their experiences by remarking that 'nothing really happened'. Sixty per cent of Kelly's (1988) sample did not name sexual violence at the time of the assault. Women's normalisation of their experiences can be traced back further in time, for instance as evidenced in historic cases reported by De Beauvoir (2011). Accounts of normalisation and delayed naming continue to be reported in more recent research (Hlavka, 2014; Tarzia, 2021) and are circulated through social media (for example, #MeToo) and online forums (for example, The Everyday Sexism Project, 2023).

This chapter explores the in-depth accounts of disabled women who have experienced delayed naming of sexual violence through a materialist feminist and a social model of disability lens. It is understood that 'all thought is fundamentally mediated by power relations that are social in nature and historically constituted' (Lee and Carson, 2014, p 16). Drawing on some of the work already outlined in this volume, this chapter suggests that the struggles women face are not always located with the individual's decision-making in/capacity. The feminist and social model approach adds an important dimension for thinking through the ideas of 'vulnerability', risk, agency, naming and how law frames and responds to these. Through this chapter, the reader is invited to reflect on the ways the Mental Capacity Act 2005 (MCA) perpetuates a medicalised or individualised focus on disability, while masking some of the social factors which are present in experiences of sexual violence.

The discussion argues that the concept of 'mental incapacity' is problematic, and it does not capture the experiences of disabled women cited in this chapter. It is evidenced that delayed naming is caused by structural inequalities and that current constructions around mental incapacity lead to an over-focus on impairment, which blames the victim for the disadvantaged position she finds herself in. The conclusion of this chapter relates the discussion back to the overall themes of this volume by exploring whether an analysis of *A Local Authority v JB*[1] (*JB*) and the evidence heard in that case goes any way towards challenging these structures and societal norms.

## The process of naming sexual violence

The research reported in this chapter uses the term 'sexual violence' to encompass all/multiple forms of rape and sexual assault, as defined by the Sexual Offences Act 2003. The chapter provides detailed insights into disabled women's personal sense making of such experiences, including reflections on the structural barriers a woman faces and must overcome to become able to admit to herself that she has been victimised. The word 'victim' is deliberately used throughout this chapter, rather than 'survivor', as, in order to begin the journey towards becoming a survivor,

1 [2021] UKSC 52.

the process of naming is fundamentally about admitting to oneself that one has been victimised.

The term 'naming' is rejuvenated from past key publications (for example, Felstiner et al, 1980; Kelly, 1988; Kelly and Radford, 1990) to revive crucial debates, while also highlighting their continued relevance to the lived experiences of the disabled women we spoke to across England and Wales in 2022. Naming is defined as a transformative sense-making process by which the victim is 'saying to oneself that a particular experience has been injurious' (Felstiner et al, 1980, p 635). It involves 'defining as unacceptable what was acceptable and insisting that what was naturalised is problematic' (Kelly, 1988, p 139). The way this is used here also encompasses what Felstiner et al (1980) refer to as 'naming' and 'blaming': a woman who has successfully named sexual violence has, beyond giving her experiences a descriptive label, also externalised blame. 'To report an incident to the police, the event must be defined by women as a crime' (Kelly, 1988, p 140). In doing this she uses a descriptive label for the crime experienced and she is aware that the law protects her.

The descriptive 'rape', for example, is defined by law as follows:

1. A person (A) commits an offence if—
   a. he intentionally penetrates the vagina, anus or mouth of another person (B) with his penis,
   b. B does not consent to the penetration, and
   c. A does not reasonably believe that B consents.
2. Whether a belief is reasonable is to be determined having regard to all the circumstances, including any steps A has taken to ascertain whether B consents.

The Sexual Offences Act also introduced equality for disabled victims before the law. Previously, the Sexual Offences Act 1956 distinguished between rape of a woman, which carried a maximum sentence of lifetime imprisonment, and 'intercourse with a defective' (someone who was deemed unable to consent). This carried a maximum sentence of two years (McCormack, 1991). Such lenience in sentencing reflected the sentiment that 'defectives' experience suffering to a lesser degree (Painter and Farrington, 2005; Weeks, 2017). Person (B) now includes all women, regardless of impairment. Yet, the concepts of consent and of a 'reasonable belief' are still contestable, as further evidenced by Sandland (see Chapter 1 in this volume). This raises broader debates about the application of the Sexual Offences Act 2003 to disabled women (Saunders, 2010). Moreover, in spite of the removal of the marriage exemption clause, Bennice and Resick (2003) claim that today's victims of marital rape are still affected by a lengthy history of legal, cultural and professional invalidation.

It is perhaps unsurprising that the Sexual Offences Act 2003 is rarely enforced. In England and Wales 'only 5% of rapes that were given an outcome by the police in the year ending December 2021 resulted in a charge' (Baird, 2022, p 17). There is attrition caused by the police; for example, not pursuing a case, as police either think it does not have merit or that the Crown Prosecution Service (CPS) would not be able to prosecute, due to lack of evidence. Further attrition occurs with the CPS itself, where they decide not to prosecute. Leverick (2020, p 273) believes that even when cases do reach court. 'jurors take into the deliberation room false and prejudicial beliefs about what rape looks like'. This raises important questions as to the extent to which sexual violence, particularly against disabled women, is seen as a 'mental capacity' issue, rather than a criminal offence. The next section moves the reader's gaze from the individual to the broader social factors that impact on disabled women, sexual violence and women's sense making. It will also contextualise jurors' false beliefs as rape myths.

## Disablist and sexist barriers to naming of sexual violence

In this chapter disability and impairment are defined through/using the social model of disability. Impairment is a 'characteristic, of the mind, body or senses within an individual which is long term and may, or may not, be the result of disease, genetics or injury' (Oliver et al, 2012, p 16). The MCA focuses on the medical and individual aspects of impairment: 'a person lacks capacity in relation to a matter if at the material time he is unable to make a decision for himself in relation to the matter because of an impairment of, or a disturbance in the functioning of, the mind or brain'.[2]

In contrast, this chapter is much more interested in disability, which is defined as a social condition, which is imposed on a person on top of their impairment. It is 'the disadvantage or restriction of activity caused by the political, economic and cultural norms of a society which takes no or little account of people who have impairments and thus excludes them from mainstream activity' (Oliver et al, 2012, p 16).

## Disablism, sexism and 'the enemy within'

There are two facets to the individual model of disability. The medical model of disability focuses on impaired bodies and minds. The assumption is that impairment is a biologically determined entity, which requires medical intervention. A further facet of the individual model 'deals with

[2] Mental Capacity Act 2005, section 2(1).

disabled people's "adjustment" to impairment and nondisabled people's "attitudes" towards people with impairments' (Priestley, 1998, p 80). Reeve (2002, p 495) explains that the psycho-emotional dimensions of disability 'affect what disabled people can *be*, rather than what they can *do*, and include being hurt by the reactions of other people, being made to feel worthless and unattractive'. These 'have their roots in the negative attitudes and prejudices about disabled people within society'. Keith (1996, p 71) explains: 'The assumptions about what using a wheelchair means [...] [are] so overwhelmingly negative and so very different to how I want to see myself, that unless I have ways of understanding and dealing with these encounters, they have the power to destroy me.'

The psycho-emotional position provides the logical basis for the concerns of disabled feminist writers who emphasise the importance of personal experience and identity (Morris, 1991; Thomas, 2006). These writers invariably attempt to resolve their concerns by combining an analysis of the psycho-emotional with the social (Priestley, 1998). Feminists have also exposed psycho-emotional dimensions of internalised sexism, which induces female self-hatred and has been referred to as the 'enemy within'. This concept also works to explain internalised disablism, as demonstrated in Keith's (1996) earlier quotation where she discussed negative assumptions that have 'the power to destroy' her sense of self. For victims of sexual violence the 'enemy within' is strengthened by internalised rape myths.

Rape myths 'deny or reduce perceived injury or [they] blame the victims for their own victimization' (Burt, 1980, p 217). One rape myth is that 'only "certain women" are raped, primarily women with "bad" reputations and those from socially marginal or minority groups' (Lonsway and Fitzgerald, 1994, p 136). This includes disabled women, who have historically been portrayed as 'vulnerable', innocent and asexual and, paradoxically, as sexually deviant, promiscuous and as a potential sexual threat (Parmenter, 2001). The notion of 'vulnerability' remains in professional discourse today (for example, McCarthy et al, 2019), in spite of cosmetic changes to the language used by the current Safeguarding Policy (Office of the Public Guardian, 2015), the Care Act 2014 and the Social Services and Well-being (Wales) Act 2014 from 'vulnerability' to 'at risk'.

The problem with pathologising disabled women as 'sexually vulnerable' is that it focuses explanations for increased victimisation rates on individuals who are targeted and not on the social conditions and power imbalances that put some groups at increased risk. Likewise, sexual consent capacity should be approached as a socially determined concept, for instance because, as will be discussed shortly and is discussed in other chapters of this volume, social and situational factors can impede knowledge and understanding about sex and violence (Clough, 2014).

## Externalising blame

Social approaches to gender and disability have a socially constructed and a material (socially created) dimension. Firstly, disability and gender can be approached as social constructs. Priestley (1998, p 81) asserts that, 'while people of difference have existed in all societies, the degree to which they are integrated or excluded will vary according to predominant cultural perceptions of that difference'. Moreover, 'social labelling and role expectations are the determinant factors in the construction of disability', gender and victimhood. Millett (1970) unpacked the glorification of male sexual violence across the literature and this is still present within recent debates around misogynism in the criminal justice system (Wistrich, 2022) and the police force (Turner, 2024).

Rape myths, including presumed 'vulnerability', are attitudes that affect women and men in all positions of society, including those who work with victims of sexual violence, as evidenced by the End-to-End Rape review (HM Government, 2021; Ministry of Justice, 2022). Rape myths have been linked to secondary victimisation, such as condemnation, disbelief that the event occurred or inaction from officials (Russell and Hand, 2017). In other words, the social construction of victimised women as 'other' leads to the creation of material discrimination and oppression.

The socio-materialist position of disability represents the philosophical basis which has been central to the mobilisation of the UK's disabled people's movement since the late 1970s. It 'can be regarded as the material relations of power arising from the development of political economy and/or patriarchy within a specific historical context' (Priestley, 1998, p 80). Socialist feminists use this position to expose patriarchal structures, which create material barriers for women (Bryson, 2021). For instance, what counts as violence has historically been determined by those in power, and boundaries have shifted over time. Sandland provides examples in Chapter 1 of the impact this had (and still has) on legal conceptualisations of sexual crimes. For instance, until 1976 the law required 'the presence of force and resistance before a court would find that a rape had occurred', which will have excluded the vast majority of rapes as defined by victims themselves (for example, Kelly, 1988).

Across time, women's attempts to speak about their lived experiences of victimisation have been dismissed and silenced. For instance, Sigmund Freud misinterpreted claims of child sexual abuse made by his patients as symptoms of repressed incestuous desire (Rush, 1980). Women who had been misunderstood in this way have been conceptualised as 'mad' (for example, Kristiansen, 2004; Hall, 2011). Even today women with labels of 'learning disabilities' and 'challenging behaviour' are over-medicated with sedatives (Branford et al, 2018) and their capacity to make sexual decisions is routinely questioned under the MCA. However, many women who are described as 'challenging' display such behaviour in response to trauma from gendered violence (Morris et al, 2020; de Vogel and Didden, 2022).

Hollomotz (2011) argued that what starts as a myth of sexual 'vulnerability' can lead to the creation or exacerbation of situational risk. This works as follows: those who are deemed vulnerable are often over-protected. Individuals may be given little agency in their daily lives and denied opportunities to practise decision making about mundane issues. Many disabled women are thus socialised into compliance. They have little meaningful choice or agency in their lives, and they routinely have to bear 'poor social care practice', which often overlaps with and borders on the abusive (Fyson and Patterson, 2020).

Women with mobility impairments are unlikely to escape intimate partner violence if they do not have practical support (Bowstead, 2020). Some types of violence happen only or predominantly to disabled people. This includes institutional abuse (Department of Health and Social Care, 2012; Social Care Institute for Excellence, 2023), domestic abuse by paid or informal carers (Saxton et al, 2001; Stay Safe East, 2020), as well as disability hate and mate crime (Thomas, 2011; Roulstone and Mason Bish, 2012; Doherty, 2017), cuckooing, home takeovers and criminal exploitation (Macdonald et al, 2022). Support needs may be exploited by the abuser (Saxton et al, 2001). For instance, partner-carers may deny access to mobility aids or other enabling facilities (Stay Safe East, 2020).

Access to essential safety information is a further aspect of materiality, as highlighted by Squires and Morgan (see Chapter 5 in this volume). Disabled young people are often disadvantaged in sex education, in that information is often not made explicit enough and accessible (McCann et al, 2019; Strnadová et al, 2022). British sex education does not teach about the importance of pleasure and consent (Sundaram and Sauntson, 2016; Young Women's Movement, 2023).

For those who are routinely 'othered' and targeted for being different, the concept of sexual consent takes on a different shape. Hollomotz (2011) reported a different threshold for what constitutes violence in segregated institutional settings for disabled people. For example, she evidenced how the attempts of disabled people who were seeking to report violence were at times ignored or labelled as 'drama' or 'challenging behaviour', leading them to understand that they have to 'put up with it' (Hollomotz, 2011, p 90), thus they internalised that raised thresholds on what is considered to be harmful apply to them. It follows that disabled women's 'enemy within' is strengthened by the interplay between disablism and sexism.

Making sense of sexual violence is complicated, regardless of the positionality of the sense maker (for example, marginalised women versus jurors). Siblings who grew up in homes characterised by patriarchal violence can have different views of whether it was violence (Hardt and Rutter, 2004). Even when faced with material evidence, such as injuries or witness accounts, they have the agency not to perceive their experience as injurious. Hence, naming is something each person has to do for themselves.

Women's delayed naming of sexual violence is a social problem which is still not fully understood. This chapter provides qualitative evidence on disabled women's reflections on the experiences of and social causes for delayed naming. The following section provides a brief overview of the project's research methods, the sample of women cited in this chapter and the analytical approach.

## Methodology

This chapter presents a secondary data analysis of a dataset that was created during a qualitative research project commissioned by the Ministry of Justice as part of a wider research programme that aimed to better understand the support needs of disabled victim-survivors of sexual violence (Hollomotz et al, 2023).[3] We conducted 30 semi-structured interviews and two focus groups with a total of 39 disabled victims across England and Wales. Of these, 36 were female born and identified either as women (34), non-binary (1) or trans (1). The accounts of these 36 respondents are included in this chapter. For ease of reference this chapter uses the term 'disabled women' when referring to these respondents, because all identified as 'women' at the time of the sexual violence.

All participants self-identified as disabled prior to the sexual violence incident/s. They had a range of impairments, including physical, neurological, sensory, cognitive and mental health conditions, and many had multiple impairments. Ages ranged from 21 to 66. Further demographic characteristics are summarised in Table 7.1. All respondents had given informed consent to participate in this study and all but one[4] understood they had experienced violence.

The research was co-produced by two universities and two organisations of deaf and disabled people. This partnership enriched the research process by holding it accountable at all stages to the social model of disability and to disabled women, who were viewed as 'expert knowers' of their own lives (Stone and Priestley, 1996). Listening to the voices of disabled women was ethically and morally the right thing to do in the context of recommissioning rape crisis services, because the intention was to use these voices to inform commissioning requirements. However, considerations for the 'greater good'

---

[3] The views expressed are those of the authors and are not necessarily shared by the Ministry of Justice (nor do they represent government policy).

[4] Tara's experiences are extensively documented in a dedicated subsection of our forthcoming monograph (Hollomotz and Burch, forthcoming).

**Table 7.1:** Overview of respondent characteristics

| Characteristic | Count (n) | % |
|---|---|---|
| Sexuality | | |
| Straight | 20 | 56 |
| Other | 13 | 36 |
| Preferred not to say | 3 | 8 |
| Ethnicity | | |
| Caucasian | 26 | 72 |
| BME | 10 | 28 |
| Religion | | |
| Christian | 16 | 44.5 |
| No religion | 16 | 44.5 |
| Muslim | 3 | 8 |
| Spiritual practitioner | 1 | 3 |
| Employment status | | |
| Employed | 14 | 39 |
| Unemployed | 20 | 56 |
| In education | 1 | 3 |
| Carer | 1 | 3 |
| Living situation | | |
| Independent living | 25 | 70 |
| Group living | 11 | 30 |

should never outweigh the rights of the individual (British Sociological Association, 2017). Even though we had ethical motivations for conducting the research, our primary concern was to safeguard those we involved. Talking about the process of naming sexual violence was, in many cases, the most sensitive part of the interviews. We did not press further when respondents were quick to move on from this topic. On occasion, we suggested to move on when women found this topic emotionally challenging. Almost all decided to continue, as they valued the opportunity to reflect back on the hurdles they had overcome and also on those transformative moments of realisation.

The first stage of the analysis presented what Denzin (1989) would describe as a 'thin description'. This gave an overview of detailed accounts of women unpicking what hindered them from understanding disturbing sexual experiences as violence. They described thoughts and feelings that amounted to a shared narrative of internalised oppression. Creating this overview was an important first step, but 'thick' description (Denzin, 1989) was needed that could go beyond surface-level appearances. Achieving this required persistence, much discussion with the wider research team and with experts by experience who had undergone the process and/or who worked with those who had. The analytical framework that was set out in the introduction to this chapter was developed to help understand the contexts and histories from which violence arose. Further context was added from re-reading full transcripts reflexively (Mason, 2018). In this way, seemingly unrelated experiences, such as Sarah's account of boarding a bus, could be used to build up 'thick' descriptions around respondents' histories. Gradually, the analytical gaze was refocused towards structural issues within 'institutions of the society, and not merely the personal situation and character of a scatter of individuals' (Mills, 1959, p 9). In short, the data was analysed thematically through immersive and reflexive reading (Mason, 2018) and by applying the sociological imagination (Mills, 1959) as a critical lens through which 'thick' descriptions (Denzin, 1989) of internalised sexism and disablism and structural inequalities emerged.

## Findings

The findings are subdivided into four thematic sections. They cover the enemy within, structural inequalities, transformative processes and some reflections on the perpetrators. This latter section is rounded off by comparing what we know about these perpetrators to the *JB* case.

### *"No, it wasn't that bad, it was all okay": the enemy within*

Regardless of whether the injury was perceived at the time of the assault, all respondents described immediate, material impacts. They experienced sexual violence as uncomfortable, disturbing, confusing, as crossing agreed boundaries with a sexual partner or as painful, violent or something they did not want to do. Many of the women described lengthy periods of not admitting it was violence, even to themselves. Olivia described that, after she spoke to a friend who had gently pointed out to her that her boyfriend's sexual demands might be problematic, "initially I felt quite angry with them. Inside I was just like: 'You're judging me', but my head managed to go: 'No, hang on a minute, I know this person well enough to know that they care.'"

Olivia alluded to fears of losing face (Ho, 1976), resulting in her working hard on what Goffman (1959) terms 'impression management'. This encompasses the sum of total conscious and unconscious actions an individual takes to influence how others perceive her. Olivia explained: "It's a hard thing to admit because you feel stupid afterwards." To avoid 'feeling stupid', respondents who had ongoing relationships with their abuser kept up the performance of the obedient spouse and minimised the violence: "Even though everyone was telling me it was abusive, there was a bit of me which had been the part that had defended me and kept me alive and sane during the relationship that was like: No, it wasn't that bad, it was all okay, it was just … this was normal behaviour" (Grace).

August reported a fear of change: "Even if what I know is harmful to me, it's better than it being unknown and scary." Feelings of having let oneself down by not resisting (enough) contributed to women blaming themselves for what has happened. Many minimised or romanticised their experiences to justify them. Some reported that this caused further psycho-emotional injuries. For instance, self-blame is positively associated with post-traumatic stress disorder (PTSD) symptoms (Bernstein et al, 2022) and this was reflected in the high incidence of PTSD in respondents who reported delayed naming in our sample. Self-blame also alters one's sense of reality. Some women worked hard not to be seen as weak and dependent in order to counteract disablist stereotypes. Some manage these impressions so successfully that, as Goffman (1959, p 28) described, they became 'sincerely convinced that the impression of reality which [s]he stages is the real reality'. However, 'minimisation in order to cope denies the reality of the violence that has been experienced' (Kelly, 1988, p 146).

Even after a personal experience of sexual violence, internalised rape myths can reaffirm a woman's 'false sense of security' that she is 'somehow immune to rape' (Lonsway and Fitzgerald, 1994, p 137). Janet had internalised the myth that rape cannot happen in marriage (Rape Crisis, 2023), but she found it "obvious" that she had not consented when her husband raped her after she left him. Yet she did not name the sexual violence *within* marriage for another decade. Instead, Janet felt blamed by her community: "It was me that would be looked at that I'd done something wrong. And obviously a big failure for being divorced." Hence, even beyond marriage, Janet performed, to some extent, what De Beauvoir (2011) referred to as abject submission by shouldering the blame for her position. Her lack of self-regard posed a barrier to Janet becoming able to externalise blame.

Delayed naming became less of an issue, the closer a woman's experiences mapped onto prevailing rape myths. For instance, Sarah explained: "A total stranger broke into my house at night and raped me at knifepoint. There was no thought process to be had. […] I called the police immediately the attacker left." The stark deviation from her daily reality enabled Sarah's instant naming. All other respondents who experienced sexual violence by a stranger reported instant awareness. Even Sharie, who was prostituted against her will over several years while she lived in supported living understood that she "didn't want to do it" at the time, but her difficulty was that she did not know how to get out of the situation.

In contrast, defining assault by a friend or partner as rape is obscured by the fact 'that it involves naming a man one has, or once had, positive feelings for as a rapist' (Kelly, 1988, p 149). This is further exacerbated by the widespread myth that 'real' rape is an attack at night, in a public place, by a stranger who uses force (preferably a weapon) (Kelly and Radford, 1990). Several respondents explicitly compared their experiences with this myth. For instance, Bea observed: "I didn't realise that sexual violence was something that could ever happen to me. I bought into the myth that perpetrators were strangers, lurking in the alleyway at night. And that wasn't my experience at all. The perpetrators were people that I have lived with under the same roof."

Women found making sense of sexual violence intertwined with other forms of intimate partner violence deeply confusing. Yvonne reflected that rape was a regular occurrence in her marriage: "It was a very abusive, coercive relationship. 'No' didn't work with him." She stated she had been married for about two decades "before I realised I was in an abusive relationship. Because I thought an abusive relationship was when you got beaten up." Similar sentiments were shared by others. Janet explained how sexist gender-role expectations impacted on her sense of agency within marriage: "I believed that things that had happened throughout the whole marriage were normal, because he was the first person I'd been with. And every time we had troubles my mum would say: 'You're not doing what he needs in the bedroom.' [...] I felt that with the Christian background we were supposed to submit to our husbands."

Instead of finding fault with the husband, or indeed with unequal distribution of power within the relationship, Janet's mother reinforced patriarchal expectations of abject submission. Her mindset confirmed Ahmed's (2017) claim that hegemonic norms shape women's thinking about themselves and the social roles they feel they have to play. Noor linked delayed naming to social isolation and an inability to speak openly about women's intimate experiences within an ethnic minority community: "I think it's much more hidden in our community because it's seen as wrong and bad and it's usually the female's fault and there's this stigma and negativity attached to it. [...] That's often part of the reason why you can't talk about it."

Fatimah fled a violent relationship and narrowly escaped an honour-based killing (Gill et al, 2014). She instantly named the physical violence and honour-based nature of the assassination attempt. Realisation about marital rape came years later: "I didn't know that marital rape was a thing." Julie explained why, even though she found specific sexual acts disturbing, painful and "very violent", she did not feel she could stop this from happening: "It happened frequently. [...] I did not feel like I could approach that with this particular partner. When it happened again, I was just like: 'Ah, well. I didn't say anything last time so does that mean that I've given this implied consent?' (nervous laugh) Which, obviously, I had not."

Julie's use of the term 'obviously' referred only to the present. It was clear to her at the time of the interview, but not while she was in the relationship. She also alludes to the vagueness around 'consent' and her partner's means to 'reasonably believe' that she had consented. She takes responsibility for not having made her position clearer. Her account aligns with the rape myths: 'If she didn't scream, try to run away or fight back then it wasn't rape' and 'If she didn't say "no" then it wasn't rape' (Rape Crisis, 2023). Sylvia did not think that her experiences, for example being made to have sex while she was in excruciating pain following surgery, entitled her to support. She struggled to find a label that could describe her experiences of being coerced and threatened into submission by her husband:

> 'I kind of just felt like that it hadn't actually happened, [...] what was I on about because it wasn't rape and it wasn't x, y, z. And I had nothing to complain about kind of thing. I didn't feel like I deserved to approach anyone to get that help. [...] I didn't want to go to the police either.'

The relationship with Nancy's ex-husband was underpinned by coercive control. He took over her bank account, controlled her clothes choices, where and when she went out and with whom. There was just one instance of sexual violence in this relationship, which Nancy did not name until after she left: "I didn't realise it myself; my friend told me on a night out when I talked to her about my experience." On her wedding night, "I'd had lots to drink, so I just passed out". When she woke up her husband

> 'showed me a video of him having anal sex with me. [...] I felt so uncomfortable about it, I said, "Are you sure that happened?" [...] He just kept saying how much I loved it, apparently. [...] I said, "I would never have agreed to that", cos I didn't like that. That's not something that I would have done. But he was like: "Oh no, you did!" and I was like: "No, I really wouldn't!"'

An unconscious woman cannot consent to sex,[5] nor to being video recorded. Hence, the CPS could press charges for two separate offences under the Sexual Offences Act 2003 and the Voyeurism (Offences) Act 2019. Moreover, Nancy believed her husband had 'reasonable cause' to know she would not have consented, even when conscious. While she was incapacitated he crossed sexual boundaries they had agreed when Nancy had capacity to consent.

Even before she named the sexual violence, Nancy realised that this incident marked a turning point in their relationship: "I'd always think back to that night, and I'd think, (sighs) 'that was the start of it'. As soon as he'd married me, that was the start of it." Long before Nancy was ready to

[5] Sexual Offences Act 2003, section 75(2)(d); *R v Bree* [2007] EWCA Crim 804.

name, she experienced rape and voyeurism as an incision, which resulted in permanent change to her relationship with the abuser.

In summary, respondents had internalised the stranger rape myth, which persists in spite of statistical evidence that suggests that perpetrators of female rape victims are most likely an intimate partner (46%) (Office for National Statistics, 2023). The persistence of this myth clouded women's judgement. We also observed a delay in naming sexual violence that co-occurred alongside other forms of gendered violence, and this reflects findings from past research (Thiara et al, 2012). For respondents who experienced intersecting forms of intimate partner violence the 'enemy within' seemed strongest in resisting naming the most intimate aspects of their relationships.

### *"It's an accumulation of it all": structural inequalities*

Some women explained that they feared negative consequences from their partner if they resisted sexual violence. For instance, Tara wondered: "If I don't take part, he's going to hate me. [...] If I say one hundred per cent: 'No!' is there going to be a row? Is he going to get mad, like he normally does?" Others confirmed that the sexual violence got worse, often in tandem with coercive control and/or physical violence once they started resisting violent sexual practices: "I used to say to him when we first met, 'You've rescued me from myself', (cries) and he used to love that. But then I started to realise what he was like, and then he used to say, 'You've changed'" (Nancy).

Delayed realisation within an existing relationship was a counterfeit means for some of these women to keep themselves safe. In some situations, this was simply the best the women were able to do, due to the structural inequalities they faced in accessing support, which could have helped escape sooner, as outlined throughout this section.

For women who experienced sexual violence within the context of a relationship or who experienced repeat victimisation, injurious experiences had become normalised. Noor hypothesised that "disablement plays into abuse and rape", which "often make it harder for us to speak out and often means we're in these situations for a lot longer than non-disabled people". She understood that race, culture, social class, disability and gender intersect, forming her unique experience of socially created risk. Lesley asserted: "I've experienced a significant level of violence compared to a lot of people, and I believe that that's because I'm different."

Carly reflected on an experience of sexual assault in a public place: "I realised that I was being targeted because I was alone and because I am disabled. I think I must give off some sort of vulnerability or ... people seem to sense it; I seem to be a target." Carly had a strong sense of justice. This quotation should not be read as Carly believing that she is 'vulnerable'.

Instead, she felt that this was how others perceive her. Sarah added: "Even just something as simple as boarding the bus in my wheelchair. I'll get a lot of watch consulting and finger tapping and just general tutting. People don't understand how aggressive that is." Burch (2021) described similar incidents of disabled people negotiating experiences of hate in the context of their everyday lives, for instance, being challenged over their entitlement to use accessible toilets.

Our respondents echoed Adichie's (2014) claim that if we see or do something over and over, it becomes 'normal'. Intersecting incidents of being repeatedly targeted created a history that disabled women carried with them before they experienced sexual violence. Nancy explained: "I take antidepressants, but it's not solely because of him, even though he's part of it. [...] It's an accumulation of it all." Repeat victimisation has been associated with an internalisation of low expectations (Sin, 2012), as illustrated by Carly: "I just felt that I was somebody who was there to be abused."

Paula is non-verbal. She experienced repeated sexual violence by a carer within a communal establishment during COVID-19 lockdown and beyond. A relative who was interviewed alongside Paula recalled how Paula tried to tell a relative: "she was trying to show [relative] that something was happening [relative] didn't really go to ask the right questions because [relative] didn't think to ask that something like that would be happening". Paula's communication pad did not include words for intimate body parts or violence. Her attempts to point at her vulva were misread as her reporting stomach pain.

Due to Paula displaying significant distress over a prolonged period, she was eventually referred to a clinical psychologist with expertise in speech and language therapy, learning disability and sexual violence. She provided Paula with communication aids that gave her the words she needed to name sexual violence. However, the delay in her communication attempts being understood meant that Paula had to endure months of regular sexual violence, while her calls for help were misread. This case illustrates Kelly's (1988) claim that language or the absence of words to describe sexual violence is a means of controlling women and that this is often exacerbated for deaf and disabled women. Censorship of cue words on communication boards was flagged by Kennedy (1996), and it is unacceptable to see that this has not yet changed, at least for Paula. This is a clear instance of societal barriers to positive sexual education and facilitation of sexual agency, deeply rooted in those historical notions of sexual vulnerability and protection, which are also covered in Chapter 5 by Squires and Morgan. It is also evidence of failures to take aspects of the legal framework under the MCA seriously, given that it requires support to be provided before making any decisions, and for communication around decisions.

Earlier, Janet was cited in stating that she believed her sexual inexperience was a contributing factor to her assuming violent sex was 'normal'. Grace linked this to youth: "At that age without questioning, I had just assumed that if you're in a relationship, consent was kind of there." Noor made a similar observation: "I didn't really understand. I think you're just a bit naïve, aren't you? When you're in the thick of it, you don't really know what's going on. Especially if you've lived in a bubble your entire life. If you're from [ethnic minority] community, you're not expected to be in situations like that."

Noor was not naïve. She was simply yet another woman who had not been afforded the opportunity to learn essential safety information, which also resonates with Bates's contribution (Chapter 4) in this volume. Similarly, Tara was negotiating the boundaries between sex she had consented to and new, painful practices being "sprung on her". She explained that she understood that once she had consented to sex at the onset, she was then not able to change her mind, implying that she believed the myth that sexual consent is given once and for all (Hunt, 2023).

Safety information needs to work against these prevailing rape myths, but disabled women's access to resources and services is at times mediated by their abusers (Breckenridge, 2018), and institutions will at times systemically silence victims as they come forward (for example, Jay et al, 2022). Gina was hospitalised with a rare illness. When she tried to report rape by a ward nurse to hospital staff, they implied that Gina must have imagined the sexual encounters. They also alluded to the myths that women lack a 'sense either of truth or of accuracy' (De Beauvoir, 2011, p 653), which implies that their accounts are invalid because they are not lucid or articulate enough. This infers an allegation of 'madness', which in turn intersects with disablist assumptions around mental incapacity.

Perpetrators manipulated impairment effects at times to discredit their victims. For instance, Julie struggled with remembering exact dates, times and sequences of events: "If I ever said anything along the lines of: 'I didn't like this thing that you did', immediately they would be like: 'I don't remember that. When exactly did it happen? What time? What day?'" This disoriented Julie and planted doubt about her version of events.

Rose recalled that questions about her mental capacity were at the forefront of officers' minds throughout her interactions with the police: "They asked me whether I had a learning difficulty, mental health issues, that sort of thing. I'd answered that, but the whole thing about whether or not I had learning issues seemed to keep coming up."

Rose was taken aback by officers' persistent questioning. Other women, especially those who did indeed have impairments affecting cognition, found it harder to assert themselves against claims about mental incapacity. Consequently, even though respondents identified as disabled and experienced real impairment effects, we can question whether all their impairments, as perceived by those they interacted with, were 'real' or constructed.

At times impairments were mislabelled and misidentified. Fatimah explained: "I've had the wrong diagnosis. I've been told I've got characteristics of PTSD and characteristics of emotionally unstable personality disorder." The diagnosis given to Fatimah was borderline personality disorder (BPD). This diagnosis is associated with structural stigma in healthcare, which inhibits the opportunities and resources offered to people living with BPD and significantly affects access to services (Klein et al, 2021). This was also Fatimah's experience: "I've still not come to terms with what's happened, I'm still fighting [to access treatment]." Hence, not recognising impairment effects related to PTSD resulted in misbelieving, doubting and shifting emphasis to the individual under the BPD label. Fatimah was made to feel that she was the problem.

Women are disproportionately labelled in this diagnostic category. They outnumber men by a ratio of three to one (Bjorklund, 2006). There is a causal relationship between trauma and BPD, and it can be argued that labelling traumatised women with a diagnostic label that is often perceived negatively by healthcare professionals individualises social problems. Instead of focusing on patriarchal violence as the cause for a woman's expressions of emotions and behaviours consistent with the presentation of BPD, she becomes the problem for expressing trauma. Carly described how her presenting as a woman in severe distress to victim support services resulted in her being denied access to these services: "They didn't think that I'd be suitable for counselling. I'd need to do stabilisation training first." Being turned away from talking therapies is a common experience for people with BPD (Klein et al, 2021).

This and the previous section have explored how delayed naming affects women at the individual level and the underlying structural inequalities responsible for this delay. The next section explores how the transformation towards naming became possible.

### *"Actually, this isn't good. This isn't normal": transformative processes*

Quinn was drug-raped. Afterwards, they sensed something was wrong, but they were too disoriented to make full sense of what had happened: "I called the Samaritans. And I've started talking to her and she was the one who went: 'I think something's happened to you.' And then when she said that it started clicking." With this support Quinn's naming was close to instant. Olivia recalled a helpful conversation with a friend: "They were really patient with me and they were like: 'Olivia, do you realise what you were, what you're describing? Do you realise that this isn't nice behaviour towards you?' [...] It was only through having that trust and that deep conversation that my head slowly began to realise that, actually, what was happening wasn't right."

Nina remembered that she started naming through talking to her victim support counsellor: "[Husband] was getting me to do sexual things. And I thought that it was normal. But I spoke to [name] and she made me realise that none of it was normal." Janet explained how counselling gave her new insights: "I think it was the way he questioned about the whole relationship. [...] And the way that he would actually feed back, 'Hang on a minute, that's not right. Did you say he did this?'" Julie adds that she found a person in authority externalising blame very powerful: "It wasn't until it was coming out of my mouth in front of that healthcare professional that I was like: 'Actually, this isn't good. This isn't normal.' [...] When a doctor says: 'That behaviour's unacceptable', it just felt like it landed, I took it more seriously." Nina, Janet and Julie explicitly referred to how they redefined what they viewed as 'normal' or 'acceptable' sexual practices.

Respondents described how their understanding of 'sexual violence' (and that it exists at all) changed over time and was socially negotiated. Through talking to peers, the women realised "you are not the only one" (Gina). They discovered commonalities in their experiences, externalised blame and named sexual violence. Nancy reflected that her role as a professional working in the voluntary sector coincidentally exposed her to materials she could relate to, and which brought on realisation: "I started running domestic abuse projects. It opened my eyes to what had happened. I was thinking: 'Gosh, that's me'." Sylvia experienced something similar: "My friends said that things weren't right, but I could not see that. The thing that opened my eyes was doing a course with one of my volunteer groups on confidence and assertiveness. It kind of, just opened my eyes to actually being able to see what was going on wasn't right."

Information about legal terminology that describes different types of sexual violence is not readily made available to women and girls. Several respondents learned to distinguish different types of violence through police questioning when they reported the crime. For instance, Kate asserted a deviation from the intercourse she had consented to: "The thing with that sexual assault is he tried to strangle me and ... I consented to sex, but I hadn't consented to that." Kate understood that she had the right to reject strangulation. Lesley remembered how she acquired the language and conceptual knowledge to make sense of her experience:

> 'I spotted a leaflet in the school nurse's office [on child molestation] and I was like: "Is this what's been happening to me?" I know that I didn't like it, but I didn't have the language to even understand it entirely. I knew that I wanted it to stop, and I knew that I was really scared. I was just like: "So there's a word for this?"' (Lesley)

As with Paula, an expert had given Lesley access to a vocabulary that enabled her to describe her experiences. The majority of respondents whose naming was delayed recalled similar key moments when they acquired new information about the boundaries of acceptable behaviour. Noor listed a vast range of information sources she found helpful in enabling naming: "You don't realise until peer-to-peer people start having conversations about similar things or you hear about campaigns or there's stuff you see on TV or in soaps, or you see someone else in the situation and then you think, you have a light-bulb moment really and you realise: 'Oh, that's you. It's happening to you.'"

Grace was the only respondent who discussed being sexually harassed in public spaces by devotees. She discussed several isolated incidents, including being harassed on public transport, in a nightclub and on the streets. Devotees are a mostly male community, which is made up of individuals who are sexually attracted specifically to disabled people, due to a fetishisation of impairment (Chambers, 2023). Grace reports public ignorance about devotees as a barrier to reporting:

> '[I have had devotees push] the wheelchair back up against a wall, like put their hand over the control panel and then started asking personal questions about how I care for myself and my hygiene. There's been a couple of them that whilst doing that have had one fiddly hand in a pocket at the same time, because it's their kink.'

Keith (1996) also hinted at strangers' invasive personal questions, such as about toileting, but without labelling this as sexually intrusive. Not all of us within the research team had heard the term 'devotee'. Although Ruth Bashall[6] confirmed that she has previously heard such incidents discussed, the fact that this could be named as a form of sexual violence was new to her when Grace brought this up with us. She explained that, in her experience, this is more generally perceived as yet another form of mundane derogation and everyday hate (Burch, 2021).

Grace explained that the police officer was puzzled when she reported one of the incidents: "It's weird having to explain to a cop what a fetishist is. And that they exist." Hereafter, she did not report a second, unrelated incident. Public ignorance appeared to have silenced Grace in her attempts to seek access to justice. Devotee harassment is not something we asked about in

[6] Ruth Bashall was a co-researcher on this project. She was the founder and former chief executive of Stay Safe East, a user-led organisation that is run by and for disabled victim-survivors of domestic and sexual violence and hate crime: https://www.staysafe-east.org.uk/.

the interviews. It is likely that other respondents had similar experiences, which they had not categorised as sexual violence, hence they did not feel this was relevant to bring up. It follows that a social definition or name is needed, which 'makes clear that others may share this experience, thereby undermining the isolation of feeling that you are the only one' (Kelly, 1988, p 141).

Lack of awareness of the specific forms of sexual violence also contributed to a delay in naming for one respondent who experienced an anti-lesbian hate crime known as 'corrective rape' (Brown, 2012; Doan-Minh, 2019). The respondent identified a lack of available information about the link between homophobia and sexual violence as a barrier:

> 'The perpetrator knew that I identified as a lesbian. And they tried to convert me by doing what they did. [...] Even the understanding of homophobic hate crime ... the examples that I have come across are generally being called slurs on a night out. And I rarely ever hear about my experiences.'[7]

When a woman names sexual violence after a delay, this often happens after she has accessed information that was new to her about the laws, different kinds of violence and her rights and from her comparing her interpretations of her experiences with those of others.

## "He was really fricking charming": reflections on the perpetrators and the *JB* case

Our respondents described their abusers' positionality as more powerful than their own. For instance, Grace explained: "He was really fricking charming and because I was an absolute gibbering wreck afterwards. He'd just tell [the police] that I had mental health problems and be all nice and calm with them whilst I'm in floods of tears." Gina described the rapist as "very good looking, very charismatic, the wonderful caring male nurse, that persona. And very popular with the other nurses and with the patients." She contrasted this with how she felt about herself: "It's because I'm so obese and so ugly that I wasn't believed." One further respondent described the perpetrator as a "local celebrity": "He's a very prominent figure and he has been to a few Paralympics. I didn't want to get him into trouble. When we split up, [our social networks] were trying to blame everything on me, and that I had

7 This account of violence is not linked to the respondent's pseudonym, to keep it detached from other identifying information.

ruined his life."[8] Sharie's experience of being prostituted for several years while she lived in supported living meets the criteria of modern slavery:[9]

> 'I was abused by so many guys. They would come in taxis to the house, pay me for sex, and I said: "Right, that's not good." But I was about eighteen, twenties, and then at that time when I was abused it was not good. They always used to pay me for sex, and they used me and abused me, came in taxis, car, taxis, car, taxis, cars.'

Sharie suggests that she understood she "didn't want to do it" at the time. She implied that her mental illness, as well as her young age, reduced her autonomy: "So many ways I was abused by men, fucking stupid men. That's how I have thoughts." There is a declaration of powerlessness, which was also reflected in many of the accounts cited in the earlier section on structural inequalities. This disempowerment also affected justice outcomes and whether women would be believed.

Gina and Paula both reported their perpetrators, who worked within health and social care settings. Nonetheless, at the time of the interview both perpetrators continued to work in their respective roles as nurse and personal care assistant. Although Paula was promised by the police that her abuser would receive a mark on their DBS[10] record, several months later she found the perpetrator had returned to delivering frontline care. Both cases are indicative of institutional denial (Greer and McLaughlin, 2013). In terms of justice outcomes for our respondents, only two of the stranger rapists had been convicted, along with several of the perpetrators against the women who participated in a focus group at a women's refuge. This is consistent with national low conviction rates. These reflections on the perpetrators will now be compared to what we know about the *JB* case in order to explore whether the *JB* case may facilitate justice in situations similar to those cited in this chapter.

At the time of the Supreme Court judgment JB was a 38-year-old male 'with a complex diagnosis of autistic spectrum disorder combined with impaired cognition' who received close supervision within a small community-living group. Hence, JB seemed to be in a marginal social position, which contrasts with the social standing of the violent men our respondents described. However, service users constitute the single largest

[8] This account of violence is not linked to the respondent's pseudonym, to keep it detached from other identifying information.

[9] Modern Slavery Act 2015.

[10] Disclosure and Barring Service: https://www.gov.uk/government/organisations/disclosure-and-barring-service

group of perpetrators of sexual violence within specialist learning-disability services (McCarthy and Thomas, 1996). Hence, the concern about protecting 'more vulnerable' women from JB is not unfounded. Nonetheless, there are some concerns around how the evidence against JB was built. For instance, in the Supreme Court (2021) judgment in *JB*, the following exchange is described as a 'graphic illustration' of JB's understanding of the concept of consent:

| | |
|---|---|
| Dr Thrift: | If a woman gets drunk at a party and has sex with a man there, is she fair game for anyone else? |
| JB: | I'd say she was fair game yes. Especially if she's done it with one person. Yes if she drinks enough she's bound to do it with the second one too. |

Dr Thrift was testing whether JB agreed with the common rape myths that women who drink alcohol are responsible for rape, which is a view shared by many of the mock jurors in a study by Finch and Munro (2007). Hence, JB agreeing is troubling, but consistent with views that prevail among many of us, most of whom would not act on them.

Had the foregoing exchange taken place as part of social research, the present researcher would advise that data with such potential response bias should be discarded from the dataset (Hollomotz, 2018). JB was confronted with a leading question, as well as a hypothetical scenario. We know that such questions are best avoided with people with learning difficulties and/or autism, as they find abstract thought challenging. It is documented that some disguise a lack of understanding through 'yeah saying', also termed acquiescence (Hollomotz, 2018). In other words, this snapshot into the evidence provided on JB's perspective indicates that he was not given a fair chance to explain his position and that we may therefore question the validity of his responses.

Reports cited by the Supreme Court also suggest that 'JB would make a "beeline" for highly vulnerable women', which is a highly subjective assessment that says more about views held by the observers than about JB's behaviours. We do not know how judgements were made about other women's 'vulnerability' and what exactly the nature of JB's 'beeline' is. Such evidence reflects the common notion that practitioners are so keen to avoid any risk of sexual abuse that they view all interactions through the lens of mental in/capacity. JB's behaviours may thus also be explained through the counterfeit deviance theory (Hingsburger et al, 1991; Griffiths et al, 2013). In brief, this puts forward the view that some males who are effectively blocked from experiencing positive sexual relationships by risk-averse social care providers turn to satisfying their sexual desires through violence. Hingsburger (1995) explained the mindset that if all sex is 'bad', what difference does it make whether the other party consents or not?

We are unable to test this theory, because epistemologically speaking the quality and nature of evidence available on JB is different to that available on our respondents. Our respondents were able to articulate their views on a voluntary basis in a safe space. We approached them as experts on their own lives (Stone and Priestley 1996). We made clear that we were there to listen, not to judge, and that we were committed to the social model of disability. The circumstances of JB's court hearing present a stark contrast, but they are consistent with how other disabled people described their experiences of court. For instance, one witness explained: '"I didn't feel like I had my say, I felt like I was led (…) I felt like it came down to how clever the lawyers were, the barristers were, and not to the actual facts"' (Beckene et al, 2020, p 74). Beyond attributing causality to his impairment, little effort was made to understand why JB behaved the way he did. JB was approached as deviant and the observers of his behaviour were treated as the experts who were able to make sense of this deviance. For instance, the judgment report itemises that:

> The nature and degree of Asperger's syndrome experienced by JB accounts for his inappropriate sexual behaviours, such as being obsessionally fixated on a particular woman, sending inappropriate sexual messages, inappropriate touching, and targeting the vulnerable. This syndrome […] also accounts for his behavioural difficulties from childhood […]. JB attempted to strangle a classmate at the age of ten [and] when he was aged 12/13.[11]

This echoes the medical pathology model of disability – one that is seen in section 2 of the MCA – but it also lacks substantive evidence. A systematic review of published literature regarding autism spectrum disorder (ASD) and violence concludes, 'while no conclusive evidence indicates that individuals with ASD are more violent than those without ASD, specific generative and associational risk factors may increase violence risk among individuals with ASD' (Im, 2016, p 32). Known social factors associated with violence among young people with ASD include sleep difficulties, higher parental income and parent-reported social and communication problems (Kanne and Mazurek, 2011; Im, 2016).

The *JB* case pathologises JB's lack of appreciation for the need of his sexual partner's consent and attributes this to impairment effects. However, from what our respondents described, such an understanding was not present in

---

[11] *A Local Authority v JB* [2021] UKSC 52 at para 20.

at least some of the non-disabled men who raped them. Let us examine Nancy's experience of rape and voyeurism on her wedding night. Sadly, this is not uncommon. Brutal sexual initiation of the bride by the groom on her wedding night has been normalised across history and cultures (De Beauvoir, 2011). Albeit he had 'reasonable cause' to know Nancy would not consent, it is possible that the groom romanticised his actions against this historic backdrop of male entitlement and that he did not, in fact, *understand* that she did not consent. Some of our women were cited earlier, stating that they once believed that their sexual consent was not required. The fact that this mindset can prevail among different men and women, among victims and abusers, even among wo/men in positions of power, such as in the criminal justice system (Wistrich, 2022) and in the police force (Turner, 2024), indicates that causes for confusion around consent are located beyond the individual biology associated with JB's ASD.

## Discussion

Over three decades on from Kelly and Radford's (1990) publication, the majority of our respondents reported, at least initially, internalised harmful rape myths which resulted in self-reproach. Women kept reassuring themselves that all was 'normal', keeping up the echo on their foresisters' ancient soothing tune that 'nothing really happened' or, as one of our respondents had put it: "No, it wasn't that bad, it was all okay [...] this was normal behaviour." However, the fact that most had eventually become able to name sexual violence is a success to be celebrated. Concurrently though, others will continue to suffer without realising that their experiences may be named, while struggling with internalised sexisms and disablism amalgamating to an 'enemy within'.

Respondents reported strong emotional reactions at the time and in the aftermath of their injurious experiences, including disassociating, feeling disturbed, uncomfortable, confused or an altered sense of self. However, none of the respondents who experienced sexual violence in the context of an ongoing relationship described resistance in the moment. When justifying a delay in naming, respondents alluded to the notion 'that rape victims had to have resisted their assailants in order for their claims to be accepted. Any abatement of struggle was interpreted as the woman's consent to the intercourse under the logic that a real rape victim would protect her honour virtually to the death' (Crenshaw, 1991, p 1270).

This myth hinders naming, because 'the further away a woman's experience was from the limited definition offered by myths about sexual violence, the more likely it was that she would not define it as sexual violence at the time of the assault' (Kelly, 1988, p 148). Psychological treatment approaches for victims of sexual violence are 'often informed by feminist frameworks that recognise the need for re-establishing appropriate boundaries in relationships, promoting self-determination, and empowerment of the victim to move from victim to survivor. Feminist-informed approaches [aim] to help the victim understand that such violence is a societal problem and not an individual problem, thereby reducing self-blame and guilt' (Regehr et al, 2013, p 11).

This approach has significant advantages over focusing on mental in/capacity, as conceptualised under the narrow frame of the MCA, which 'has the potential to leave people in vulnerable and abusive situations, as it only "protects" those who are "incapable"; those deemed to be capacitous and thereby autonomous, are left outside of its remit, even if they are vulnerable' (Clough, 2014, p 387).

In the Introduction to this volume Clough and Pritchard-Jones refer to professionals' dilemmas about distinguishing 'a good intimate relationship, as compared to a bad one'. Sandland's discussion in Chapter 1 could be used to argue that such an ambition is utopic, as he evidences that even prosecutors and legal scholars have difficulty in distinguishing the 'good' and 'bad', as the legal and practical tools they have available to do so are ill equipped for this task. These sense-making struggles across different stakeholders' evidence that cause difficulties in naming sexual violence are not located at the individual level.

## Conclusion

The paradoxical scapegoating of the male who inspired this collection (JB) detracts attention away from the social causes that make it possible for some men (but not others) to rape women (and get away with it). While it is important that the *JB* case and discussions around it problematise the importance of establishing sexual consent, the focus on JB's impairments as the cause of impaired understandings around women's consent is inherently disablist. JB is pathologised for his lack of discretion to disguise his agreement with prevailing rape myths. With rape convictions being at an all-time low, it is surprising that we have the time to police a man who *may* offend when we do not appear to have the resources to effectively prosecute those who *have* offended.

To this day, legal practices protect from a minority of sexual crimes that are in line with prevailing rape myths, such as the requirement for women to demonstrate active dissent. The burden of proof lies with the prosecution, not the defence, firstly to assert that they did not consent and secondly to prove that 'A does not reasonably believe that B consents'.[12]

12 Sexual Offences Act 2003, section 1(1)(c); however, this is also subject to the evidential and conclusive presumptions in sections 75 and 76 of the Act.

Absence of material expressions of dissent therefore provides scope for the defence to argue that 'A did indeed reasonably believe that B consented'. Thus, the legal requirement for victims to express dissent does not reflect the reality of rape victims' description of their responses to rape and it must be seen as a contributing factor to the low conviction rates in England and Wales.

Moving forward, the question whether, in the context of a society where misogyny, rape myths and sexism are at times normalised, it is even possible to comprehend female consent is essential, rather than optional. Future legal reform must be driven by the reality of women's lived experiences, so that the terminology and expectations that are set out by the law map onto these. Women who have experienced sexual violence across a range of contexts need to redefine the parameters of sexual violence and key terms to be used in assessments of issues, such as 'rape' and concepts used to establish this, such as 'consent'.

**Acknowledgements**

The chapter is dedicated to the memories of Ruth Bashall and Susie Balderston, who listened patiently to many half-formed ideas about naming and pointed me to the bits that mattered. Special thanks to Abigail Gorman, who advised us that naming is the first and often most difficult step towards healing and survival. Without you, we wouldn't have asked about this! Most of all, I would like to thank the respondents for sharing their deep insights into this difficult subject.

## References

Adichie, C.N. (2014) *We should all be feminists*. New York: Vintage.

Ahmed, S. (2017) *Living a feminist life*. Durham, NC: Duke University Press.

Baird, V. (2022) *2021/22 annual report by Dame Vera Baird QC Victims' Commissioner for England and Wales*. London: Office of the Victims' Commissioner.

Beckene, T. et al (2020) 'Experiences of going to court: Witnesses with intellectual disabilities and their carers speak up', *Journal of Applied Research in Intellectual Disabilities*, 33(1), 67–78.

Bennice, J.A. and Resick, P.A. (2003) 'Marital rape: history, research, and practice', *Trauma, Violence, & Abuse*, 4(3), 228–246.

Bernstein, E., Kanefsky, R., Cook, M. and Newins, A.R. (2022) 'Acceptance of rape myths and psychological symptoms: the indirect effect of self-blame', *Journal of American College Health*, 1–5. https://doi.org/10.1080/07448481.2022.2086005

Bjorklund, P. (2006) 'No man's land: gender bias and social constructivism in the diagnosis of borderline personality disorder', *Issues in Mental Health Nursing*, 27(1), 3–23.

Bowstead, J.C. (2020) 'Private violence/private transport: the role of means of transport in women's mobility to escape from domestic violence in England and Wales', *Mobilities*, 15(4), 559–574.

Branford, D., Gerrard, D., Saleem, N., Shaw, C. and Webster, A. (2018) 'Stopping over-medication of people with intellectual disability, autism or both (STOMP) in England part 1–history and background of STOMP', *Advances in Mental Health and Intellectual Disabilities*, 13(1), 31–40.

Breckenridge, J.P. (2018) 'The relationship between disability and domestic abuse', in N. Lombard (ed), *The Routledge handbook of gender and violence*. Abingdon: Routledge, pp 133–144.

British Sociological Association (2017) *BSA statement of ethical practice*. The British Sociological Association. Available at: https://www.britsoc.co.uk/media/24310/bsa_statement_of_ethical_practice.pdf (Accessed 22 September 2023).

Brown, R. (2012) 'Corrective rape in South Africa: a continuing plight despite an international human rights response', *Annual Survey of International & Comparative Law*, 18, 45–66.

Bryson, V. (2021) *Futures of feminism*. Manchester: Manchester University Press.

Burch, L. (2021) 'Everyday hate and affective possibility: disabled people's negotiations of space, place and identity', *The International Journal of Disability and Social Justice*, 1(1), 73–94.

Burt, M.R. (1980) 'Cultural myths and supports for rape', *Journal of Personality and Social Psychology*, 38(2), 217.

Chambers, G.C. (2023) 'Disabled sexuality and negotiations with sexual partners', *Sexuality and Disability*, 41(2), 357–386.

Clough, B. (2014) 'Vulnerability and capacity to consent to sex-asking the right questions', *Child & Family Law Quarterly*, 26, 371–396.

Crenshaw, K. (1991) 'Mapping the margins: intersectionality, identity politics and violence against women of color', *Stanford Law Review*, 43(6), 1241–1299.

De Beauvoir, S. (2011) *The second sex*. New York: Vintage Books.

de Vogel, V. and Didden, R. (2022) 'Victimization history in female forensic psychiatric patients with intellectual disabilities: results from a Dutch multicenter comparative study', *Research in Developmental Disabilities*, 122, 104179.

Denzin, N.K. (1989) *Interpretive interactionism*. Newbury Park, CA: Sage.

Department of Health and Social Care (2012) *Winterbourne View Hospital: Department of Health review and response*. Available at: https://www.gov.uk/government/publications/winterbourne-view-hospital-department-of-health-review-and-response (Accessed 26 July 2023).

Doan-Minh, S. (2019) 'Corrective rape: an extreme manifestation of discrimination and the state's complicity in sexual violence', *Hastings Women's Law Journal*, 30, 167.

Doherty, G. (2017) *What is the nature and extent of mate crime offending against disabled people and how effective are institutional responses?* University of Leeds.

Feder, G.S. and Howarth, E. (2014) 'The epidemiology of gender-based violence', in *ABC of domestic and sexual violence*. John Wiley & Sons, pp 1–4.

Felstiner, W.L., Abel, R.L. and Sarat, A. (1980) 'The emergence and transformation of disputes: naming, blaming, claiming', *Law and Society Review*, 15(3–4), 631–654.

Finch, E. and Munro, V.E. (2007) 'The demon drink and the demonized woman: socio-sexual stereotypes and responsibility attribution in rape trials involving intoxicants', *Social & Legal Studies*, 16(4), 591–614. https://doi.org/10.1177/0964663907082737

Fyson, R. and Patterson, A. (2020) 'Staff understandings of abuse and poor practice in residential settings for adults with intellectual disabilities', *Journal of Applied Research in Intellectual Disabilities*, 33(3), 354–363.

Gill, A.K., Strange, C. and Roberts, K. (2014) *'Honour' killing and violence: Theory, Policy and practice*. Basingstoke: Palgrave Macmillan.

Griffiths, D., Hingsburger, D., Hoath, J. and Ioannou, S. (2013) '"Counterfeit deviance" revisited', *Journal of Applied Research in Intellectual Disabilities*, 26(5), 471–480. https://doi.org/10.1111/jar.1203

Goffman, E. (1959) *The presentation of self in everyday life*. New York: The Overlook Press.

Greer, C. and McLaughlin, E. (2013) 'The Sir Jimmy Savile scandal: child sexual abuse and institutional denial at the BBC', *Crime, Media, Culture*, 9(3), 243–263.

Hall, K.Q. (2011) *Feminist disability studies*. Bloomington: Indiana University Press.

Hardt, J. and Rutter, M. (2004) 'Validity of adult retrospective reports of adverse childhood experiences: review of the evidence', *Journal of Child Psychology and Psychiatry*, 45(2), 260–273.

Hingsburger, D. (1995) *Just say know! – Understanding and reducing the risk of sexual victimisation of people with developmental disabilities*. Barrie, ON: Diverse City Press.

Hingsburger, D., Griffiths, D. and Quinsey, V. (1991) 'Detecting counterfeit deviance: differentiating sexual deviance from sexual inappropriateness'. *Habilitation Mental Health Care Newsletter*, 10, 51–54.

Hlavka, H.R. (2014) 'Normalizing sexual violence: young women account for harassment and abuse', *Gender & Society*, 28(3), 337–358.

HM Government (2021, June) *The end-to-end rape review report on findings and actions*. Available at: https://assets.publishing.service.gov.uk/government/uploads/system/uploads/attachment_data/file/1001417/end-to-end-rape-review-report-with-correction-slip.pdf (Accessed 9 April 2024).

Ho, D.Y.-f. (1976) 'On the concept of face', *American Journal of Sociology*, 81(4), 867–884.

Hollomotz, A. (2011) *Learning difficulties and sexual vulnerability: A social approach*. London: Jessica Kingsley Publishers.

Hollomotz, A. (2018) 'Successful interviews with people with intellectual disability', *Qualitative Research*, 18(2), 153–170.

Hollomotz, A., Burch, L. and Bashall, R. (2023, 26–01). *Formal support needs of disabled victim-survivors of sexual violence: A qualitative research report*. Available at: https://www.gov.uk/government/publications/formal-support-needs-of-adult-victim-survivors-of-sexual-violence (Accessed 17 February 2024).

Hunt, E. (2023) *We need to talk: The truth about sexual violence and my fight for justice*. London: Mardle.

Im, D.S. (2016) 'Template to perpetrate: an update on violence in autism spectrum disorder', *Harvard Review of Psychiatry*, 24(1), 14.

Jay, A., Evans, M., Frank, I. and Sharpling, D. (2022) *The report of the Independent Inquiry into Child Sexual Abuse*. London: HMSO.

Kanne, S.M. and Mazurek, M.O. (2011) 'Aggression in children and adolescents with ASD: prevalence and risk factors', *Journal of Autism and Developmental Disorders*, 41, 926–937.

Keith, L. (1996) 'Encounters with strangers: the public's responses to disabled women and how this affects our sense of self', in J. Morris (ed), *Encounters with strangers: Feminism and disability*. London: The Women's Press, pp 69–88.

Kelly, L. (1988) *Surviving sexual violence*. Cambridge: Polity Press.

Kelly, L. and Radford, J. (1990) 'Nothing really happened: the invalidation of women's experiences of sexual violence', in M. Hester, L. Kelly and J. Radford (eds), *Women, violence and male power: Feminist activism, research and practice*. Maidenhead: Open University Press, pp 19–33.

Kennedy, M. (1996) 'Sexual abuse and disabled children', in J. Morris (ed), *Encounters with strangers: Feminism and disability*. London: The Women's Press, pp 116–134.

Klein, P., Fairweather, A.K., Lawn, S., Stallman, H.M. and Cammell, P. (2021) 'Structural stigma and its impact on healthcare for consumers with borderline personality disorder: protocol for a scoping review', *Systematic Reviews*, 10(1), 1–7.

Kristiansen, K. (2004) 'Madness, badness and sadness revisited. Ontology control in "mental health land"', in K. Kristiansen and R. Traustadóttir (eds), *Gender and disability research in the Nordic countries*. Lund: Studentlitteratur, pp 365–393.

Lee, L.L. and Carson, A. (2014) 'Intimate violence in a specialist college setting: can students with learning difficulties manage themselves?', *British Journal of Learning Disabilities*, 42(1), 6–16. https://doi.org/10.1111/bld.12004

Leverick, F. (2020) 'What do we know about rape myths and juror decision making?', *The International Journal of Evidence & Proof*, 24(3), 255–279.

Lonsway, K.A. and Fitzgerald, L.F. (1994) 'Rape myths: in review', *Psychology of Women Quarterly*, 18(2), 133–164.

Macdonald, S.J., Donovan, C., Clayton, J. and Husband, M. (2022) 'Becoming cuckooed: conceptualising the relationship between disability, home takeovers and criminal exploitation', *Disability & Society*, 1–21, https://doi.org/10.1080/09687599.2022.2071680.

Mason, J. (2018) *Qualitative researching* (3rd edn). London: SAGE.

McCann, E., Marsh, L. and Brown, M. (2019) 'People with intellectual disabilities, relationship and sex education programmes: a systematic review', *Health Education Journal*, 78(8), 885–900.

McCarthy, M. and Thompson, D. (1996) 'Sexual abuse by design: an examination of the issues in learning disability services', *Disability & Society*, 11(2), 205–217.

McCarthy, M., Bates, C., Triantafyllopoulou, P., Hunt, S. and Milne Skillman, K. (2019) '"Put bluntly, they are targeted by the worst creeps society has to offer": police and professionals' views and actions relating to domestic violence and women with intellectual disabilities', *Journal of Applied Research in Intellectual Disabilities*, 32(1), 71–81.

McCormack, B. (1991) 'Sexual abuse and learning disabilities', *British Medical Journal*, 303(6795), 143–144.

Millett, K. (1970) *Sexual politics*. New York: Columbia University Press.

Mills, C.W. (1959) *The sociological imagination*. New York: Oxford University Press.

Ministry of Justice (2022, 16-06). *End to end rape review progress report: One year on*. Available at: https://www.gov.uk/government/publications/end-to-end-rape-review-progress-report-one-year-on (Accessed 9 April 2024).

Morris, D., Camden-Smith, C. and Batten, R. (2020) 'Self-reported experiences of intimate partner violence in a female forensic intellectual disability population', *Advances in Mental Health and Intellectual Disabilities*, 14(1), 1–13.

Morris, J. (1991) *Pride against prejudice: Personal politics of disability*. London: The Women's Press.

Office for National Statistics (2019, 02-12). *Disability and crime, UK: 2019*. Available at: https://www.ons.gov.uk/peoplepopulationandcommunity/healthandsocialcare/disability/bulletins/disabilityandcrimeuk/2019 (Accessed 29 November 2021).

Office for National Statistics (2023, 23-03). *Sexual offences victim characteristics, England and Wales: year ending March 2022*. Available at: https://www.ons.gov.uk/peoplepopulationandcommunity/crimeandjustice/articles/sexualoffencesvictimcharacteristicsenglandandwales/yearendingmarch2022 (Accessed 22 June 2023).

Office of the Public Guardian (2015) *Safeguarding policy: Protecting vulnerable adults*. Available at: https://www.gov.uk/government/publications/safeguarding-policy-protecting-vulnerable-adults (Accessed 9 April 2024).

Oliver, M., Sapey, B. and Thomas, P. (2012) *Social work with disabled people* (4th edn). Basingstoke: Palgrave Macmillan.

Painter, K. and Farrington, D.P. (2005) 'Wife rape in Great Britain', in R. Muraskin (ed), *Women and justice*. Abingdon: Routledge, pp 85–103.

Parmenter, T.R. (2001) 'Intellectual disability – quo vadis?', in G.L. Albrecht, K. Seelman, D. and M. Bury (eds), *Handbook of disability studies*. Sage Publications, pp 267–296.

Priestley, M. (1998) 'Constructions and creations: idealism, materialism and disability theory', *Disability & Society*, 13(1), 75–94.

Rape Crisis (2023) *Myths vs facts*. Available at: https://rapecrisis.org.uk/get-informed/about-sexual-violence/myths-vs-realities/ (Accessed 25 September 2023).

Reeve, D. (2002) 'Negotiating psycho-emotional dimensions of disability and their influence on identity constructions', *Disability & Society*, 17(5), 493–508. http://dx.doi.org/10.1080/09687590220148487

Regehr, C., Alaggia, R., Dennis, J., Pitts, A. and Saini, M. (2013) 'Interventions to reduce distress in adult victims of sexual violence and rape: a systematic review', *Campbell Systematic Reviews*, 9(1), 1–133. https://doi.org/https://doi.org/10.4073/csr.2013.3

Roulstone, A. and Mason Bish, H. (2012) *Disability, hate crime and violence*. Abingdon: Routledge.

Rush, F. (1980) *The best kept secret: Sexual abuse of children*. New York: Prentice-Hall.

Russell, K.J. and Hand, C.J. (2017) 'Rape myth acceptance, victim blame attribution and Just World Beliefs: a rapid evidence assessment', *Aggression and Violent Behavior*, 37, 153–160. https://doi.org/https://doi.org/10.1016/j.avb.2017.10.008

Saunders, C. (2010) 'Making it count: Sexual offences, evidential sufficiency, and the mentally disordered complainant', *Liverpool Law Review*, 31, 177–206.

Saxton, M., Curry, M.A., Powers, L.E., Maley, S., Eckels, K. and Gross, J. (2001) '"Bring my scooter so I can leave you": a study of disabled women handling abuse by personal assistance providers', *Violence Against Women*, 7(4), 393–417. https://journals.sagepub.com/doi/10.1177/10778010122182523

Sin, C.H. (2012) 'Making disablist hate crime visible', in A. Roulstone and H. Mason-Bish (eds), *Disability, hate crime and violence*. Abingdon: Routledge, pp 147–165.

Social Care Institute for Excellence (2023) *Safeguarding adults review: Whorlton Hall*. Available at: https://www.scie.org.uk/news/mediareleases/whorlton-hall-review (Accessed 12 July 2023).

Stay Safe East (2020) *Stay Safe East statement on the Domestic Abuse Act*. Available at: https://staysafe-east.org.uk/wp-content/uploads/2021/05/Stay-Safe-East-statement-on-the-Domestic-Abuse-Act-FINAL-version-converted.pdf (Accessed 12 July 2023).

Stone, E. and Priestley, M. (1996) 'Parasites, pawns and partners: disability research and the role of non-disabled researchers', *British Journal of Sociology*, 47(4), 699–716.

Strnadová, I., Danker, J. and Carter, A. (2022) 'Scoping review on sex education for high school-aged students with intellectual disability and/or on the autism spectrum: parents', teachers' and students' perspectives, attitudes and experiences', *Sex Education*, 22(3), 361–378.

Supreme Court (2021, 24 Nov). *A Local Authority (Respondent) v JB (by his Litigation Friend, the Official Solicitor) (AP) (Appellant)*. Available at: https://www.bailii.org/uk/cases/UKSC/2021/52.html (Accessed 9 April 2024).

Tarzia, L. (2021) 'Toward an ecological understanding of intimate partner sexual violence', *Journal of Interpersonal Violence*, 36(23–24), 11704–11727.

The Everyday Sexism Project (2023) *The everyday sexism project*. Available at: https://everydaysexism.com/ (Accessed 19 October 2023).

Thiara, R.K., Hague, G., Bashall, R., Ellis, B. and Mullender, A. (2012) *Disabled women and domestic violence: Responding to the experiences of survivors*. London: Jessica Kingsley.

Thomas, C. (2006) 'Disability and gender: reflections on theory and research', *Scandinavian Journal of Disability Research*, 8(2–3), 177–185.

Thomas, P. (2011) '"Mate crime": ridicule, hostility and targeted attacks against disabled people', *Disability & Society*, 26(1), 107–111. http://www.informaworld.com/10.1080/09687599.2011.532590

Turner, A. (2024) 'Sexism and misogyny as traits of police culture: problems, red flags and solutions', *International Journal of Police Science & Management*. https://doi.org/10.1177/1461355724122

Weeks, J. (2017) *Sex, politics and society: The regulations of sexuality since 1800* (4th edn). Abingdon: Routledge.

Wistrich, H. (2022) 'Misogyny in the criminal justice system', *The Political Quarterly*, 93(1), 64–68. https://doi.org/https://doi.org/10.1111/1467-923X.13100

Young Women's Movement (2023) *Bold girls ken*. Available at: https://www.youngwomenscot.org/bold-girls-ken (Accessed 6 July 2023).

8

# Reflections from Practice: The Legal Labyrinth of Sexual Capacity – Balancing Rights with Risks

*Lorraine Currie and Neil Allen*

## Introduction

The previous three chapters vividly reveal the challenge for practitioners and those seeking to reform law and policy: namely, how should the law strike the 'right' balance between sexual freedom and freedom from sexual abuse so as to promote sexual autonomy and prosecute sexual offences? They raise essential issues and pose challenges to the empowerment and protection aims of what many see as a rights-based, person-centred Mental Capacity Act 2005 (MCA). Drawing upon the United Nations Convention on the Rights of Persons with Disabilities (UNCRPD), the ultimate challenge in relation to international norms is how to preserve legal capacity in sexual relations on an equal basis with those without disability.

### *'Equal basis with others'*

Squires and Morgan refer in Chapter 5 to a 'gloriously ordinary life' sought by disabled people where 'We all want to live in the place we call home with the people and things we love, in communities where we look out for one another, doing things that matter to us'. In Chapter 6 Sorinmade and Peisah discuss the psychological and physiological benefits of sexual expression in later life, while looming large is the risk of being consigned to celibacy, even despite having a fully capacitous partner. They underline the highly risk-averse approach taken to meeting the intimate desires of those with disability, and the relative ease with which their most intimate affairs and activities are shared with family, using the justification of safeguarding.

In wider society age has a different resonance: consider Mick Jagger who had his youngest child at the age of 73 and got engaged to his 36-year-old partner when he was 79. Then there is Al Pacino, who fathered his youngest child at age 83 with his 29-year-old partner, making him one of the oldest fathers on record. Think about the wonderful female role models such as Judi Dench and Maggi Smith both still working at age 88, and the likes of Bob Dylan aged 82 and Bruce Springsteen a mere child at 73, Paul McCartney at 78 and Ringo Starr at 80: all still performing. Joan Collins is still touring at 90. Sexually active, glamorous, partnered many times; their relationships, actions and behaviour are not policed, except perhaps in the court of public opinion.

---

**Practice example**

Take John, living in a care home with dementia. Another resident, Jean, has taken to John and follows him around. She makes sexual advances towards him; they have been seen cuddling and her pants were found in his pocket. Jean has been assessed to lack mental capacity to engage in sexual relations. John is not too bothered about this new relationship, but Jean is insistent and very amorous. John is a mellow chap all round. The care home staff don't know how to manage the situation. The social worker eventually concludes that John also lacks capacity for sexual relationships and the solution to the whole thing is to move John to a different care home.

---

If they epitomise the enjoyment of legal capacity for those without mental disability, enter a care home where the legal environment is very different. Add to that a diagnosis of dementia and your life will be different again, where the in/ability to decide on sexual intimacy represents a cliff edge with a dramatic drop into the underworld of the criminal law. Having the capacity to engage in sexual relations enables sexual freedom. But if it is lacking, sexual activity is criminalised, and what could have been consensual intercourse by law becomes rape because valid consent is no longer possible. English law draws the 'IM-curtain', for 'if, in any case, there is a declaration of lack of capacity, the relevant local authority must undertake the very closest supervision of that individual to ensure, to such extent as is possible, that the opportunity for sexual relations is removed'.[1]

[1] *IM v LM* [2015] Fam 61 at [1].

Carers, too, risk prosecution if they 'cause' or 'incite' someone with mental disorder to engage in sexual activity even if they have capacity.[2] Yet, 'the courts must tread especially carefully where an organ of the state proposes that a citizen's ability to perform, in a non-abusive way, the sex function should be abrogated or curtailed', for this 'involves a very profound aspect of civil liberties and personal autonomy'.[3]

This illustrates the point made in Chapter 5 by Squires and Morgan, that 'sexual expression and wellbeing is a basic human right, but for many older and disabled people there is a lacuna between the standards set out in law, and their experience'. Care staff and social workers often see these situations as 'problems to solve' and mental incapacity as the gateway to solving them. Finding mental incapacity is often seen as the means to control behaviour through best-interests decision making, whereas person-centred, strengths-based practice would in fact encourage support to manage risk whether capacitous or incapacitous.

Social care staff who are working with Jean could spend time not only assessing her capacity to engage in sexual activity but to try to understand her deeper needs, how to meet them and, as necessary, work to identify risks and develop plans to manage them. Care staff could be working to foster closeness, friendship or intimacy which, as Sorinmade and Peish note in Chapter 6, meets the person's 'basic human instincts and needs, ranging from sexual needs to the need for companionship, physical contact and the relief of loneliness', while staying within guidelines and civil and criminal law.

On the other hand, promoting rights can easily become a cliché, such as when a young person's care plan talks of 'private time' as a pseudonym for masturbation, but this raises the question of privacy in general. Their room should be private, their home providing a sanctuary, however they choose to spend their time, on an equal basis with their non-disabled counterparts. Wider examples remind us that writing in the first person does not make practice person-centred; for example a sign on a young person's door which says, 'I can go out, when my name is on the rota' does not move us nearer to the 'gloriously ordinary life'. In practice, issues of sexual capacity are rarely straightforward because it is often linked to issues of contact and risk, pregnancy and risk, sexual exploitation/wider vulnerability, or sexual practices which challenge the norm.[4]

2 *Secretary of State for Justice v A Local Authority* [2021] EWCA Civ 1527.

3 *D Borough Council v AB* [2011] EWHC 101 at [11].

4 Such as autoerotic asphyxiation: see Re *AA (Court of Protection: Capacity to Consent to Sexual Practices)* [2020] EWCOP 66 and *Re AA (Capacity: Social Media and Internet Use)* [2021] EWCOP 70.

## Supporting intimacy

### Practice example

A special college for 18-plus-year-olds had a great curriculum around sex education and rights. However, not everyone on campus received the same education. A member of the catering staff was overheard to say, "They're lovely when they come there, then they tell them about sex and it spoils them". The catering staff on site were keen to perpetuate the view that those with a learning disability are to remain as children and not develop sexual selfhood and identity. While the wider curriculum promoted rights and sexual identity, this was not being carried across the whole staff group.

Another specialist college had a person-centred approach to sexual education and advice, but this was not followed up in subsequent care and support planning. Tom formed a sexual relationship with another young man, and they quickly became inseparable. Tom's family planned to buy him a house in the local area which he could share with his friend after his time at college. However, when Tom's parents found out that his friend was more than a friend, they withdrew this offer. The social worker had a brilliant relationship with Tom and had concluded that he had capacity for key decisions. His parents wanted an independent assessor to assess capacity for sex, accommodation and care.

Young people with intellectual disability often do not receive the same degree of information, education and advice around sexual matters at the same age as their non-disabled counterparts. This can sometimes be linked to infantalising young people because of their disability. A review by the National Development Team for Inclusion in 2016 considered the barriers to people with learning disabilities developing sexual/romantic relationships and found barriers related to the support provided, particularly 'the limited information, resources and training available to support people to develop relationships' (Harflett and Turner, 2016, p 8). This included a lack of accessible information for people with learning disabilities and their families and a lack of training for teachers. Daly, Heah and Liddiard (2019, p 5) argue, 'Where sexuality education is offered to disabled young people, it has been criticised by disabled scholars for its focus on normative bodies and normative bodily experiences, which can serve to alienate and further marginalise disabled children and young people, as well as propagate dis/ableist myths.'

This serves as a great example of the MCA 2005 being used as a gateway to rights or to restrictions. The parents in this case scenario hoped that a finding of a lack of mental capacity would allow them to make the decisions about where Tom lived and with whom he had a relationship. Clearly, they hoped that he would be found not to have capacity, but this was not the case. Although the social worker had a person-centred, strengths-based approach, the council were overly influenced by the parents when looking for accommodation for Tom alone, rather than seeing him as part of a couple. The right to form relationships and to exercise sexual preferences must be appreciated by everyone on the journey of support. Social care professionals are ideally placed to challenge decisions which they do not feel promote the person's rights.

Squires and Morgan challenged this approach in Chapter 5, finding that social work practice has too often been risk averse and deficit orientated, focusing on regulating rather than enabling the intimate lives of disabled and older people. At the same time they point out that social work has a critical role to play in challenging the marginalisation of disabled people's sexual rights.

## Protection from abuse

Hollomotz (Chapter 7) illustrates further how sexual violence can transcend the boundaries and binaries erected by the MCA 2005 and Sexual Offences Act 2003. She notes from her research that expressions of trauma were misattributed through diagnostic overshadowing. While traumatic experiences can result in a mental impairment, such as trauma arising from year-long treatment in intensive care,[5] the functional test comes first, and to approach it otherwise risks the unconscious bias of such overshadowing.[6] Rather than situating the issue at the individual level, what societal changes – or law reforms – are required to address these concerns?

Arguably the Supreme Court's decision in *JB* situates capacity and consent in that broader social context by taking into account the wider legal system, including the protection of others. The relevant information is less disability specific and more in tune with the mutual consent that is expected of the population at large when it comes to sexual relations. It also means that, as in *Hull City Council v KF*,[7] someone could have capacity to decide on sexual relations in a general sense but lack such capacity in relation to a specific abusive partner because of the additional risks involved. If reformers were to abolish the mental impairment requirement in order to create a 'Capacity

[5] *University Hospitals Birmingham NHS Foundation Trust v ST* [2023] EWCOP 40.

[6] See also *A Local Authority v RS* [2020] EWCOP 29, where indulging in risky behaviour in pursuit of sexual interests, which allegedly led to a registered sex offender forcing RS to have sex, was held to amount to the taking of unwise decisions as opposed to being capacity related.

[7] [2022] EWCOP 33.

Act', that would arguably move domestic law at least in the direction of what the UNCRPD and its associated Committee expects. It must be recognised, however, that interfering in disabled people's lives on an equal basis with those without disability might lead to difficult outcomes.

Take, for example, the woman with intellectual disability who married her convicted husband in prison while he was serving a 13-year term of imprisonment for serious sexual offences against a woman with mental disabilities. It was not in dispute that, were the couple to resume married life together following his release on licence, he would pose a serious risk to her, although there was no evidence that serious harm had ever been suffered. Without her mental impairment causing her inability to decide the matter, 'We must leave PC free to make her own decision, and hope that everything turns out well in the end'.[8] Is the risk of sexual abuse the price to pay for her enjoying legal capacity on an equal basis with others?

Do those subject to domestic sexual abuse and violence who wish to remain with the perpetrator lack capacity to make such decisions? Should a 'Capacity Act' – without any mental impairment requirement – be available whereby enforced separation and injunctions could be deployed in the name of the victim's best interests? Or does the criminal law not provide the equal basis for intervention?

## Mental capacity as an on-off switch for support?

### Practice example

Sally is a young woman with a moderate intellectual disability, an experience of childhood trauma and a fixed belief that nothing bad can ever happen to her. Her only desire is to have a baby. She does not want a partner, marriage or a home; she just wants a baby. The social worker assessed her to have capacity for sex but struggled to engage her in any discussion of contraception (why would she, she wanted a baby). For historical reasons Sally lives in a care home. Care home staff are very worried. Sally is making contact with lots of different men on dating sites with one aim only: sex for reasons of achieving a pregnancy. Staff felt powerless because Sally was found to have capacity. They tried to help her understand risk, but she was unable to entertain the concept, due to her fixed belief that nothing bad can ever happen to her. Staff apply for a Deprivation of Liberty Safeguards authorisation, seeing this as a way of minimising contact with men. The authorisation is not granted, as Sally is found to have mental capacity.

[8] *PC v City of York Council* [2013] EWCA Civ 478 at [64].

This scenario and the previous case of *PC* highlight the challenges for social work when someone has the relevant mental capacity but is potentially at risk of abuse. In Sally's example social workers were trying to balance supporting her own wishes – to have a baby – against the potential risk of abuse from meeting with strangers without any ability to assess risk. Care home staff felt powerless to impose a regime of support and risk assessment because she had mental capacity in many areas. Could the inherent jurisdiction be deployed to fill this gap?

The inherent jurisdiction is best understood as the ability of the High Court to make declarations and orders to protect vulnerable adults who are unable to make decisions because of some reason other than a mental impairment. Such a cause may, for example, be the undue influence of others, or some other form of coercion or constraint which falls short of a mental impairment and therefore outside the scope of sections 2–3 of the MCA 2005. Described as 'the great safety net', it can as a last resort be used by High Court judges to fill the gaps, where the approach taken is facilitative rather than dictatorial, the aim being to provide the person with the space and opportunity to make their own decisions without such a malign influence over them.

These types of cases ideally need discussion in a legal planning forum to help identify the correct legal route. For example, the inherent jurisdiction should be considered only once all other legal avenues have been considered and exhausted. In domestic abuse cases, for example, the forum would need to consider whether this could be addressed by the section 42 of the Family Law Act 1996,[9] the section 76 of the Serious Crime Act 2015,[10] a Domestic Violence Protection Order, a Stalking Protection Order or other civil remedy such as the Protection from Harassment Act 1997. This type of forum helps to share discussion of risk across a range of professionals and disciplines and can give a clear legal steer as to the options available. This model helps practitioners to develop plans to mitigate risk and promote rights.

## The time continuum

Criminal law tends to act retrospectively. It is difficult to deploy criminal legal rules to mitigate the *risks* of sexual abuse or violence in a relationship. Only if the crime has been at least attempted if not committed can the law sanction the perpetrator's conduct. The MCA 2005, however, is forward looking, where

[9] Non-molestation orders which victims, but not public authorities, can seek. So, if the victim wishes to remain in contact with the perpetrator this will not be an option.

[10] The criminal offence of controlling or coercive behaviour where A and B live together and 'are members of the same family'.

capacity involves comprehending the reasonably foreseeable consequences and where best interests can take account of risks. Where available, it has the attraction of being able to deploy a best-interests framework *before* any such risks actually materialise so as to prevent the sexual harm in the first place. The difficulty, however, is 'Asking whether a person can consent to sex in the abstract is a little like asking whether they can put their name on a piece of paper. Well it all depends on whether the piece of paper is a birthday card or a will' (Herring and Wall, 2014, p 626). As Baroness Hale noted in a criminal case, 'One does not consent to sex in general. One consents to this act of sex with this person at this time and in this place.'[11]

Sorinmade and Peisah note in Chapter 6 that legal safeguards are there for the 'here and now' consent in sexual relations. If consent is the safeguard against sexual abuse, they ask whether consent too can be forward looking. Should capacitous people be able to make advance decisions in respect of future intimacy? Or give such legal authority to, for example, health and welfare lasting powers of attorney to decide in the future 'then'? Would this be a better form of supported decision making advocated by Squires and Morgan? While Parliament recognises people's (legally binding) right to decide in advance to refuse healthcare in the future,[12] and to make (non legally binding) advance statements as to what they would like, it has yet to recognise advance consent.

If a capacitous person can make decisions based on the reasonably foreseeable consequences, and if the Court of Protection can make anticipatory declarations and best-interests decisions if there is a real risk of the person losing capacity in the future, one can see a 'forward-looking' argument for advance consent to sexual relations. But it would, we suggest, require parliamentary consideration because of the competing policy issues at stake. Some may see advance consent as a 'safeguard for sexual autonomy', while others may see it as a 'licence to rape'. Alternatively, as Sorinmade and Peisah recommend, should section 27 MCA 2005 be amended to permit best interests decisions on sexual relations?

## Conclusion

The reasonably foreseeable consequences of contact between two people can span a significant scale of intimacy, which means the 'matter' requiring a decision can vary dramatically depending on the context. Some forms of intimacy carry significant risks and implications, such as pregnancy or assault; others may be minimal such as a kiss or hand holding. For mental capacity

11 *R v Cooper* [2009] UKHL 42 at [27].

12 MCA 2005 ss 24–26.

enthusiasts, to silo contact and sexual capacity sometimes feels instinctively wrong. For you can have the bread without it being a sandwich but you cannot have a sandwich without having the bread. One alternative route for reform that has been discussed across the chapters is to separate 'mental' from 'capacity' and steer the rudder of English law more towards the UNCRPD destination of equal-basis legal capacity. It would mean there would be no need for diagnostic overshadowing because no 'mental' impairment would be required. 'Incapacity' to engage in sexual relations would be key, and it would leave nothing – it would not need anything – to causally bite onto. Whether the inability to decide was because of dementia, intellectual disability or domestic abuse would not matter.

If the law were reformed along these lines, it could dramatically increase the scope of State intervention. It would, for example, mean the 'Capacity Act' could be used in cases of domestic violence if the victim was unable to comprehend the risks of the perpetrator. But in these, as in inherent jurisdiction cases, having the legal authority to intervene is one thing; working out practically what to do is quite another. For example, judges can impose injunctions against the accused with a threat of imprisonment for breach, but what if the victim wants to remain in contact? Injuncting the victim is hardly facilitative of their autonomy.[13] How can such injunctions be effectively policed other than in the most draconian of circumstances, which may involve detaining the person against their will to protect them?

Situations like this engage so many issues for social care professionals. The balance between Article 5 and Article 8 ECHR, UNCRPD rights, complex capacity assessments, decisions about whether judicial oversight is needed and, if so, which Court, looms large. Practitioners are often aware only of their own cases and may not know of numerous others their council has either taken to court or had legal advice on. Learning from practice provides support for individual practitioners, sharing positive experiences of supported decision making, such as the following example, can help to reduce the fear of 'getting it wrong', and sharing positive examples can promote where practice is getting it right.

---

**Practice example: support which sees mental capacity as only part of the story**

Social workers supported a team of personal assistants to produce a risk management plan for internet dating and dates. Alison had capacity to engage in sex but needed

[13] See *Redcar & Cleveland Borough Council v PR & Ors* [2019] EWHC 2305 (Fam) at [46] for the limited circumstances in which injunctions against the vulnerable person are permitted.

support to access dating sites, support to understand risk and support to get to and from dates. The social worker helped the team to understand their roles; for example, in providing support with finding and joining websites (logging on, setting passwords, creating a profile) and then left the choosing of suitable partners to Alison. A risk management plan was drawn up, beginning with an initial date in Starbucks, where Alison and the date were both visible to the personal assistant who waited in the car park. The risk management plan considered what would happen if they both wanted to leave and at what point the personal assistant would intervene. As any relationship developed the risk management plan developed with it to ensure Alison's protection, but also to empower her to develop safe and healthy relationships. This approach was almost 'blind' to the capacity/incapacity question but sought to involve Alison in decision making and provide essential support to meet potential partners within a framework where she was appropriately protected. Alison ultimately met her partner and they have now been together for four years.

## References

Daly, A., Heah, R. and Liddiard, K. (2019) 'Vulnerable subjects and autonomous actors: the right to sexuality education for disabled under-18s', *Global Studies of Childhood*, 9(3), 235–248.

Harflett, N. and Turner, S. (June 2016) *Supporting people with learning disabilities to develop sexual and romantic relationships*. Available at: https://www.ndti.org.uk/assets/files/Supporting_people_to_develop_relationships_Report.pdf (Accessed 26 February 2024).

Herring, J. and Wall, J. (2014) 'Capacity to consent to sex', *Medical Law Review*, 22(4), 620–630.

# Conclusion

*Beverley Clough and Laura Pritchard-Jones*

As shown throughout this edited collection, not only has the law around capacity, consent and sexual relationships recently undergone shifts in the form of the Supreme Court case of *A Local Authority v JB*,[1] but it is an area of increasing importance for professionals and practitioners working in areas such as social work, health, or supporting victims of sexual abuse. The aim of this collection has not been to resolve any of the legal or practical issues that these authors confront, but to open – or in some cases, reopen – some of the existing discussions and debates on mental capacity and sex, as well as offering new perspectives on them. In doing so, this collection has shown that such conversations and debates must not focus solely on the doctrinal questions which have historically tended to preoccupy lawyers but must also consider the challenges and opportunities the legal framework poses for disabled adults, as well as professionals working in health, social care and sectors beyond.

It is undoubtedly the case that *A Local Authority v JB* (*JB*), as well as many of the other decisions from the lower courts outlined in the Introduction and throughout the chapters, have precipitated a renewed focus on mental capacity and sex, often driven by legally and factually complex cases where there may be concerns about sexual abuse. The clarification as to what is considered relevant information under the Mental Capacity Act 2005 offered by the Supreme Court in *JB*, as well as the relationship between the civil and criminal law frameworks, is – in many ways – to be welcomed. This is not least because of the historic 'spasmodic trail' – to use Sandland's words in Chapter 1 – of predominantly criminal case law that governed this area prior to the introduction of the Mental Capacity Act 2005 (MCA). Such a spasmodic trail likely reflected society's unwillingness to countenance the idea that disabled adults might have sex lives, and that these sex lives might – moreover – be genuinely consensual and therefore

1 [2021] UKSC 52.

not criminal. However, the earlier chapters in this volume have sought to unpack some of the unresolved questions that *JB* leaves, and to demonstrate the extent to which the decision of the Supreme Court may leave more ambiguity than it has resolved. Likewise, the chapters in Part II point to the ways in which the law – both criminal and civil – may, at best, fail to grapple with some of the very real dilemmas that face practitioners working in this field and, at worst, may in fact exacerbate them, and in turn exacerbate some of the vulnerabilities experienced by those individuals who may fall under – or outside of, in the case of Hollomotz's Chapter 7 – the law's current gaze.

## The law as a help or a hindrance?

One of the points which Sandland introduced in Chapter 1 was the 'underdevelopment' of the law in the context of sex and mental capacity. In some ways, it may be that the jurisprudence under the MCA means that we have now gone the other way. There is an ever-growing body of case law now in this context which, as with *JB*, can take the law and practice in new and challenging directions; something Ruck Keene, Enefer and Cusack refer to in Chapter 2 as 'juridification'. The development of the civil and criminal law here represents an attempt to empower professionals and disabled adults, while also recognising the need to protect some adults from criminal sexual exploitation. However, this volume has brought to the surface more nuanced questions as to what role the law does – and should – play in navigating this tension. For some authors – for example, Sorinmade and Peisah in Chapter 6 – it is clear that the law, in requiring 'here and now' capacity, leans too heavily towards protection and unwarranted intrusion into the lives of disabled adults. In doing so, it potentially compromises the rights of some disabled adults to have meaningful sexual or intimate relationships, and for whom continued relationships of this kind might provide meaning and happiness and reduce isolation and loneliness. Ruck Keene, Enefer and Cusack's Chapter 2 concludes with linked sentiments; just because the MCA *allows* us to question a person's capacity to engage in sex, does not necessarily mean that we *should*. Can it therefore be said that the MCA – from its sparse origins in the common law in the 1990s that was used to justify its very existence – has encroached too much on these 'decision spaces' (Series, 2022) that it was arguably never intended for, thus representing too great a safeguarding power? As Series suggests, '"safeguards" are also the cutting edge of power … law's tools for resistance and liberation can also normalize and legitimate disciplinary power' (Series, 2022, p 162). Is the way the law has developed in this area overly focused on safeguarding against sexual abuse and exploitation, to the exclusion of all else, and does this reinforce professional power over disabled adults?

There is thus a pressing need to be attentive to the ways in which power is utilised and deployed in this context, and the effects of this on the lives of disabled people.

Likewise, Hollomotz's Chapter 7 throws into sharp relief the fact that the law in its current form, with its emphasis on a causative nexus between the functional inability to make a decision and the disturbance in the functioning of the mind or brain perhaps adopts an overly medicalised and individualised approach towards sexual relationships and capacity. In doing so, it masks from view the wider social forces at play in situations where a disabled person may have experienced sexual violence or exploitation. In effect, Hollomotz demonstrates that 'mental capacity' is clearly a messier concept than the MCA currently recognises or can contain. Impairments and abuse often coexist, and the courts have been clear that it is only where an inability to make a decision is because of the former that the MCA will step in. In many ways this is a good thing; it is unlikely that a legal framework which removes decision-making powers or agency from a person could be seen as empowering for adults who have been the victims of sexual abuse. However, it may also lead us to question the extent to which there are sufficiently robust legal measures in place to allow for the identification of and response to sexual violence outside the MCA. Lindsey and Brennan's Chapter 3 perhaps goes some way to remedying this by drawing attention to the hybrid orders available under the Sexual Offences Act 2003 as a possible solution.

Similarly, the reflections from practitioners in Chapters 4 and 8 draw important attention to the broader context within which the law sits. Likewise, the insights provided by Hollomotz as to the ways in which certain communication technologies do not contain words for intimate body parts or activities starkly highlight the constraints within which capacity assessments are situated, and may not enable a true reflection of disabled people's experiences. This also points to a broader theme as to the key role that professionals (and technologies) can play in facilitating and scaffolding sexual relationships and education, which is prominent in many of the chapters. Another aspect of this, as recognised by Squires and Morgan in Chapter 5, is that we need to be attentive to the fact that 'disabled and older people's private lives are subjected to invasive restriction and enquiry', and to recognise the part that the law does and can play in this. The case of JB provided glimpses into the intense ongoing restrictions that are placed on his ability to have social interactions, not just in regard to sexual relations. Lindsey and Brennan (Chapter 3) point to the different legal tools that are there for professionals, yet we can also see through the chapters by Bates (Chapter 4), Squires and Morgan (Chapter 5) and Peisah and Sorinmade (Chapter 6) that sometimes, turning to a particular tool such as the MCA – often driven by fears of liability – may result in unwarranted further intrusion in the lives of disabled people and their sexual autonomy. In exploring these ideas in future research there may be a need to consider the broader legal landscape or powers and obligations here, and to consider whether the current tools offered by either the criminal or civil law do enough to adequately respond to the particularities of the issues raised in this volume.

## Decision specificity as a new battleground?

In one sense, the MCA is a clear reflection of its origins in the common law of tort and medicine in the 1990s, as well as the need for a defence for practitioners against liability. The MCA developed from a legal framework which emphasises the need for capacitous consent in order for professionals to avoid liability, and it is precisely these origins which meant that the earlier case law around sexual capacity focused on capacity to *consent to* sex, which *JB* has now shifted to the language of *engage in* sex (Pritchard-Jones, 2021, p 146). As this volume demonstrates, this relatively small shift in framing has significant consequences. As Clough questions, 'how does a particular representation (of a problem, of an object) configure our responses?' (Clough, 2022, p 16). While the essence of the MCA remains focused on a person's ability to make a particular decision at a particular time and this continues to configure the responses by the courts and practitioners, *JB* demonstrates that the exact parameters of a decision – or the matter – are malleable. What these decisions are, and should be, and the extent to which they should continue to be subdivided into different domains such as sex, social media and internet use, as opposed to broader decisions about contact, is an emerging battleground for the courts, and may very well feed into the perception of the MCA as being too heavily focused on safeguarding at the expense of other imperatives.

We can see this malleability in the face of safeguarding concerns play out in cases such as *A Local Authority v AW*,[2] which involved AW, a 35-year-old man with learning disabilities and autism and who enjoyed using sexual websites, dating sites and chat rooms to watch sexual acts and to meet other men. AW was driven in particular by his desire to find a boyfriend. While AW could appear highly capable, he was also extremely vulnerable socially, especially in the way he used the internet to meet men and in his sexual relationships. There were considerable safeguarding concerns about the impact this might have on AW, including the fact that he had previously been assaulted on multiple occasions, with at least one of these assaults being sexual. Moreover, AW had also engaged in inappropriate and criminal behaviour; he had assaulted a minor and had assaulted staff at his

2 [2020] EWCOP 24.

living accommodation, and there were also allegations that he had behaved inappropriately towards women, including being aggressive, and following another woman home. AW was deemed to lack capacity in relation to making decisions regarding contact with other people, using social media and the internet, and making decisions about disclosure of personal information to others, but had capacity in relation to consenting to sexual relations. As Cobb J highlighted in the Court of Protection, 'this suite of conclusions reflects a potential anomaly … namely [that AW has] the decision-making facility to embark on sexual relations whilst, at the same time, he is not able to judge with whom it is safe to have those relations'.[3] To put this simply, AW may have capacity to have sex with another man, but not to have contact with them.[4] The ways that decisions about contact, sexual relationships, intimacy and residence are closely intertwined struggle against the neat categories of decisions envisaged by the MCA and the ways that professionals and others are expected to apply it in practice.

In AW's case, the best interests care package proposed a person-specific contact risk assessment to establish whether AW has the capacity to have contact with any individuals with whom he wishes to embark on a sexual relationship, and a specific support plan drawn up as appropriate where that is the case. In this sense, suggestions alluded to by Ruck Keene, Enefer and Cusack in Chapter 2, as well as by Currie and Allen (Chapter 8) in their reflections on the later chapters, may suggest that, within the parameters of the current legal framework, one option might be to have capacity to engage in sex as part of a broader capacity assessment about contact with another person. Future research must take such a suggestion seriously, exploring what such a shift might look like legally and in practice. Whatever its merits, such a suggestion does throw into sharp relief the fact that the MCA – as the later chapters show – is only as good as those who act as the network of support around people in a situation such as AW's. Mental capacity legislation alone is not equipped to remedy some of the – to use Hollomotz's term (Chapter 7) – social incapacities that disabled people face in their intimate lives. In AW's case, the evidence presented to the Court was that the local authority, AW's support workers and his current residential facility were all supportive of AW's needs and had agreed a care plan that genuinely 'seeks to strike a balance between offering AW protection, while affording him privacy and a degree of autonomy'.[5] What good practice looks like in supporting adults with cognitive disabilities to have sexual

---

3 *Ibid.*, at [28].

4 Also see *Hull City Council* v *KF* [2022] EWCOP 33, where Poole J grappled with this issue of contact and sexual capacity.

5 *Ibid.*, at [43].

and intimate relationships, while also navigating risk, is an important aspect of turning the empowering ethos underpinning the legislation into practical outcomes for people with disabilities, and is explored further in the chapters in Part II.

Nonetheless, situations such as in *AW* highlight the problems underpinning the decision-specific approach to capacity. By driving the decision-specific tests for contact and sexual relationships in different directions, the MCA potentially holds a person whose capacity is called into question to a higher standard of decision making than most of the rest of the population, and thereby moves away from the approaches envisioned by the United Nations Convention on the Rights of Persons with Disabilities (UNCRPD). The application of the legal framework here risks adversely impacting on the lives of disabled people in a way that non-disabled people will not experience. The regulation of the minutiae of interpersonal interactions and decisions which occurs for many people with intellectual and cognitive impairments, and the separation of these into 'silos', simply does not occur for many non-disabled people. While the potential for discrimination was robustly discounted by the Supreme Court, the impact of the law in this area on the lives of disabled people requires careful examination and emerges in a number of contributions in this volume.

## Persistence of protection and vulnerability

A further prominent theme across the chapters is the persistence of ideas of protection and vulnerability, which can be traced from the legal cases and frameworks mentioned by Sandland (Chapter 1) right through to the current judgments. While these tensions are thus clearly at the forefront of the development of law in this area, they also seem to take on different meanings and implications as law and practice has developed. Vulnerability was prominent, particularly in gendered ways, in the early legal frameworks encountered in Chapter 1, and theoretical works have sought to challenge and rethink how vulnerability is responded to through law (Clough, 2014). However, many of the chapters demonstrate the way in which our contemporary legal and policy landscape perpetuates an individualised – or, indeed, medicalised – idea of vulnerability as stemming from impairments and warranting exceptional legal responses, in turn 'othering' those who are deemed vulnerable.

The evolution of ideas of protection is also interesting here. Protection seems to pull in different directions as the law and social ideas around disability and sexuality have developed. Protection of society was a clear undercurrent in the earlier statutes and case law mentioned by Sandland, particularly in relation to the eugenic underpinnings. Yet the move towards the MCA was seen as signalling an orientation towards empowering and/or protecting the individual, as seen in Ruck Keene, Enefer and Cusack's Chapter 2. However, *JB* demonstrates the re-emergence of a more explicit public protection imperative, and one which warrants careful scrutiny. It is clear that while the language of empowerment, autonomy, protection and risk is a permanent feature of the discourse in this context, the subtle shifts in meaning or orientation can signal how precarious these concepts are in practice, as well as how significant the implications can be in the day-to-day lives of disabled people.

It is worth elaborating here on some recent judicial pushback to this move towards public protection as part of the MCA mentioned in the Introduction. In *Re PN*,[6] Poole J was faced with factually similar circumstances to *JB*, whereby *PN* was a man with autistic spectrum disorder (ASD) and learning disabilities, and had a history of sexually inappropriate behaviour. Applying *JB*, PN was found to have mental capacity to consent to sex, and Poole J made a striking observation that,

> following *JB*, there may be a natural desire to protect those with whom P might want to have sexual relations, in particular in cases where P has a history of sexual offending. Lord Stephens repeatedly refers to the MCA 2005 protecting not just P, but others – at [92], [106], and [107]. However, it seems to me, although the issue of the consent of others to sexual relations has entered the list of relevant information, the *Court of Protection must not allow the desire to protect others unduly to influence a clear-eyed assessment of P's capacity.* The unpalatable truth is that some capacitous individuals commit sexual assault, even rape, but also have consensual sexual relations. An individual with learning disability, ASD, or other impairment, may act in the same way, but it is only if they lack capacity to make decisions about engaging in sexual relations that the Court of Protection may interfere. If P would otherwise have capacity, then the court should not allow its understandable desire to protect others to drive it to a finding that P lacks capacity, thereby depriving P of the right they would otherwise have to a sexual life. The Court of Protection should not assume the role or responsibilities of the criminal justice system. One of the core principles of the MCA 2005 is that 'a person is not to be treated as unable to make a decision merely because he makes an unwise decision' – s1(4). Deciding to act in a way that might be a criminal offence would be an 'unwise' decision. Such decisions might contribute to a determination of a lack of capacity, but P is not to be treated as unable to make a decision

[6] [2023] EWCOP 44.

> merely because they may make a decision to act in a way that might amount to a criminal offence.[7]

This interesting intervention may pave the way for yet further refinement and debate around the role and boundaries of protection in this context, particularly in relation to ideas of vulnerability and empowerment. It remains to be seen how the Court of Protection itself continues to navigate this personal versus public protection dichotomy that emerges from cases such as *JB*.

## Future research agendas

But where next? What avenues for further discussion and research does this volume open? Some of these avenues are clearly linked to the narrower field of sexual relationships and intimacy. However, some of the questions raised by the authors in this volume transcend this narrow field and raise fundamental questions more broadly about the law, the experiences of disabled adults and the extent to which law can – or should – be used either as a tool to drive change in practice or to regulate the minutiae of decisions that adults – *all adults* – make on a daily basis.

It is undoubtedly the case that more research must be done on this, and even more so to understand the voices of those whose lives have been touched by the MCA in this way. Existing research has begun to consider this in the everyday domains of an adult's life, and the extent to which the supported decision-making paradigm articulated by the UNCRPD has been, and can be, translated into practice (Harding and Taşcioğlu, 2018). However, more is needed specifically around experience of the MCA in the context of intimate relationships. If the MCA is used on the ground in an increasingly paternalistic and protectionist way to control and regulate sexual decision making, then is it time to revisit safeguarding laws? In the 1990s, the Law Commission – in its original consultation that led up to the MCA – proposed separate public law safeguarding powers which were ultimately not taken forward. If the MCA is being used to do much of the heavy lifting in cases of sexual abuse, is it time to revisit these proposals, rather than leaving safeguarding to the MCA? Lastly, on the interface between protection and empowerment, there is a need to look at the existing criminal law framework. Do the tools as outlined in the Sexual Offences Act 2003 adequately respond to many of the concerns raised in this volume?

---

[7] *Ibid.*, at [11], emphasis added. A similar point was made in *A Local Authority* v *ZZ* [2023] EWCOP 61, whereby Burrows J stated that '[a]lthough the protection of the public is a relevant consideration in MCA and Court of Protection cases, it is not the primary purpose of this jurisdiction'. At [49].

These are all distinct issues, yet underpinning all of them is the need to consider how law and legal tools in this context might be imagined differently, if driven and understood through the voices and experiences of disabled people. Some of the more controversial proposals presented and discussed in this volume – such as advance or substitute decisions for sex or intimacy – would, in fact, require a wholesale rethinking of the parameters and form of both the criminal and civil law. Similarly, how might core concepts such as consent, sexual intimacy, support, risk, protection, vulnerability, be reconceptualised through a more explicit orientation towards and engagement with disabled people? Ending with a provocation from Sandland's Chapter 1, where it was noted that there was a questionable understanding of intellectual disabilities in the 19th century, we might want to consider how far we have moved on from that, and to note the importance of the UNCRPD here for pushing this urgent re-evaluation of law and practice.

## References

Clough, B. (2014) 'Vulnerability and capacity to consent to sex: asking the right questions?', *Child and Family Law Quarterly*, 26(4), 371–397.

Clough, B. (2022) *The spaces of mental capacity law: Moving beyond binaries*. Abingdon: Routledge.

Harding, R. and Taşcioğlu, E. (2018) 'Supported decision-making from theory to practice: implementing the right to enjoy legal capacity', *Societies*, 8(2), 25–42.

Pritchard-Jones, L. (2021) '*A Local Authority V JB* [2020] EWCA Civ 735 and *A Local Authority v AW* [2020] EWCOP 24: rethinking sexual capacity?', *Medical Law Review*, 29(1), 143–156.

Series, L. (2022) *Deprivation of liberty in the shadows of the institution*. Bristol: Bristol University Press.

# Index

References to endnotes show both the page number and the note number (77n33).

Printed and bound by CPI Group (UK) Ltd, Croydon, CR0 4YY

15/09/2026

14962385-0006